To Follow the Lambe Wheresoever He Goeth

Monographs in Baptist History

VOLUME 5

SERIES EDITOR
Michael A. G. Haykin, The Southern Baptist Theological Seminary

EDITORIAL BOARD
Matthew Barrett, The Southern Baptist Theological Seminary
Peter Beck, Charleston Southern University
Anthony L. Chute, California Baptist University
Jason G. Duesing, Southwestern Baptist Theological Seminary
Nathan A. Finn, Southeastern Baptist Theological Seminary
Crawford Gribben, Trinity College, Dublin
Gordon L. Heath, McMaster Divinity College
Barry Howson, Heritage Theological Seminary
Jason K. Lee, Southwestern Baptist Theological Seminary
Thomas J. Nettles, The Southern Baptist Theological Seminary
James A. Patterson, Union University
James M. Renihan, Institute of Reformed Baptist Studies
Jeffrey P. Straub, Central Baptist Theological Seminary
Brian R. Talbot, Broughty Ferry Baptist Church, Scotland
Malcolm B. Yarnell III, Southwestern Baptist Theological Seminary

Ours is a day in which not only the gaze of western culture but also increasingly that of Evangelicals is riveted to the present. The past seems to be nowhere in view and hence it is disparagingly dismissed as being of little value for our rapidly changing world. Such historical amnesia is fatal for any culture, but particularly so for Christian communities whose identity is profoundly bound up with their history. The goal of this new series of monographs, Studies in Baptist History, seeks to provide one of these Christian communities, that of evangelical Baptists, with reasons and resources for remembering the past. The editors are deeply convinced that Baptist history contains rich resources of theological reflection, praxis and spirituality that can help Baptists, as well as other Christians, live more Christianly in the present. The monographs in this series will therefore aim at illuminating various aspects of the Baptist tradition and in the process provide Baptists with a usable past.

To Follow the Lambe Wheresoever He Goeth

The Ecclesial Polity of the English Calvinistic Baptists 1640–1660

Ian Birch

FOREWORD BY
Stephen Holmes

PICKWICK *Publications* · Eugene, Oregon

TO FOLLOW THE LAMBE WHERESOEVER HE GOETH
The Ecclesial Polity of the English Calvinistic Baptists 1640–1660

Monographs in Baptist History 5

Copyright © 2017 Ian Birch. All rights reserved. Except for brief quotations in critical publications or reviews, no part of this book may be reproduced in any manner without prior written permission from the publisher. Write: Permissions, Wipf and Stock Publishers, 199 W. 8th Ave., Suite 3, Eugene, OR 97401.

Pickwick Publications
An Imprint of Wipf and Stock Publishers
199 W. 8th Ave., Suite 3
Eugene, OR 97401

www.wipfandstock.com

PAPERBACK ISBN: 978-1-4982-0901-4
HARDCOVER ISBN: 978-1-4982-0903-8
EBOOK ISBN: 978-1-4982-0902-1

Cataloguing-in-Publication data:

Names: Birch, Ian.

Title: To Follow the Lambe Wheresoever He Goeth: The ecclesial polity of English Calvinistic Baptists 1640–1660 / Ian Birch.

Description: Eugene, OR: Pickwick Publications, 2017 | Monographs in Baptist History 5 | Includes bibliographical references and index.

Identifiers: ISBN 978-1-4982-0901-4 (paperback) | ISBN 978-1-4982-0903-8 (hardcover) | ISBN 978-1-4982-0902-1 (ebook)

Subjects: LSCH: Baptists—England—History—17th century. | England—Church history—17th century. | subject | subject

Classification: BX6276 B5 2017 (print) | BX6276 (ebook)

Manufactured in the U.S.A.   01/10/17

To Elizabeth, James, and Joanna

Contents

Foreword by Stephen Holmes | xi
Acknowledgments | xiii
List of Abbreviations | xiv
Introduction | xv

1. "Casting Balls of Wildfire into the bosom of the Church": The Emergence of English Particular Baptist Churches to 1660 | 1
   1.1. From Jacob to Jessey
   1.2 Particular Baptist Expansion, 1644–1660
      1.2.1. Publishing
      1.2.2. Preaching
      1.2.3. Disputations
      1.2.4. Missionary Evangelism
   Summary

2. "A True Visible Church of Christ": The Contours of Calvinistic Baptist Ecclesiology | 32
   2.1 The Rule of Christ
   2.2 A Believer's Church
   2.3 Baptism, Infant Baptism, and Church Membership
   2.4 A Gathered Church
   2.5 A Visible Church
   2.6 A Separate Church
   Summary

3. "To follow the Lambe wheresoever he goeth": The Church of King Jesus | 65
    3.1. The Forerunner, Henry Jacob
    3.2. "Christology" in Early Particular Baptist Confessions
    3.3. *Munus Triplex Christi* and Ecclesiology in Thomas Collier
        3.3.1. Collier on Christ's Priesthood
        3.3.2. Collier on Christ as Prophet
        3.3.3. Collier on Christ's Kingship
    Summary

4. "A Holy and Orderly Communion": Theology and Practice of Discipline among Early Particular Baptists | 96
    4.1 The Purity of the Saints in Particular Baptist Confessions
    4.2 Church Discipline in Hermeneutical Perspective
    4.3 Church Discipline in Early Particular Baptist Records
        4.3.1. Occasions of Discipline in Baptist Records
        4.3.2. Pastoral Procedure in Discipline
    4.4 Theology of Discipline among Particular Baptists
        4.4.1. The Authority of the Church
        4.4.2. The Glory of Christ
        4.4.3. Purity of the Body of Christ
    Summary

5. "An Intolerable Usurpation": Theology and Practice of Ministry among Early Particular Baptists | 129
    5.1 The Choosing of "Meet Persons": Baptist Lay Ministry
    5.2 Offices of Ministry in Particular Baptist Churches
    5.3 The Calling of Ministers in Baptist Congregations
    5.4 Ordination among Early Calvinistic Baptists
    Summary

6. "The Counsel and Help of One Another": Independency and Interdependency: Particular Baptists in Association | 161
   6.1 The Origins of Particular Baptist Associations to 1660
      6.1.1 The Origins of Associations in the Association Records of the English Particular Baptists
   6.2 Theology of Particular Baptist Associations
   6.3 Associational Authority and Local Ecclesiology
   Summary

Conclusions | 192

Bibliography | 207
Index | 225

Foreword

IT IS HARD TO imagine the ordinary life of the congregation Henry Jacob founded in Southwark in 1616. For three decades they met illegally, rarely numbering more than a few dozen, seeing some of their number arrested and imprisoned, enduring multiple schisms amongst the few that remained, seeking through all such setbacks to find an agreed way to follow the Lord 'in ways known and to be made known'.

In the early 1630s, the very future of the church must have seemed precarious. There was a lasting schism over the issue of fellowship with parish churches, leading to a breakaway congregation pastored by John Spilsbury. Jacob's successor as pastor, John Lathrop, was imprisoned about this time, and plea-bargained his release into exile, taking a good chunk of the congregation across the Atlantic with him. The main congregation was left without a minister for three years after his departure, and when they finally called Henry Jessey, six more of their number left in protest, and joined Spilsbury's congregation.

This last sad departure of six believers, however, marks one of the great turning-points in Protestant history, akin to Wesley's Aldersgate experience or what happened at Azuza St. These six had come to the conviction that the ordinance of baptism should be given to believers only, not to infants; their departure and joining with Spilsbury marks the probable beginning of the very first Calvinistic Baptist congregation.

Today, Baptists are regularly described as the largest Protestant denomination, numbering comfortably over 100 million. Almost all Baptists are, via various twists, turns, and ingraftings, the spiritual descendants of those six believers, Spilsbury, and those with whom they covenanted together. (Although the beginnings of the General Baptists under Smyth was earlier, and although the two traditions developed in parallel for some decades, it was essentially the Particular Baptists and those descended from them or joining with them who blossomed and spread into the worldwide movement of today.) From that early beginning, in two decades they spread across the UK, organised, and defined themselves as a self-conscious denomination.

Because of the temporal priority of General Baptist beginnings, historians have focused their interest there, and neglected the Jacob-Lathrop-Jessey church and its baptistic offshoots. For all of us who stand in historic Baptist traditions today, however, this is the 'rock from which we were hewn'; Sabine Staresmore, Richard Browne, and the rest are our mothers and fathers in the faith. For others less personally connected, this is still the origin of one of the most significant ecclesial traditions of modern times, and the arguments and agreements of those few believers have become remarkably determinative for church history. The story deserves to be told, and to be told well.

Dr. Birch tells it well. His interests are theological, asking what ideas shaped these early Calvinistic Baptists. Of course, social and economic historians will have something to say (as will historians of gender; the remarkable Independent preacher and church planter Katherine Chidley stands in the background of this story, and other women rise to remarkable positions of leadership and influence in the newly-formed Baptist churches in the early years). It is right, however, to give intellectual history, and particularly historical theology, the primary word; these early Baptists were seeking to obey the call of Jesus, often putting themselves in great personal hardship and danger to do so, and simply out of respect for them, the primary interpretation of their story must be theological.

If their intentions were theological, however, they lacked a theologian. There is no magisterial writer who interprets their vision for them and for others in this early period (or, to be honest, in any later day). The arguments which they were prepared to break fellowship over, to suffer persecution for, must be reconstructed from slogans, sermons, and suggestions. Much of the strength of Dr. Birch's account is his patience with these fragmentary and unsystematic sources, and his patient weaving together of the threads that we have to make a convincing tapestry, a picture of the underlying belief system.

With Dr. Birch as our sure guide, we discover a community committed to following Jesus as King, to creating and maintaining pure communities of faith, to enabling all to minister so that the body may be built up, to connecting together in love and fellowship. There is much to celebrate in this vision; no doubt there are also questions to be asked of it. Dr. Birch enables us to see and appreciate the vision of these early Particular Baptists that was historically to prove so powerful over the centuries; for that, we owe him a great debt. He tells his story clearly, convincingly, and compellingly; this is an excellent book, which I commend unreservedly.

Stephen Holmes

Acknowledgments

I WOULD LIKE TO place on record my gratitude to the many people who have helped make the research and writing of this book possible. In particular I am indebted to the guidance and wise comments of my PhD supervisor Revd. Dr. Stephen Holmes of the Divinity Department of the University of St Andrews. His own interest and writing in early Baptist theology has made for a stimulating partnership throughout the course of my writing. Advice and suggestions for lines of enquiry have also been sought and given by Professor John Coffey, and Dr. Larry Kreitzer, and for these I am most grateful.

In my pursuit of sources and original documents the library staff at my home institution, the University of the West of Scotland, have been of considerable help. In the initial stages of the research a profitable week was spent at the Angus library at Regents Park College, Oxford.

Parts of the work were read by my colleague Revd. Dr. James Gordon, whose sharp eye for grammar and punctuation has enabled me to avoid numerous errors. The remaining faults are of course my own.

Support for the work has come from the Scottish Baptist College, the Baptist Union of Scotland, my parents and friends. I hope that seeing the work completed is an appropriate reward for their support.

My wife and children have been patient, supportive, encouraging throughout, and without them, especially Elizabeth, this work would not have been possible.

Abbreviations

ARPB   *Association Records of the Particular Baptists*
BQ   *The Baptist Quarterly*
EEB   Stephen Wright, *The Early English Baptists, 1603–1649.*
EED   C. Burrage, *The Early English Dissenters in the Light of Recent Research (1550–1641)* 2 vols.
HBB   W. T. Whitley, *A History of the British Baptists* 2nd.
HEB   A. C. Underwood, *A History of the English Baptists.*
JEH   *The Journal of Ecclesiastical History*
JTS   *The Journal of Theological Studies*
ODNB   *Oxford Dictionary of National Biography*
TBHS   *Transactions of the Baptist Historical Society*

Introduction

IN 1641, THOMAS EDWARDS wrote to members of the Long Parliament to alert them to what he considered the major issue of the time:

> Tis not unknown to You, Right Noble and Worthy Senators, that the Great and Present Controversie of these Times is about the Church, and Church Government.[1]

Edwards, an Anglican clergyman at the time but soon to become a virulent Presbyterian, recognized that the political instability of the early 1640s had provided an opportunity for religious sects, notably "Anabaptism, Brownisme, &c.,"[2] to flourish. The settling of a national church government was therefore a matter of urgency so not to incur Divine displeasure upon a nation which had known God's grace.[3] Edwards's appeal added to the growing momentum in Parliament for ecclesiastical reform.

In the eighteen months between the calling of the Long Parliament, in November 1640, and the outbreak of Civil War in August 1642, while most members of Parliament believed in the necessity of church reform few, if any, had a clear program for national church polity. Kirby observes, "[Puritans] were more accustomed to dissent, not to constructive thinking."[4] When asked what he would put in place of the bishops Oliver Cromwell replied, "I can tell you, sir, what I would not have, though I cannot, what I would."[5] A range of opinions were canvassed in a flurry of published pamphlets. Disenchanted Puritans had established contact with Scottish radicals

---

1. Edwards, *Reasons against the Independent Government*, Epistle Dedicatory.
2. Ibid.
3. Ibid., A3.
4. Kirby, "English Presbyterians," 420.
5. Kenyon, *Stuart Constitution*, 252.

and their agenda for reform had in view the Presbyterianism of the Scots. Robert Baillie came to London in 1640 to promote the Covenanter cause and agitate against episcopacy.[6] Less radical reformers in the House longed for a return to an idealized Jacobethan age of Prayer Book Protestantism. This moderate Anglicanism was represented in the *Grand Remonstrance* presented by the Commons to the King on 1 December 1641.[7] They stated,

> our intention is, and our endeavours have been, to reduce within bounds that exorbitant power which the prelates have assumed unto themselves, so contrary to the Word of God and to the laws of the land, to which end we passed the bill for the removing them from their temporal power and employments.[8]
>
> And we desire to unburden the consciences of men of needless and superstitious ceremonies, suppress innovations, and take away the monuments of idolatry.[9]

While the Grand Remonstrance expressed Parliament's intention to bring about church reform, it was equally clear that religious tolerance for sectaries was not intended. They stated,

> We do here declare that it is far from our purpose or desire to let loose the golden reigns of discipline and government in the Church, to leave private persons or particular congregations to take up what form of Divine Service they please, for we hold it requisite that there should be throughout the whole realm a conformity to that order which the laws enjoin according to the Word of God.[10]

For a moment it appeared that the momentum for ecclesiastical change was with the conservatives who favored a reformed Church of England with a modified episcopacy. Pym, the *de facto* leader of the opposition to the King in parliament, recognized that the unity of the Commons might be threatened by this article, and under his influence provision was made for an assembly to consider the question of reform of Church government:

> And the better to effect the intended reformation, we desire there may be a general synod of the most grave, pious, learned and

---

6. Coffey, "Toleration Controversy," in Durston and Maltby, *Religion in Revolutionary England*, 44.

7. See Gardiner, *Constitutional Documents*, 202–32.

8. Article 183. Ibid., 229.

9. Article 184. Ibid., 229.

10. Article 184. Ibid., 229. For the wider debate see Coffey, *Persecution and Toleration*, 137–39.

judicious divines of this island, assisted with some from foreign parts professing the same religion with us, who may consider of all things necessary for the peace and good government of the Church, and represent the results of their consultations unto the Parliament, to be there allowed of and confirmed, and receive the stamp of authority, thereby to find passage and obedience throughout the kingdom.[11]

By the mid-1640s three visions of the church were being worked out simultaneously, Presbyterianism, Independency and a variety of forms of sectarianism. This thesis is a historical and theological engagement with one element of the ecclesiastical controversies of the 1640s and 1650s, the emergence and polity of the sect later known as the English Particular Baptists.

In 1962 Glen Stassen, then a PhD candidate at Duke University, noted that Baptist historiography had largely ignored the origins and theology of the English Particular Baptists, a lacuna he judged to be a serious issue for Baptist confessional scholarship. He stated:

Whatever the reason for this lack, its consequence is that the most profound Baptist theology of this period [the seventeenth century] just simply seems not to have been investigated. This injustice cries for righting.[12]

This present work is a contribution to this omission,[13] particularly in relation to the developmental phase of English Particular Baptist ecclesiology, 1640–1660. The approach is situated within the discipline of historical theology, and contextualizes the theology of the church developed and promulgated by the English Calvinistic Baptists within an account of their rise and consolidation.

Around the year 1640 a Calvinistic Independent congregation, led by Henry Jessey, generated a group of members who separated themselves from the main body in order to administer believer's baptism by immersion. By the time of the restoration of the monarchy in 1660, after a period of considerable growth, the English Calvinistic Baptists had established a strong sense of distinct identity, and were about to face renewed persecution as episcopacy was re-established as the national, compulsory form of

---

11. Article 185. Gardiner, *Constitutional Documents*, 229.

12. Stassen, "Anabaptist Influence," 322.

13. Renihan has published a doctoral dissertation examining the later ecclesiology of the Particular Baptists, which discusses the subsequent phase of development— *Edification and Beauty: The Practical Ecclesiology of the English Particular Baptists, 1675–1705*.

church.¹⁴ These dates form the boundaries of this enquiry into the doctrine of the church in the thought and practice of the English Calvinistic Baptists.

This book concentrates exclusively on the ecclesial polity of the Calvinistic Baptists. This is for two primary reasons. First, the development of the General Baptists has been studied in some depth in recent work. Notably, Stephen Wright, *The Early English Baptists, 1603–1649*, James Coggins, *John Smyth's Congregation: English Separatism, Mennonite Influence, and the Elect Nation*, Stephen Bratchlow, "Puritan Theology and General Baptist Origins," Lonnie Kliever, "General Baptist Origins: The Question of Anabaptist Influence," Mark Bell, *Apocalypse How?*, Barry White has written manifold articles.¹⁵ Traditionally, the English Particular Baptists have received less detailed attention that the older General Baptists. Second, I have focused on only one Baptist group because despite having in common the practice of believer's baptism by immersion, and congregational church government, the two groups developed separately and independently throughout the period studied here.¹⁶ Though similar in a number of features the two groups had little to do with each other.¹⁷ At the individual level characters like Thomas Lambe defied theologically classification as either a General or Particular Baptist, though ecclesially he associated with the Generals.¹⁸ At the level of organized communities convictions were forged separately, with little or no reference to the other.

The task of enquiring into early Calvinistic Baptist ecclesiology is made more difficult than chronicling contemporary alternative polities, for example, that of Presbyterianism or Independent Congregationalism, since the nature of their theological writings is non-systematic. The exception to this is the First London Confession of 1644, but even here articles of faith are brief, creedal statements, not developed theological argument. Baptists had no Baxter, Marshall or Owen. Baptist writings are occasional, often apologetic, and sometimes homiletic. The theology available in these sources is therefore not always fully developed. The investigation of this enquiry is

---

14. See Morrill, "Church in England," in Morrill, *Reactions to the English Civil War*, 89–114.

15. E.g. White, "English General Baptists," 16–27; see also *The English Baptists of the Seventeenth Century*.

16. This was not an absolute demarcation, and there were exceptions to the general rule, especially in the early 1640s. See Wright, *EEB*, 94.

17. See Howard, *Looking-Glass*, 5–6. Howard reports that those who switched from the Particulars to the Generals, or *vice versa* were required to be baptized again, since they were regarded as having been baptized into the wrong faith. Brown, *Political Activities*, 4.

18. In *A Treatise of Particular Predestination* Lambe affirmed his commitment to both general redemption and particular election. Lambe, *Treatise*, 2–4.

therefore necessarily eclectic in its use of sources, drawing from a number of writers, preachers, and evangelists to identify theological commitments energizing their work of bringing into being new congregations, conformed to the Rule of Christ. The risk of this approach is assessing whether the views of one Baptist represent the views of the movement, or are only idiosyncratic. In regard to major issues of Baptist ecclesial polity I therefore seek to provide corroborating evidence.

The book divides thematically into three sections. The first section considers the historical context for the emergence of the English particular Baptists. Chapter 1 is foundational for later theological analysis, and explores the origins of Baptist churches derived from the semi-separatist congregation formed by Henry Jacob in Southwark in 1616, up to the Restoration of 1660. The theme is one of emergence and growth, in a period of relative religious freedom caused by political turmoil, especially from the calling of the Long Parliament. As Baptist churches were formed, divided, multiplied, and associated throughout this period, theological convictions both drove the process forward, and were further forged in debate and defense of their congregational ecclesiology. The first part of the chapter uses the Stinton manuscript[19] as a basis for describing the rise of the Calvinistic Baptists in London, and the second part of the chapter sets out the primary reason for their relative success in surviving persecution, spreading their ideas, and planting new congregations.

Chapter 2 builds on the historical foundation of the first chapter, and describes the theological features of Baptist congregationalism in its emergent phase. The Baptist form of church was typically sectarian and voluntarist, Reformed, congregational, prioritizing experiential faith and the visible church. Calvinistic in soteriology, Particular Baptists were committed to a church separate from state control, and state sponsored religious conformity. This apparent political posture was the result of conversionist experience, which inspired Baptists to acknowledge Christ alone as immediate head of every congregation, as of every believer. Spiritual conversion was an experience of the unmediated power of Christ to effect inner renewal of life. Sins were forgiven, assurance of salvation secured, without any human mediator or sacramental means of grace. Since Christ was immediately present to the soul of saints, surely his kingly presence must be likewise available to the church. Building on this personal, experiential, understanding of the Gospel Baptists determined to have a church conformed to the purposes

---

19. A full transcription of the so-called Stinton Repository with historical introduction is available in *TBHS* 1 (1908–9), 193–245. See White, "Who Really Wrote," 3–10, 14.

and precepts of King Jesus, that is, "the Rule of Christ,"[20] the immediate head of every congregation of saints gathered in his name.

Chapter 3 develops further the theological commitments of the Particular Baptists, focusing on what I consider to be their primary and controlling conviction, namely devotion to the kingship of Jesus over his people. In particular, attention is given to the influence of the *munus triplex* doctrine in shaping early Baptist Christology. This model provides the basis for speaking about ecclesiology in Christological perspective, a foundational principle in Particular Baptist ideology.

Chapters 4, 5, and 6 consider the practical outworking of ecclesiological core beliefs in congregational life. The focus will be upon the formation of holy communities and the implementation of congregational discipline. Since Baptists rejected the *corpus mixtum* model of the Church, though affirmed in Reformed theology and operated by Anglicans and Presbyterians, in favor of a believer's Church, gathered under the reign of Christ, the question they faced was how to maintain the purity of the body of Christ.

In chapter 5, Baptist ecclesiology will be examined in relation to ministry. The variety of offices and organization of officers in Baptist congregations, as set out in their publications will be discussed in relation to other models of ministry functioning in the period. Finally, the Baptist understanding of church in trans-local reality will be surveyed. The primary basis for this analysis will be the *Association Records of the Particular Baptists*, a compilation of documents, mainly from the 1650s, providing access to the thoughts and processes of early Baptist leaders, churches and associations in the development of what was more accurately called *consociation*. This chapter brings to a conclusion the account of earliest Particular Baptist ecclesiology, which began with the independent church of Henry Jacob, and led to the formation of a number of sectarian congregations, but eventually settled into a denominational form of inter-related churches, sharing common convictions, expressed confessionally in subscribed documents of 1644 and 1687, by which they were bound together. By 1660 it can be said that the identity and unity of these churches was consolidated, ensuring their distinct identity through the persecution of the Restoration, and beyond the Act of Toleration.

Throughout the work I have adopted the contemporary style of dating. In the period covered in this thesis England was using the Old Style, or Julian calendar. The year officially began on 25 March. In this text, the Old Style is maintained in order to reflect dates given in original documents. Spelling, punctuation and formatting have followed the original sources in

20. For example, Kiffin, *Brief Remonstrance*, 6.

citations given in the text. This accounts for the variation in the names of Thomas Collier, sometimes spelled Colyer, and William Kiffin, sometimes spelled Ciffyn, Cufin, or Kiffen.[21] The spellings are used randomly in the original sources, since spelling in the seventeenth century was not standardized, therefore except for citations where I have remained true to the original text for the sake of accuracy, I have adopted the spellings "Collier" and "Kiffin." On occasions where discussion of sources takes place in the body of the material, modernization of spelling has been used to maintain the flow of the argument.

---

21. In the most detailed work on Kiffin to date, Kreitzer employs the spelling "Kiffen," however the majority of documents I have consulted, and the majority of modern commentators, use the spelling Kiffin. See Kreitzer, *William Kiffen and his World (Part 1)*, 8–9.

1

"Casting Balls of Wildfire into the bosom of the Church"[1]

The Emergence of English Particular Baptists to 1660

Introduction

ENGLISH PARTICULAR BAPTISTS APPEAR as an identifiable collective organization in the mid seventeenth century. The date by which it can be stated certainly that there existed a group of at least seven Independent churches practicing believer's baptism and holding to Calvinistic tenets of theology is October 1644, the occasion of the publication of the First London Confession.[2] The unity of these churches is expressed in the preface to the Confession where they stated,

> though wee be distinct in respect of our particular bodies, . . . yet are all One in Communion, holding Jesus Christ to be our head and Lord.[3]

---

1. Featley, *Dippers Dipt.*, Preface.

2. There were other Calvinistic Baptist churches which did not sign the London Confession in 1644, for example, and somewhat ironically, the congregation of Henry Jessey, the "mother Church of the Independents." Shakespeare, *Baptist And Congregational Pioneers*, 178. Jessey's church at this time still practiced infant baptism and could not sign the article on ordinances. See Whitley, *TBHS* 1, 235, n. 17.

3. Lumpkin, *Baptist Confessions*, 155.

2   To Follow the Lambe Wheresoever He Goeth

Prior to 1644 it is only with caution that we can speak of the English Particular Baptists as a collective entity.⁴ Murray Tolmie has suggested that the concept of "proto-denomination" be employed to describe a group of churches fully evolved ideologically, but organizationally incomplete.⁵

In this chapter I will draw on near contemporary documents⁶ to trace the emergence of English Particular Baptists from the mother church founded by Henry Jacob to the restoration of the monarchy, in order to provide the necessary context to examine the doctrine of the church among these believers.

1.1 From Jacob to Jessey

The emergence of English Particular Baptists may be traced back to the congregation of Independent Puritans⁷ founded by Henry Jacob in Southwark,⁸ London, in 1616.⁹ The formation of the church is recorded in a document known as Stinton Numb: 1, where it states:

> The Church Anno 1616 was gathered
>
> Hereupon yᵉ said Henry Jacob wᵗʰ Sabine Staismore, Rich Browne, David Prior, Andrew Almey, Wᵐ Throughton, Jno Allen, Mʳ Gibs, Edwᵈ Farre, Hen Goodall, & divers others well-informed Saints haveing appointed a day to seek yᵉ Face of yᵉ Lord in fasting & Prayer, wherein that particular of their Union

---

4. See Hill, "History and Denominational History," 65–71. Wright, *EEB* 11.

5. See Tolmie, *Triumph of the Saints*, 50. Mark Bell notes the denominational features of Interregnum Baptists, particularly their aspiration to national association. See Bell, "Freedom to Form," in Durston and Maltby, *Religion in Revolutionary England*, 183. Author's emphasis.

6. The so-called Stinton Repository. See "Introduction," n. 18.

7. This is the term used by Burrage for Jacob's church. See Burrage, *EED* 1, 287. Other terms such as "non-separating Congregationalist" and "semi-separatist" (Tolmie), "moderate separatist" and even "Jacobite" (Watts) are also used to convey their distinct churchmanship. The terminology is compared in Watts, *Dissenters* 1, 52–3, 94–99; also Duesing, "Henry Jacob (1563–1624): Pastoral Theology and congregational ecclesiology," 298 n. 5.

8. It is interesting to think that the General Baptist congregation of Thomas Helwys, now led by John Murton, was meeting at the same time in Newgate, but since Jacob did not have anabaptist convictions they would be of no importance to him. See Burrage, *EED* 1, 259.

9. The story of the foundation of Jacob's church is told in detail in Burrage, *EED* 1, chapter 13; White, *English Separatist Tradition*, 165–68; Tolmie, *Saints*, chapter 1; Watts, *Dissenters* 1, 50–62. Additional material may be found in von Rohr, "*Extra Ecclesiam Nulla Salus*," 107–21.

togeather as a Church was mainly commended to ye Lord: in ye ending of ye Day they were United, Thus, Those who minded this present Union & so joyning together joined both hands each wth other Brother and stood in a Ringwise: their intent being declared, H Jacob and each of the Rest made some confession or Profession of their Faith & Repentance, some, ware longer some ware briefer, Then they Covenanted togeather to walk in all Gods Ways as he had revealed or should make known to them.

Thus was the beginning of that Church of which proceed, they within a few Days gave notice to the Brethren here of the Antient Church.

After this Hen Jacob was Chosen & Ordained Pastor to that Church, & many Saints ware joined to them.[10]

The *Confession* affirmed Jacob's willingness to submit to all civil authority,[11] both godly magistrate and government. He did not advocate separation of church and state, but sought freedom and toleration to be an independent congregation, that is, "Christs visible politicall Church under the Gospell."[12] What Jacob desired was an end to human tradition in the church, and liberation from the authority of priests and bishops.[13]

The basis on which Jacob's pioneering "independent" church[14] formed was clearly covenantal, the members committing themselves as a gathered congregation. It is less clear to what extent it was their intention to be a separatist conventicle. The argument for separatism derives from the detail that a few days following the first gathering of the church Jacob consulted with "the Brethren here of the Antient Church,"[15] a strictly Separatist congregation with Barrowist convictions.[16] Jacob's approach may suggest he de-

---

10. *TBHS* 1, 209. Biographical details of early members are given by Tolmie, *Saints*, 13.

11. Jacob affirmed his willingness to swear the oath of the king's Supremacy, and the oath of Allegiance. Jacob, *Confession*, E3.

12. Ibid., article 3.

13. Ibid., D5.

14. Crosby recounts the forming of Jacob's church from a manuscript of William Kiffin, "There was a congregation of Protestant *Dissenters* of the *independent* Persuasion in *London*, gather'd in the year 1616, whereof Mr. *Henry Jacob* was the first pastor." Kiffin's memoire speaks of independence not separatism. Crosby, *History of the English Baptists*, 1:148. Indeed, the earliest reference to "independency" was in regard to Henry Jacob's polity. See Ha, *English Presbyterianism, 1590–1640*, 7.

15. *TBHS* 1, 210. The background to this church is given in Watts, *Dissenters* 1, 34–40; see also *TBHS* 1, 210 n. 6.

16. The opinion of the Ancient Church regarding the Church of England is known

sired friendly relations, and possibly hoped that they would join with him, but they did not.[17] This implies that the Ancient Church did not recognize Jacob's ecclesiastical polity as commensurate with their own separatism, for even as late as 1624 they regarded "Mr Iakobs people [as] Idolators in their going to the parish assemblies."[18] Furthermore, on the formation of his own congregation Jacob submitted to re-ordination,[19] and in *A Confession and Protestation* listed twenty-eight Articles, "wherein onely wee dissent from the publique Ecclesiatical order, and doctrine in England."[20]

In fact, Jacob's attitude towards the Church of England was far from hostile, and he refused to separate entirely from the National Church.[21] In *A Confession and Protestation* Jacob rejected "the slander of schism . . . and also of separation" on the basis that his own church recognized the parish churches of England as true churches "in some respect."[22] He stated clearly that he did not refuse to attend the parish church "on occasion."[23] Thus, while Jacob accused the Church of England of false worship, irregular ordination and unjustified episcopal jurisdiction, making impossible his remaining within the National Church, "all communion with them could not be severed without schism from Christian fellowship."[24] Jacob's "independent" church therefore maintained communion with the parish churches, a policy which planted in his congregation an ambiguity which proved an enduring source of tension as the church grew, causing a series of secessions in the 1630s and 1640s. Jacob left the Church in 1622 for Virginia,[25] and John Lathrop[26] succeeded as pastor in 1624.

---

through a Clement Gamble, who betrayed them in 1588–89. See Burrage, *EED* 1, 126.

17. Ibid., 314.

18. Ibid.

19. Stinton No. 1, in *TBHS* 1, 210–11.

20. Jacob, *Confession*, A4.

21. Jacob's initial convictions were Puritan, and non-separatist, as made evident in his discussions with Francis Johnson in 1599. See Jacob, *Defence of the Churches*. His involvement in the Millenary Petition of 1603 sought the Reformation of the Church, not separation from it. For an overview see Dale, *History of English Congregationalism*, 215–17.

22. Jacob, *Confession*, Title page, and article 8.

23. Ibid., B4.

24. Tolmie, *Saints*, 11. Ha describes Jacob's achievement as a "Third Reformation" following the "Second Reformation," namely the protracted Presbyterian assault on episcopacy. Ha, *English Presbyterianism*, 7.

25. *TBHS* 1, 212; Burrage, *EED* 1, 319–20 corrects the date in the margin of the Kiffin manuscript to 1622, as also Whitley in *TBHS* 1, 212–13 n. 10.

26. Lathrop's background is outlined in Tolmie, *Saints*, 16–17.

The first division over the issue of strict separation occurred in 1630[27] when a church member, possibly Sabine Staresmore,[28] had a child baptized in a parish Church to the consternation of a number of members.[29] John Duppa, Daniel Chidley the elder,[30] and others urged renouncing the offending couple, and demanded the church "[d]etest & Protest against ye Parish Churches." The church, however, could not agree on the question of separation, some being unwilling to either affirm or deny the truth of parish churches, "not knowing w^t in time to come God might further manifest to them thereabout." Yet, for peace sake, they all renewed their covenant around a commitment to

> Walke togeather in all ye Ways of God So farr as he hath made known to Us, or shall make known to us, & to forsake all false Ways.[31]

It must have been immediately following this covenant renewal that Duppa, Dyer, and Chidley the elder, with others, organized their own separatist congregation.[32] While their ecclesiology was characterized by radical separatism, they rejected infant baptism on the grounds that the Church of England was a false Church, and their baptism therefore not valid, not yet on the basis of convictions about believer's baptism.

On 12th September 1633 a number in the Lathrop church expressed dissatisfaction over the continuation of semi-separatist policy of relations with Parish churches and sought "dismission."[33] Three reasons for the secession are given in the Jessey memorandum.[34] First, the secessionists denied the "Truth of ye Parish Churches," secondly, "ye Church being now become so large y^t it might be prejudicial." This reason reflects the discovery of the church, arrest and imprisonment of some of the members in April 1632.[35]

27. *TBHS* 1, 219.

28. This is proposed by Burrage, *EED* 1, 177 and 321, but opposed by Tolmie, *Saints*, 201 n. 43. My own reading of the evidence, in A. T., *A Christian Reprofe*, 20, supports the suggestion of Burrage.

29. This is recorded in the "Covenant Renewed" appended to Stinton No. 1. *TBHS* 1, 225.

30. On Chidley see Gentles, "London Levellers," 282–84.

31. *TBHS* 1, 225. See also Rohr, "*Extra Ecclesiam*," 115.

32. Gentiles in the article cited above, mistakes the progress of the Duppa church with the misfortunes of the Lathrop church continuing.

33. *TBHS* 1, 220.

34. For citations See ibid.

35. Whitley gives details of the named members arrested by Tomlinson and subsequently tried based on the records of the Star Chamber and High Commission. See ibid., 214 n. 12.

Thirdly, the secessionists desired to "become an Entire Church & further yᵉ Comūnion of those Churches in Order amongst themselves." This suggests a desire on the part of the leavers to foster relationships with the strict separatist groups formed by the previously exited Duppa and How. These propositions were agreed by the mother church resulting in ten members of Lathrop's congregation initially, and seven later, forming their own stricter congregation.[36]

Among the names of those who left the Lathrop church was Samuel Eaton, and here a supplementary detail is significant: "Mr Eaton with Some others receiving a further Baptism."[37] The precise date and circumstances of this "further baptism" are unknown, except that it was performed by John Spilsbury, and almost certainly by effusion.[38] Furthermore, it cannot be said that Eaton's baptism was "believers' baptism" since the cause of his "anabaptism" was a form of extreme separatism and a rejection of the infant rite he received in a false church, now regarded as invalid. It is incorrect to say, as Burrage states, that the rebaptism was due to antipaedobaptist views,[39] since infant baptism continued to be practiced among them for some time.[40] The argument ran, that if the parish church was a false church its baptism was invalid, and their baptism therefore was not valid.[41]

In 1634 the pastor of the mother church, John Lathrop, petitioned for release from prison on the basis that he would leave England. In June that year he was freed, and with about thirty members of his congregation went

---

36. Ibid., 220,

37. Ibid.

38. See ibid., 221 n. 24. White speculates that Eaton may have been baptized while in prison. See "Samuel Eaton," 12.

39. It appears likely that by 1636 Eaton had come to hold that believer's baptism was the only true form since he was preaching against infant baptism, not merely baptism in an apostate church, during his final imprisonment in Newgate jail in this year. The evidence is the petition of a fellow prisoner, Francis Tucker, a clergyman imprisoned for debt. The petition is transcribed in Burrage, *EED* 2, 325–26. See White, "Samuel Eaton," 13 also the commentary to the Jessey memoranda by Whitley, *TBHS* 1, 221 n. 23.

40. White also suggests Eaton had come to a conviction about believer's baptism by this date, but again this appears to be unlikely. White's argument is based on the conflation of the Jessey memoranda and Stinton no. 2 which makes the evidence appear stronger than it is in reality. See "Samuel Eaton," 12 and 14.

41. See Whitley, *TBHS* 1, 220 n. 23. Following his arrest on 29 April 1632 Eaton suffered greatly at the hands of the authorities, including two long spells of imprisonment. It is likely that this served to harden his attitude into a complete repudiation of the Church of England. See White, "Samuel Eaton," 12. On the reasons for Eaton's baptism see also Bell, "Freedom to Form," in Durston & Maltby, *Religion in Revolutionary England*, 187.

to New England.[42] The church remained without a pastor for three years until the arrival of Henry Jessey.[43] Jessey was a clergyman who had been ejected from his living at Aughton in Yorkshire in 1633 for non-conformity. A year after Jessey joined the church, a number of remaining members who were moving to more radical views about baptism realized the new pastor would not facilitate their desire for believer's baptism and departed the mother church and joined the group overseen by John Spilsbury.[44] The Kiffin Manuscript records:

> 1638. Mr Tho: Wilson, Mr Pen, & H. Pen, & 3 more being convinced that Baptism was not for Infants, but professed Beleivers joined wth Mr Jo: Spilsbury ye Churches favour being desired therein.[45]

The Jessey memorandum explains the departure in this manner:

> 1638. These also being ye same Judgement wth Sam. Eaton & desiring to depart & not to be censured our interest in them was remitted with Prayer made in their behalf June 8th 1638. They having first forsaken Us & Joyned wth Mr Spilsbury.[46]

It is evident from both records that by 1638 discussions in the Jessey church about *who* should be baptized had resulted in an antipaedobaptist contingent coming to a consensus. Thus it can be said that a church which was Calvinistic and Baptist was formed in London not earlier than 1633 and not later than 1638. In terms of the evolution of the first Particular Baptists J. H. Shakespeare accurately stated,

> In 1638 there was either the first Calvinistic Baptist Church, with John Spilsbury as its pastor, containing Samuel Eaton, Mark Lucar, and others, or that in the same year, there were two Calvinistic Baptist Churches in London, the one under John Spilsbury and the other under Samuel Eaton.[47]

---

42. Lathrop's fortunes are described in Paul, "Henry Jacob," 100–104.
43. For details of Jessey see, Wright, "Jessey, Henry," in *ODNB*.
44. How Spilsbury became the leader of this group is unknown. Between 1633 and 1638 he either became the pastor of an independent group with Anabaptist convictions to which Eaton and the other attached themselves, or he had risen to leadership in Eaton's congregation. See Underwood, *HEB*, 58. Tolmie, *Saints*, 25 advances the theory that Spilsbury came out of the Duppa church.
45. Ibid., 231.
46. Ibid., 221.
47. Shakespeare, *Baptist and Congregational Pioneer*, 183.

By May 1640 the Jacob-Lathrop-Jessey church had expanded and could no longer meet in one place without jeopardizing the safe concealment of the congregation. The congregation divided into two "by mutual consent," the last separation before the Civil War, one half continuing under the pastoral leadership of Jessey and the other half under Praisegod Barebone.[48]

In the same year, 1640, Richard Blunt and a number of Spilsbury's church held conference together with a few of Jessey's church and became convinced that baptism by pouring, or sprinkling, was not the method employed by the Apostles, but that true baptism:

> ought to be by dipping ye body into ye water, resembling Burial & riseing again. 2 Col: 2:12 [sic] Rom 6:4.[49]

"Sober conference" was held by the church over this matter, but Spilsbury remained unconvinced, despite Blunt's position being argued from New Testament texts.[50] Those, however, who had come to immersionist views discussed how best to proceed, and conferred with those of Jessey's church who had independently arrived at similar convictions. One decision they made, circa 1641, was to separate from Spilsbury's church and form two congregations united in principle but gathered separately:

> They proceed on therein, viz, Those Persons y^t ware persuaded Baptism should be by dipping ye Body had mett in two Companies, & did intend so to meet after this, all these agreed to proceed alike together. And the Manifesting (not by any formal Words or Covenant) wch word was scrupled by some of them, but by mutual desires & agreement each Testified: Those two Companyes did set apart one to Baptize the rest; So it was solemnly performed by them.[51]

Why it was necessary for these two companies to form independently, who was their leader, where they gathered, and their status as congregations or churches or mere companies, was not detailed.[52] In terms of an emerging

---

48. *TBHS* 1, 232.

49. Ibid., 232. The number "2" prior to the Colossians reference is as transcribed in the Gould manuscript. Crosby has the reference as 2 *Colos* ii.12 and *Rom* v. 4. See *HEB* 1, 102. The origin, authenticity and meaning of the "2" remains a mystery.

50. Whitley suggests the source of the idea may have been *via* John Canne, or Mark Lucar. Whitley, "Revival of Immersion," 31–35.

51. *TBHS* 1, 233.

52. Kilcop, in a later tract dispute with an anonymous "seeker" stated that at this stage these groups of believers did not regard themselves as churches. Kilcop was defending Baptists as conforming in their organization to the primitive pattern, thus he says, "we by the aforesaid ministry were converted, and were also baptized, before we

"Casting Balls of Wildfire into the bosom of the Church" 9

sense of consocation, the relationship between the two companies was not by "formal words or covenant" but by unity of heart and mind, that is, "mutual desires and agreement," the emphasis being on common convictions about the priority of faith and baptism.

This detail in the Kiffin manuscript was a piece of historiography. Written after the Restoration it emphasized that early Baptists had understood the basis of congregating in an orderly manner, namely subsequent to conversion and baptism. Covenanting was rejected as a basis for constituting a church, though it had been sufficient for Henry Jacob in 1616.[53] This is what was meant by the statement that they desired to "Manifest" their unity and agreement by testimony, but not by a "Covenant" or "formal Words," the very word "Covenant" being disagreeable to them. It was "disagreeable" because it was based on an Old Testament concept which was familiar enough to Puritans, while the New Covenant, in the reasoning of the immersionists, was entered by faith and baptism.[54] "Testimony" highlighted the importance of *believer's* baptism, that is, visible faith preceding the sacrament, as the foundational basis for these companies, which was precisely the distinctive and unique characteristic of these emerging Calvinistic Baptist churches.

Discussions held amongst the immersionists about the mode of baptism were hampered by lack of knowledge of other practicing immersionists in England, "none haveing then so so [sic] practised in England to professed Believers."[55] The dipping of infants was legal and still practiced in parts of England, though rarely so, but this offered no help to Blunt.[56] It is also now known that the General Baptists came to convictions about the immersion of new members about this time, but relations between the two groups were poor, and either the Particular Baptists associated with Blunt did not know the General's advance in baptismal practice, or would not consult them

---

congregated." *Unlimited Authority of Christ's Disciples*, 17.

53. See the Jessey memorandum: "Those who minded this present Union & so joining together jolyned both hands each wth other Brother and stood in a Ringwise : their intent being declared, H Jacob and the Rest made some confession or Profession of their Faith & Repentance . . . Then they Covenanted together to walk in all God's Ways as he had revealed or should make known to them." *TBHS* 1, 209.

54. See ibid., 210 n. 5.

55. Ibid., 232–33. There was a man baptized by immersion known to the Particular Baptists, John Canne. He was with the Broadmead Church in 1641. See Underhill, *Records of a Church of Christ*, 18. Canne was also linked to the London church of Lathrop in 1630, according to Stinton no. 1, *TBHS* 1, 225. Canne was therefore probably the link between the Jessey church, the Collegiants, and discussions about believer's baptism by immersion. See Whitley, "Revival of Immersion," 33–34.

56. Details and accounts of infant baptism by immersion are given in Champlin Burrage, *EED* 1, 331 n. 1. See also Harrison, "Renewal of the Practice," 108–9.

on this matter.[57] What is not clear from this comment is whether the immersionists were troubled by lack of wider consultation about this matter and did not want to proceed into, for them, unchartered sacramental water. Or, whether they had settled on the necessity of immersion and desired to receive the rite from some communion already practicing this form of baptism. This was the opinion of Crosby, who stated on the authority of Edward Hutchinson, that they decided:

> to send over to the foreign *Anabaptists*, who descended from the antient *Waldenses* in *France* or *Germany*, that so one or more receiving *baptism* from them, might become proper *administrators* of it to others.[58]

This successionist version of events was repeated by Crosby in a further description of Blunt's visit to the Collegiants,[59] and his return to Kiffin, and in regard to the main details it shows some dependence on the Kiffin Manuscript. From his supposed source, Crosby writes of the English immersionists of 1642,

> those who followed this *scheme* did not derive their *baptism* from the aforesaid Mr. *Smith*, or his congregation at *Amsterdam*, it being an antient congregation of foreign *Baptists* in the *Low Countries* to whom they sent.[60]

Wherever Crosby derived this view of the origins of immersion among the Baptists it was not from Stinton's transcript of the Kiffin manuscript.

According to Stinton no.2, Richard Blunt was sent to Holland, probably in the latter half of 1641, possibly at the suggestion of John Canne, and because he understood the Dutch language. There he consulted with a group of Rynsburgers, or Collegiants, in Leyden who had revived the practice of baptism by immersion as a result of contact with the immersionist Polish Minor Brethren.[61] The Kiffin Manuscript implies that he went on this journey alone, but other evidence proves there were others in a party of

---

57. See Wright, "Baptist Alignments Part 1," 266, and "Baptist Alignments Part 2," 346–48.

58. Crosby, *HEB* 1, 100. Italics as in original. See Hutchinson, *Treatise Concerning the Covenant and Baptism.*

59. The Rijnsburger Collegiants were a lay movement of those dissatisfied with the measures advocated by the Remonstranten at the Synod of Dort. They survived 1620–1780s. See Harrison, "Renewal of the Practice," 107; also Durnbaugh, "Baptists and Quakers," 73–75.

60. Ibid., 102–3. Italics as original.

61. See Whitley, "Revival of Immersion," 31–35. Also, Williams, *Radical Reformation,* 788.

investigation.⁶² Upon his return the two immersionist companies appear to have made a decision to "proceed on therein" and according to the record,

> Those two Companyes did set apart one to Baptize the rest; so it was solemnly performed by them. Mr Blunt Baptized Mr Blacklock yt was a Teacher amongst them, & Mr Blunt being Baptized, he and Mr Blacklock Baptized ye rest of their friends that ware so minded, & many being added to them they increased much.⁶³

The administration of Blunt's baptism, the fact of which is clearly emphasized in the passage, has been the source of much speculation.⁶⁴ On the basis of Crosby, historians⁶⁵ assumed he had been baptized by the John Batte, or Jan Batten,⁶⁶ spoken of in the transcript.⁶⁷ Jessey, writing ten years after the event, stated that Blunt was not baptized when he returned to restore the practice in England, though he does not say by whom he was baptized.⁶⁸ White argued that Blunt baptized himself.⁶⁹ Burrage takes the opposite view, stating that, "it is well known that Blunt did not baptize himself." His evidence is the statement published anonymously in 1681,

> He [Shem Acher, i.e. Francis Bampfield] has been credibly informed by two yet alive in this city of *London*, who were Members of the first Church of the Baptized [i.e. immersed] Believers here, that their first Administrator [of immersion] was one who baptized himself, or else he and another baptized one another and so gathered a Church.⁷⁰

On the basis of this witness Burrage concluded that Blunt was immersed by Blacklock. The ambiguity surrounding the circumstances of Blunt's baptism has been taken as deliberate by Stephen Wright.⁷¹ Wright argues that the author's purpose in this passage may have been to reassure

---

62. See Wright, "Baptist Alignments," 279 n. 31. The sources are Praisegod Barbon, E. Hutchinson and *Anti-Quakerism*.

63. *TBHS* 1, 233–34.

64. See for e.g., Durnbaugh, "Baptists and Quakers," 73–75.

65. So Ivimey, Whitsitt, Barclay, Lofton, Scheffer, Newman, Williams and Estep. See Wright, *EEB*, 85 n. 40.

66. The exact name is disputed, but is unimportant for the immediate purpose.

67. Dutch studies of the Collegiants assert the baptism of Blunt by Batten. See Durnbaugh, "Baptists and Quakers," 75 n. 21.

68. Jessey, *Storehouse of Provision*, 188.

69. White, *English Baptists*, 61.

70. Burrage, *EED* 1, 334 n. 1.

71. Wright, "Baptist Alignments," 268.

readers that Blunt *was* baptized, thus emphasizing that Blacklock, and three future leaders of Baptist churches who signed the 1644 London Confession, Thomas Kilcop, Thomas Sheppard and Thomas Munday, were not rebaptized by an unbaptized administrator.

Stinton no. 2 records that during January 1642 some fifty-three people were baptized by these two men and the names of the baptized listed under the respective baptizer. This document in Stinton's record finishes with the comment,

> Those that ware so minded had communion together were become Seven Churches in London.[72]

One of these churches was known later by the name of its baptizer and some of the baptized as the Blunt, Emmes, and Wrighter Church.[73] Another church, referred to in Stinton no. 2, was that led by Mr Green with Capt Spencer which had begun in Crutched Fryers in 1639.[74] According to the record, it was when these seven churches were defamed as, "unsound in Doctrine as if they were Armenians" as well as holding Anabaptist convictions they joined together to publish "a Confession of their Faith in fifty-two Articles wch gave great satisfaction to many that had been prejudiced."[75] This document was published in October 1644 as a confession, an *apologia* for their life and doctrine. The substance of the Confession will be discussed throughout the work.

In the Jessey church, the issue of believer's baptism resurfaced in 1643, this time precipitated by a question about the validity of infant baptism.[76] In the Stinton manuscript no. 4, headed *Debate on Infant Baptism, 1643*, it is recorded,

---

72. *TBHS* 1, 235.

73. Edwards, *Third Part of Gangraena*, 112. On his opposition to dissenters and separatists see Hughes, *Gangraena and the Struggle for the English Revolution* also Watts, *Dissenters* 1, 87f; also Birch, "Particular Baptists in the 1640s through the Eyes of their Enemies," 25–38.

74. See *TBHS* 1, 235.

75. Ibid., 235–36.

76. For the purpose of clarity, Whitley's synopsis of the succession of baptismal questions in the J-L-J church is worth restating. In 1630 Dupper, and 1633 Lucar, asked, "Is baptism by the parish clergy sufficient, or must there be a new baptism on profession of belief? 1640, Blunt, Kilcop, Lukar, Blaiklock, Munden, Skippard asked: Is baptism anything but immersion? Now arises a complement of the first question; 1643, Knowles [i.e. Knollys]: May infants be baptized at all?" In 1644 the final question was: "Is any qualification for the administrator needful except ability to teach and evangelize?" *TBHS* 1, 240 n. 1.

> Hanserd Knollys our Brother not being satisfied from Baptizing his child, after it had bin endeavoured by ye Elder, & by one or two more; himself referred to ye Church then that they might satisfye him, or he rectify them if amiss herein; wch was well accepted.[77]

A former Church of England clergyman, Knollys, had joined the church in 1641 and subsequently had scruples about the baptism of his child, and so referred the matter to the church for their discernment.[78] After several conferences Knollys persuaded a number of the congregation to his views, some of whom joined the Church of which Kiffin was pastor, and others formed themselves into a new church with Knollys as pastor. Having no state support, Knollys provided for himself in the ministry by opening a school and joining fellow Baptist pastor William Kiffin in the woolen trade.[79] With the help of a number of assistants Knollys served his church until his death aged ninety-three.

To conclude the account of the emergence and evolution of the Particular Baptists to the publication of the First London Confession it is possible to identify several congregations born from the mother church of Jacob-Lathorp-Jessey. The earliest secession was that led by John Duppa and resulted in a church committed to strict separatist Independency. The second Independent church was formed from the division of the Lathrop church in 1633, again over the question of the need for strict separatism. Subsequent to his release from prison in 1634 Samuel Eaton became a preacher among this group, though whether he became its pastor, as Tolmie states,[80] cannot be determined with certainty. This church dissolved in 1639 following Eaton's death and some of the members appear to have returned to the Jessey church.[81] A third church was led by John Spilsbury, the origins of which remain a mystery,[82] but which by 1638 was attracting separatists from the

---

77. Ibid., 240.

78. Tolmie dates Knollys's joining of Jessey's church to 1641 based on the memoires of Kiffin, who states Knollys died on 19th September 1691 after fifty years ministry to one London congregation. Knollys states "I was then Pastor." See Kiffin, *Life and Death of Mr Knollys*, Epistle to the Reader. This is at odds with the Stinton manuscript which dates Knollys's membership to 1643–4. See Tolmie, *Saints*, 44, and *TBHS* 1, 254.

79. Kiffin, *Life and Death of Mr. Knollys*, Epistle to the Reader A3.

80. Tolmie, *Saints*, 22.

81. This is a widely held conjecture based on the association of Blunt and Kiffin with Jessey in 1640 when they were known to have been formerly with the Eaton congregation.

82. In published extracts from his PhD thesis, Thompson suggests Spilsbury was part of the Duppa split from the J-L-J church in 1630, later baptized Eaton and his group, and around 1633 had his own congregation of Reformed, baptized believers.

Jacob-Lathrop-Jessey church convinced of the need to move on to believer's baptism.[83] A fourth church appears to have been organized in 1639 on the basis of this detail in Stinton no. 2,

> 1639 Mr Green wth Capt Spencer had begun a Congregation in Crutched Fryers, to whom Paul Hobson joined who was now wth many of that Church one of ye Seven.[84]

The name Paul Hobson appears on the London Confession of 1644 as one of the signatories of one of the seven subscribing churches.

In 1641 two more companies had formed around Richard Blunt and Samuel Blacklock on the basis of a conviction regarding baptism by immersion. The manner of the progression of these two companies into churches is lost, but in time Richard Blunt became the Pastor of one, and Thomas Kilcop became pastor of the other. Following shortly after the great immersion ceremony conducted by Blunt and Blacklock, John Spilsbury also became convinced of believer's baptism by immersion and instituted the practice in his own church. Thus by the end of 1642 at least three churches in London practiced believer's baptism among its members.

What this section has shown is that in the formative period up to the publication of the First London Confession in 1644, the independent congregation founded by Henry Jacob not only survived persecution from without[85] and secession from within, but birthed around eight other separate Calvinistic Baptist churches in London.[86] In the next section the fortunes of the Particular Baptists from the time of the 1644 Confession to the restoration of the monarchy in 1660 will be outlined.

1.2. Particular Baptist Expansion, 1644–1660

In the 1640s and 1650s Particular Baptists witnessed considerable growth in numbers as their cause expanded beyond the boundaries of London, the result of preaching, public disputations, publishing and missionary evangelism. A measure of their progress was that by 1660 there were approximately

---

There are gaps in the theory, and much of it remains conjecture. See Thompson, *Outside the Camp*, 44–46.

83. This is explicitly stated in Stinton no. 2. See *TBHS* 1, 231.

84. Ibid., 235.

85. The seizure of Lathrop's congregation in 1632 by Tomlinson, the pursuivant of Laud, bishop of London, is recounted in *TBHS* 1, 214–15. Other persecutions are listed in *TBHS* 1, 222–25. See also, Orme, *Remarkable Passages*, 15–19.

86. Eight churches signed the second edition of the London Confession in 1646 and had clearly been in existence some time prior to this date.

131 Particular Baptist churches in existence.[87] The initial burgeoning of the Baptists was witnessed by the Scots Commissioner Robert Baillie who reported on the alarming increase of the Independents in London in December 1643 and added, "but the Anabaptists more, and the Antinomians most."[88] Three years later Baillie wrote again of the expansion of the Baptists in his 1646 tract, *Anabaptism the true fountain of error*,

> Their number in *England* till of late was not great; and the most of these were not *English*, but *Dutch* strangers; . . . [But] under this shelter [of Independency] the Anabaptists have lift up their head, and increased their numbers, much above all other sects of the land.
> . . . As for the members whether of these seven [churches which published their confession of faith], or of their other thirty-nine congregations (for before the penning of that confession this sect was said to be grown unto no lesse than forty six churches, and that as I take it within and about *London*) they are a people very zealous of liberty, and most to be under the bondage of the judgement of any other.[89]

The importance of personal and political *de facto* liberty[90] as a key factor in the growth of Baptists in this period of history is highlighted by McGregor, who argues that the sect type of religion, of which Baptists were a prime example, "offered élite spiritual status," to masses of people who were caught up in the social revolution of the time.[91] He contends that commitment to a sect was effectively an expression of "religious self-determination, the assertion of individual independence by wife, child or servant,"[92] that is, by those who otherwise had small opportunity for liberty of any sort. Political uncertainty in the 1640s and 1650s meant, "the Baptists were able to gather many of these victims of economic and social change into a mass evangelical movement."[93] Thus it is to economic and social factors, a sense of empowerment for the "dispossessed, underprivileged, and disinherited,"[94]

---

87. Whitley, "Baptist Churches," *TBHS* II (1920–1911), 236–54. See also Watts, *Dissenters* 1, 160 n. 3 who corrects Whitley's list at a number of points, rightly reclassifying some "Baptist" churches as Congregationalist.

88. Baillie, *Letters and Journals* I, 408, 437.

89. Baillie, *Anabaptism the true fountaine of . . . Errors*, 18, 49. The "confession of faith" referred to by is the First London Confession reprinted in 1646.

90. On the legal situation see Coffey, *Persecution and Toleration*, 134–60.

91. McGregor, "Baptists: Fount of All Heresy," 48.

92. Ibid., 47.

93. Ibid., 49.

94. Cited in Ibid., 48. The categories are from Niebuhr, *Social Sources of*

more than theological principles, that McGregor attributes the appeal of the early Baptists.

For clues about the social status of early Baptists we are mainly reliant on the propaganda of their enemies. Daniel Featley sniped in regard to Baptist gatherings, "a brewers Clerk exerciseth, A Taylor expoundeth, A Waterman Teacheth—the lowest of the people."[95] Thomas Edwards asked Parliament to consider,

> Is it fitting that well meaning Christians should be suffered to goe and make Churches, and then proceed to chuse whom they will for Ministers, as some Taylor, Felt maker, Button-maker, men ignorant, and low in parts, by whom they shall be led into sinne and errors[?][96]

It is true that Baptist proselytizing was generally most successful among the lower social strata, but it is also true that while members may have experienced a degree of empowerment once inside the church fellowship, entrance remained strictly contingent on "a declaration of an experimental work of the Spirit upon the heart."[97]

The geographical expansion of the Calvinistic Baptists throughout the 1650s is illustrated by the endeavors of the London leadership to locate, and extend pastoral care, to the burgeoning number of Baptist causes springing up throughout England, Ireland, Scotland and Wales. This is evident from the Kiffin *et al.* letter of 24 June 1653, written to a number of strategically located churches, wherein it said:

> wee intreat your care and paines in visiting the severall weake and scattered brethren in your parts, that from a thorough knowledg of, and acquaintance with, theire present standing, wee may receive information from you and our brethren in Ireland, according to their desires, from us: what churches and societies wee may groundedly communicate with, according to a rule of Christ, and what not.[98]

It is further stated:

> Our great design in this letter is to obtain a full knowledge of all the churches in England, Scotland and Wales and, therefore, wee desire you not to forget to informe us not only concerning

---

Denominationalism, especially chaps 2 and 3.

95. Featley, *Dippers dipt*, B4 Preface.
96. Edwards, *Reasons Against Toleration*, 23.
97. *ARPB*, 56.
98. Ibid., 111.

the estates of any churches that are in your country or neere adjacent that soe, if it may be possible, wee might have the full knowledge of all the churches or saints that are one with us in the sound principles of the truth.[99]

One region where Baptists prospered greatly was Ireland.[100] By 1653 there were ten Particular Baptist churches in Dublin, Waterford, Clommell [Clonmell], Killkenny, Corke, Lymrick, Galloway, Wexford, Kerry, and Carrick Fergus,[101] comprised almost entirely of soldiers settled in military precincts.[102] Influential Baptists in Ireland included Thomas Patient,[103] who in 1644 had signed the First London Confession. Having travelled to Ireland with the army in 1649, in the early 1650s Patient evangelized throughout the country,[104] and possibly organized a church at Clough Keating in Tipperary.[105] Another was Christopher Blackwood, known as "the oracle of the anabaptists in Ireland,"[106] and another, Benjamin Cox. The Baptists in Ireland cultivated their own identity, which was fervently eschatological, apart from London influence.[107]

Such apocalyptic ideas as the Irish were expressing made conservative leaders in London, like Kiffin, nervous. In January 1654, Kiffin, Spilsbery and Joseph Fansom wrote to the Irish Baptists urging patience and humble acceptance of the new political order which had brought Cromwell to power as Protector.[108]

The growth of Particular Baptists in the period 1645–60 can be attributed to a number of activities which did not go unnoticed by their enemies. Thomas Edwards issued a warning to magistrates of their strategies in his polemical diatribe *Gangraena*. Exhorting magistrates to do their duty he suggested:

99. Ibid., 112.
100. See Whitley, "The Plantation of Ireland," 276–81.
101. See *ARPB*, 119–21.
102. Whitley, "Plantation of Ireland," 279.
103. Greaves, "Patient, Thomas (d. 1666)," in *ODNB*.
104. Ivimey, *History of the English Baptists* 1, 234.
105. Whitley, *HBB*, 190. This is based on the record of Crosby, and cannot otherwise be verified.
106. Thurloe, *State Papers*, 4:90. Letter of Thomas Harrison dated 1655.
107. *ARPB*, 115.
108. See Nickolls, *Original Letters and Papers of State*, 159–60. That this letter was written to the Irish Baptists is confirmed by a report from Henry Cromwell to Secretary Thurloe on 8 March 1654. See Thurloe, *State Papers*, 2:149.

they should execute some exemplary punishment upon some of the most notorious sectaries and seducers, and upon the wilful abetters of these abominable errors, namely the printers, dispersers, and licencers, and set themselves with all their hearts to find out ways, to take some course to suppress, hinder, and no longer suffer these things: to put out some declaration against the errors and ways of the sectaries; and their sending emissaries into all parts of the kingdom, to poison the countries; as their dipping of persons in the cold water in winter, whereby persons fall sick, &c.;[109]

This statement highlights the three primary methods by which the Baptists were advancing their cause, namely publishing and pamphleteering, public disputation and missionary evangelism. To this list might be added the regular preaching of Baptist pastors which was known on occasions to attract considerable crowds.

1.2.1. Publishing

The middle decades of the seventeenth century have been described as a period of unprecedented productivity, and influence, of the published word in English cultural history.[110] The proliferation of publications in this era is attributed to the breakdown of pre-publication censorship in 1641,[111] which provided a new opportunity to disseminate ideas, beliefs, and opinions more widely.[112] In 1600 the annual output of printing in England was less than three hundred titles, in 1642 it was around three thousand.[113] Between 1640 and 1661 George Thomason collected twenty-two thousand publications comprising broadsides, tracts, pamphlets and books.[114]

---

109. *Gangraena* 1, 98.

110. Keeble, *Cambridge Companion*, 1. See also Barnard, "London Publishing, 1640–1660," 1–16; Corns, "Literature and History," in Coward, *Companion to Stuart Britain*, 166–86.

111. The zenith of publishing censorship was the Star Chamber decree of 1637. In that year, for pamphlets published against the innovations Archbishop Laud, William Prynne, Henry Burton and John Bastwick were pilloried, had their ears lopped off, fined £5000 and sentenced to perpetual imprisonment. Burton, imprisoned in Guernsey Castle, was denied ink, pen, and paper to prevent further publishing. Unregulated publishing only lasted until the Licensing Order of 14 June 1643, which again required all books and pamphlets to be approved by an appointed censor. A contemporary response to the Act was John Milton, *Areopagitica*.

112. See Coffey, *Persecution and Toleration*, 144.

113. Statistics are given in Keeble, *Cambridge Companion to Writing*, 1–2, 51.

114. See Achinstein, "Texts in Conflict," in Keeble, *Cambridge Companion*, 50–51.

Baptists were among those eager to participate fully in debates of the time by means of print, and in the period 1640 to 1660 their publications were in excess of ninety works.[115] The most prolific of authors among the Particular Baptists was Thomas Collier, his works in this twenty year period running to around thirty items.[116] Their most important publication was the *First London Confession* of 1644, reissued in 1646, 1651 and 1652. Print also gave a voice to women among the Baptists, thereby allowing them to participate in public discourse on matters religious and political.[117] Sarah Wight[118] was associated with the congregation of Henry Jessey, who edited her prophetic writings. Indeed her testimony and visions were only made available to a wider Christian readership on account of their publication under the name of Henry Jessey.[119] Elizabeth Poole[120] was another female among the Particular Baptists who exercised a prophetic ministry beyond the bounds of the church or congregation. A member of Kiffin's church from about sixteen years of age, she was expelled from the congregation for heresy and immorality[121] some time before 1648. Poole moved to Abingdon where she came into contact with John Pendarves, minister of the Abingdon Baptist congregation, and his wife Thomasine. Possibly through Pendarves,[122] Poole came into contact with the army which led to a brief season of prominence in national political affairs.[123] Her words were published in the tract *An Alarum of War, Given to the Army*. Jane Turner, connected to the church of John Spilsbury,[124] also channeled her ministry through the written word, as she expounded the experience of grace in her *conversion narrative*.[125]

---

115. The source of this estimate is Whitley, *Baptist Bibliography*, 1:17–65.

116. See Land, "Doctrinal Controversies," 341–62.

117. See Laurence, "Priesthood of She-Believers," 348; Freeman, *Company of Women Preachers*; and Mack, *Visionary Women*.

118. "Wight, Sarah (*b.* 1631)," Bullock in *ODNB*.

119. See Jessey, *Exceeding Riches*. Also, Dailey, "Visitation of Sarah Wight," 438–55.

120. See *"Poole, Elizabeth (bap. 1622?, d. in or after 1668),"* Brod in *ODNB*. The historiography of Poole's life and ministry is discussed by Kreitzer, *William Kiffen and His World (Part 2)*, 262–89.

121. Charges she denied. Mack, *Visionary Women*, 98.

122. See Kreitzer, "Fifth Monarchist John Pendarves," 112–22.

123. It is also suggested by Gentles, that Poole came into contact with the General Council via Colonel Nathaniel Rich, and Underdown suggests Cromwell was the nexus. Lack of evidence makes the question indeterminable. See Nevitt, "Elizabeth Poole Writes the Regicide," 235.

124. In his preface to her work *Choice Experiences*, Spilsbery [*sic*] described Jane Turner as "a Daughter of Zion," and "a Mother in Israel." See *To the Christian Reader*, i.

125. Turner, *Choice Experiences*.

By means of publishing Baptists found a voice for explaining and defending their theological, ecclesiastical and social commitments to the wider public. In respect of theology, Baptists were concerned to demonstrate their adherence to the Calvinist consensus, ecclesiologically to deny relations to Continental Anabaptists, and politically to assert they were no threat to the civil government.[126] Their success in winning greater acceptance was mixed, however their willingness to engage in written debate brought them further into the mainstream of public discourse.

1.2.2. Preaching

In the 1640s, Independent and Baptist preaching was referred to as, "this new kinde of talking trade, which many ignorant coxcombes call preaching."[127] Since preaching was hardly an innovation by the time of the Civil War,[128] the remark likely reflected clerical disgust at the rising popularity of unlearned, non-ordained, sectarian practitioners.[129] The target on this occasion was three men at one time associated with the Jessey congregation, Green the feltmaker, Spencer the horserubber,[130] and Barebones the leather seller. The popularity of such men is suggested in the appendix to Taylor's tract, *New Preachers*, where he describes a thousand people gathering to hear the preaching of "Mr. *Barebones* a reverend unlearned Letherseller."[131] Thomas Edwards makes reference to gatherings at Hanserd Knollys' church, next door to the parish church of St Helen Bishopsgate, where according to the neighbours, as many as a thousand gathered each Sunday to hear him preach.[132]

---

126. This is not meant to imply that theology and politics were regarded separately by Baptists, but only that these three purposes are evident individually in the First London Confession. See, Introductory Letter and *passim*.

127. Taylor, *New Preachers*, title page.

128. See Hill, *Society and Puritanism*, 16–58.

129. Taylor's primary grievance concerns the lack of ordination, which means an absence of authority to preach. Taylor, *New Preachers*, A2.

130. Green and Spencer are named in Stinton number 2 as having begun a congregation in Crutched Fryers in 1639. *TBHS* 1, 235. By 1644 Paul Hobson had joined this congregation.

131. Taylor, *New Preachers*, Appendix, entitled, "A brief touch, in memory of the fiery zeale of Mr Barebones."

132. Edwards, *Gangraena*, 1.98. Tolmie questions the accuracy of Edwards on this point, suggesting, "It is unlikely that Knollys had had a thousand members in his church ... The explanation of Edwards's information is probably that the meeting of Knollys's church ... were open to the public." Tolmie, *Saints*, 60. See also Hughes, *Gangraena*, 7.

The social and political significance of preaching in the seventeenth century was of such magnitude that control of pulpits was of great concern to Parliament[133] and on 26 April 1645, the house passed the Ordinance, "None to Preach but Ordained Ministers and Candidates," stating:

> It is this day Ordained and Declared by the Lords and Commons in Parliament assembled, That no person be permitted to preach who is not Ordained a Minister, either in this or some other Reformed Church, except such (as intending the Ministry) shall be allowed for the trial of their Gifts by those who shall be appointed thereunto by both Houses of Parliament.[134]

The impact of the Ordinance on sectarian preachers was negligible, as is evident from the case of Paul Hobson. Among Particular Baptists, Hobson was one of the most notable preachers of the time.[135] A measure of his ability is the testimony of Laurence Claxton [Lawrence Clarkson], who remembered first hearing Hobson and the impact it made on him:

> At which time *Paul Hobson* brake forth with such expressions of the in-comes and out-goes of God, that my soul much desired such a gift of preaching, which after a while *Hobson* and I being acquainted . . . so that thither I went, and there tarried a soldier with them, at which time I had a small gift of Preaching, and so by degrees increased into a method, that I attempted the pulpit at Mr. *Wardels* Parish in *Suffolk*.[136]

According to Thomas Edwards, Hobson would preach publicly in any pulpit to which he could gain access, and privately to the soldiers, and his influence spread as his regiment moved between London, Yarmouth and Bristol.[137] When based in London, Edwards records that Hobson's usual practice was, "Every *Wednesday* in *Finsbury-fields* in *Checker-alley* in the Afternoon he preaches."[138] Tolmie supposes this was at the church founded by Knollys at Finsbury Fields, and that Knollys was offering an imitation of

---

133. See Hill, *Century of Revolution*, 75–77.

134. *Acts and Ordinances*, 677.

135. Edwards, *Gangraena*, 1. 33–34. See Hill, *A Turbulent, Seditious, and Factious People*, 53. On Hobson, see Whitley, "Rev. Colonel Paul Hobson," 307–10; "Hobson, Paul (d. 1666)," Greaves in *ODNB*.

136. Claxton, *Lost Sheep Found*, 10.

137. Whitley, "Rev. Colonel Paul Hobson," 307.

138. Edwards, *Gangraena*, part 1, 34. Emphasis as per original.

the conventional weekday puritan lectures.[139] It is known that he was also active in evangelism in Exeter during 1646.[140]

In the summer of 1645, Hobson, together with Captain Beaumont, was arrested for illicit preaching in Newport Pagnell,[141] "in contempt of the Ordinance of Parliament made the last April."[142] Hobson was questioned by the Governor of Newport Pagnell, Sir Samuel Luke, who sent both Hobson and Beaumont to Fairfax for punishment. To Luke's annoyance Fairfax released Hobson with only a warning, which he promptly ignored by returning immediately to Newport Pagnell to resume preaching.[143] This was something of a test case, and henceforth no general opposition to laymen preaching arose.[144]

Enemies of Baptists, such as John Taylor, and others, realized that sectarian preaching aroused great interest and excitement among the wider public and for this reason he despaired that their conventicles were training grounds for other uneducated preachers, recording:

> as one of them told the Lords in Parliament: that they were all preachers for so they practice and exercise themselves as young players doe in private, till they bee by their brethren judged fit for the pulpit, and then up they goe, and like Mountebankes play their parts.[145]

The democratization of preaching was giving to Baptists an appeal to those who desired to participate in the practice of religion. The fervent manner of their preaching was a crucial component in their growth as it drew sizeable audiences into their circle of influence.

1.2.3. Disputations

According to Ann Hughes, disputations during the Interregnum bear witness to the "fluid marketplace that religion in England had become, and

---

139. Tolmie, *Saints*, 60.

140. White, *English Baptists*, 72.

141. Newport Pagnell was on the frontier of Parliament's Eastern Association and a fiercely contested territory during the first years of the Civil War. See Hill, *Turbulent, Seditious, and Factious People*, 45–53.

142. Edwards, *Gangraena*, part 1, 33.

143. Ibid., 89-91. See also Hill, *Turbulent, Seditious, and Factious People*, 50.

144. See Whitley, "Rev. Colonel Paul Hobson," 307.

145. Taylor, *New Preachers*, A3.

"Casting Balls of Wildfire into the bosom of the Church" 23

of the willingness of orthodox Puritans to compete in it."[146] By competing in the arena of religious truth, Baptists, along with other sectarians, proselytized for their understanding of the Gospel and their style of Church, ministry and sacraments.[147]

The starting point of the period of disputations was 1641,[148] the year in which the High Commission and Star Chamber were abolished. With the demise of the primary instruments of royal and ecclesiastical oppression, Baptists were emboldened to propagate their convictions. A disputation at Ashford in Kent on 27 July 1649, between Samuel Fisher and several clergymen on the subject of infant baptism, drew a crowd of around two thousand people. On 9 October 1674, a number of Baptists including William Kiffin disputed with Quakers regarding the Person of Christ and the inner light when, "thousands were present."[149] By means of these disputations, new members were drawn to the Baptist cause, including about a score of clergymen who left the Church of England becoming ardent propagandists of Baptist principles.[150] John Tombs[151] came to antipaedobaptist views as a result of a disputation at Bristol in 1642,[152] later becoming a disputant in defense of believer's baptism.[153]

Disputations also generated a flurry of pamphlets and sermons, thereby multiplying the effect of the controversy and drawing greater attention to the Baptist message.[154] One notorious pamphlet controversy was that conducted between John Bunyan and the Quaker Edward Burrough during 1656–57.[155] Another was that, discovered by Geoffrey Nuttall, between

---

146. Hughes, "Pulpit Guarded," in Laurence, Owens, Sim, *John Bunyan*, 49.

147. These were central to the dispute between Thomas Collier and Francis Fullwood. See Hughes, Ibid., 50.

148. See Langley, "Seventeenth Century Baptist Disputations," 216–43.

149. See ibid., 226, 236.

150. *HBB*, 70.

151. Tombs' identity as a Baptist is questionable as he remained the vicar of Leominster from 1649 until his ejection in 1662. The fluidity of church affairs during the period of the parliament of saints meant that the vicar of Leominster could bring several Baptist churches into being in the West of England, and provide men for their ministry. After his ejection in 1662 the Bishop of Hereford wrote, "The only considerable Non Subscriber is the proud Anabaptist Toms, than whom I never knew a prouder, the very child of old Marcion." See ibid., 69

152. See ibid., 69; Langley, "Seventeenth Century Disputations," 222.

153. Thomas, *History of the Baptist Association*, 10.

154. See Langley, "Seventeenth Century Disputations," 232, 237.

155. Bunyan, *Vindication of the Book*. See also Hughes, "Pulpit Guarded," 31–32.

Thomas Collier and John Smith in 1651, concerning the doctrine of the person of Christ.[156]

Arthur Langley has identified the dates of ninety-one disputations,[157] and also the various locations of one hundred and five, which included the Shire Hall in Cambridge, numerous prisons and orchards.[158] The total during the commonwealth period was sixty-one, suggesting that the liberty Baptists experienced in this period was fully exploited in the advancement of their cause.

Baptist disputations were mainly with clergymen concerning questions about infant baptism,[159] the Trinity, the Church, the Person of Christ, the parousia of Christ, universal redemption, election, the resurrection of the body, the right of private persons to undertake public preaching, Church government and discipline, Original Sin, the immortality and immateriality of the soul, and admission of the Jews into England.[160] At least thirty two were with Quakers.[161] Both Thomas Collier and Samuel Eaton feature in the polemical disputes between Baptists and Quakers during the 1650s over scripture, perfectibility and the inner light.[162]

One of the most famous verbal disputations in which Baptists engaged was that between Daniel Featley and four Baptists in Southwark in 1642, details of which were published by Featley in 1644.[163] The principal disputant for the Baptists was William Kiffin,[164] at this time pastor of the church formerly led by Samuel Eaton, and the substance of the dispute concerned the lawfulness of infant baptism according to scripture or apostolic tradition. The opening statement was made by a "Scotchman" who took the role of "opponent," setting the question to which Featley was required to respond:[165]

---

156. See Nuttall, "Thomas Collier," 40–41.

157. Hughes notes that there are many more than the ninety-one counted by Langley. Works such as Edwards' *Gangraena* and Fox's *Journal* have many accounts. See Hughes, "Pulpit Guarded," 36 n. 7.

158. Langley, "Seventeenth Century Disputations," 221.

159. For example, see White, "Two Early Propagandists," 167–70.

160. See Langley, "Seventeenth Century Disputations," 220–21; Hughes, "The Pulpit Guarded," 34; Nuttall, "Thomas Collier," 40–41.

161. Hughes, "Pulpit Guarded," *passim*.

162. Ibid., 33.

163. Featley, *Dippers dipt*, 1–19.

164. Langley states that Kiffin was veteran of six contests. "Seventeenth Century Disputations," 218.

165. For the formal structure of medieval disputations, which follows the pattern laid down by Aristotle see Mikko Yrjönsuuri, "Disputations," 205–9.

> Mr. Doctor, We come to Dispute with you at this time, not for Contention sake, but to receive satisfaction. We hold that the Baptism of Infants cannot be proved lawful by the testimony of Scripture, or by Apostolicall Tradition; if you therefore can prove the same either way, we shall willingly submit unto you.[166]

The question surprised Featley, who had anticipated a debate about ecclesiastical customs, and his initial response was to accuse his interlocutor of being an Anabaptist, "[which] is a heresy."[167] From this point the debate ranged over a number of subjects including the Trinity, the nature of the visible church, baptismal regeneration, and the nature of scripture. The disputation ended when "it grew late, and the conference broke up," neither side able to claim clear victory.[168]

Another much publicized debate was planned for December 1645, between Benjamin Cox, William Kiffin and Hanserd Knollys, and Edmund Calamy with other Presbyterians in opposition. The debate was cancelled when the Lord Mayor of London became concerned about the threat of violence. The Baptists subsequently published their arguments in the tract, *A Declaration Concerning the Publike Dispute Which should have been in the Publike Meeting-House of Alderman-Bury, the 3d of this instant Moneth of December: Concerning Infants-Baptisme. Together, with some of the Arguments which should then have been propounded and urged by some of those that are falsely called Anabaptists, which should then have disputed*.[169] A year later a debate about similar issues took place at Trinity Church Coventry, between Knollys and Kiffin, and the Rev. John Bryan DD, Vicar of Trinity Church, and the Rev. Obadiah Grew, MA, DD, Vicar of St Michael's Coventry.[170]

In her study of public disputes in 1640s and 1650s, Ann Hughes notes that most educated clergymen were reluctant participants in debates with sectaries. They often felt they were degrading themselves by disputing with the unlearned.[171] In addition, many clergymen believed that engaging Baptists in debate gave legitimacy to their opponent's views.[172] This is a tacit

166. Featley, *Dippers dipt*, 1. Italics as in original.
167. Ibid., 1.
168. Ibid., 1–19.
169. Anon.
170. See Whitley, *Baptist Bibliography* 1:21. Kiffin had no formal theological training, as became evident in the dispute with Featley when he admitted he had not so much as heard of the 39 Articles. Featley, *Dippers dipt*, 5.
171. Cited in Hughes, "Pulpit Guarded," 37. This was most certainly true of Daniel Featley, see *Dippers dipt*, 2.
172. See Hughes, "Pulpit Guarded," 37.

acknowledgment that disputations were an effective means of drawing interested and sympathetic persons to awareness of the Baptists cause.

1.2.4. Missionary Evangelism

In 1670, Captain Richard Deane wrote to Dr. Barlow, Bishop of Lincoln, recounting that:

> In the year 1649, the Baptists greatly increased in the country, and their opinions did likewise spread themselves into some of the regiments of horse and foot in the army.[173]

The expansion of the Calvinistic Baptists in 1649 noted by Captain Deane was not accidental but the consequence of a declared intention to expand their network of churches. In spring that year, seven Baptist congregations in London each determined to "set aside at least one of its members for missionary labours,"[174] to undertake pioneer, entrepreneurial evangelistic work, to establish new Baptist churches, and to unite them in fellowship with one another. The task given to these first Baptist evangelists is summarized by White:

> Such a person . . . was given authority to go out and convert those who had no Christian faith (or those who had a faulty one), to baptize his converts, to link them into congregational fellowship and bring them under congregational discipline, and then, as happened in a number of cases, to link the individual congregations into associations.[175]

According to Benjamin Cox, the essential qualifications of Baptist evangelists were not education and ordination, but the enabling of the Spirit of Christ, a sense of calling to the work, and evidence to the congregation of evangelistic gifts in the conversion of sinners.[176] In addition, Cox affirmed that evangelistic preachers were authorized to administer baptism and the Lord's Supper, as well as to gather and organize converts into churches with officers nominated to provide ministry.[177]

---

173. Ivimey, *History of the English Baptists*, 1:294.
174. White, "English Particular Baptists," 20.
175. Ibid., 21.
176. Cox, *Appendix to a Confession of Faith*, article XIX, in Underhill, *Confessions of Faith*, 58.
177. Ibid.

"Casting Balls of Wildfire into the bosom of the Church"   27

Particular Baptist missionary work as early as 1643–44 is known from the record of Luke Howard, when Kiffin, Patience, Spillman and Collier "began to have an Entrance into Kent."[178] There they made many converts, though later a number switched to the General Baptists, or held Arminian views though they remained among the Particulars, and some joined the Quakers.[179]

One of the most prominent evangelists among the Particular Baptist was Thomas Collier who preached in the West Country from 1646.[180] This we know from Thomas Edwards who described Collier as,

> A great Sectarie in the West of England, . . . and a great Emissarie [preacher], a Dipper, who goes about Surrey, Hampshire, and those Counties thereabouts, preaching and dipping.[181]

The impact and fruitfulness of Collier's ministry can be measured by the record that by 1689 the greater numbers of Particular Baptists were concentrated in London, Devon, Gloucestershire, Wiltshire, and Berkshire.[182]

In summer 1649, the London Calvinistic Baptist churches held a prayer meeting at the Glasshouse church[183] to seek the Lord that he would send labourers "into the dark corners and parts of this land."[184] An answer came in September that year when John Myles[185] and Thomas Proud came to London, apparently after a visit to Glamorgan from William Consett and Edward Drapes from the Glasshouse church in London.[186] Myles spent a fortnight in London where he frequently attended meetings at the Glasshouse church and was baptized as a believer. Being recognized as divine provision for home mission, Myles and Proud were sent back to Glamorgan to gather "a company or society of people holding forth and practicing

---

178. Howard, *Looking-Glass for Baptists*, 5. Collier is spelled "Colyer."
179. Ibid., 5–7.
180. On Collier's evangelistic career see Land, "Doctrinal Controversies," 25–30.
181. Edwards, *Gangraena* ii, 122.
182. See Land, "Doctrinal Controversies," 30.
183. White, *inter alios*, mistakenly confuses the identity of the Glasshouse church for Glaziers Hall church, Broadstreet. This was a meeting place of the General Baptists. See Owens, *The Ilston Book*, xcvii, n. 48.
184. Recounted later by John Myles and recorded in the Ilston Churchbook. See ibid., 31–32. See also White, "John Miles and the Structures," in Mansel, *Welsh Baptists Studies*, 36; also Richards, "John Myles in Wales," 362–65.
185. On Myles, or Miles, see the biographical details in Morgan, "John Myles (1621–83) and the Future of Ilston's Past," 176-84. For the sake of uniformity I have adopted Myles.
186. Owens, *Ilston Book*, 32. See also, Richards, "John Miles in Wales," 363.

the doctrine, worship, order and discipline of the Gospel according to the primitive institution."[187]

Within a fortnight of beginning their mission to South Wales in October 1649, Myles and Proud had baptized two women, and by October 1650 forty-three members had been gathered.[188] They continued to gather five congregations, and the first general meeting of the members of the first three churches was held at Ilston, Glamorgan, 6–7 November 1650.[189] In terms of evangelistic method, it is recorded that in January 1650 Myles travelled to Breconshire where he was allowed access to the pulpit of a congregation of Independents at Llanigon led by Walter Prosser and James Hughes. Prosser and Hughes were immediately won over to the Baptist cause and promised to correspond with Myles concerning the reaction of the remainder of the congregation. Subsequently the church was divided over the issue of believer's baptism and asked Myles not to return to the church until they had consulted more widely with others, notably Vavasor Powell and Walter Cradock. Initially Myles complied with their request but later the Illston church sent a letter to Llanigon, and also Myles himself, in which they asserted that because they held back on the question of baptism the church at Llanigon was "not yet in any true church order."[190] Consequently the Ilston members advised those who had come to a clear conviction about baptism to separate from the others who had not. According to the Churchbook at Llanigon, the visit of John Myles to the church proved highly significant and "there was a considerable number there baptized and joined together in the order of the Gospel," the newly baptized group forming a new congregation at Hay, about two or three miles from Llanigon.[191]

At the meeting of the three churches at Ilston on 6–7 November 1650 the representatives of Hay, Llanharan and Ilston decided, amongst other things, that David Davies, formerly minister at Gelligaer, Glamorgan, recently baptized and in membership at Ilston,[192] Walter Prosser and John Myles should by turns preach at Carmarthen town.[193] On 19 January 1651 the three churches now gathered at the newly established fourth church at

---

187. See Owens, *Ilston Book*, 31.

188. The numbers are according to the membership list in the Ilston Churchbook. See ibid., 3–4, and 32.

189. Ibid., 14.

190. Ibid., 35.

191. Ibid., 40.

192. Ibid., 36.

193. Details are given in *ARPB*, 3, also Owens, *Ilston Book*, 42.

"Casting Balls of Wildfire into the bosom of the Church"   29

Carmarthen, evidence of remarkable progress by Baptist evangelists at this time. The Ilston Churchbook records,

> there was a very considerable number baptized and joined in church fellowship . . . who now be another city of God in that town where Satan's seat was.[194]

In the West Country there is evidence that Baptists continued the practice of evangelizing in town and countryside throughout the 1650s. At an Association meeting on 5th and 6th of the 9th month, 1656, a question was raised:

> Query 1. Whether it be an absolute duty now lying on several churches speedily to send forth persons fitted for the great and good work of preaching the Gospel to the world? Answer: we judge it to be a duty and at this time much to be laid to heart and performed to send forth such brethren as are fitted to the work of preaching the Gospel to poor sinners that they might be saved.
>
> 1. That it's a duty appears by the commission of Christ, Mat 28.18f., and by the churches that first trusted in Christ according thereunto, Acts 11.22,13.1ff.,1.15-23.
>
> 2. That it's now to be performed appears by the open door that God hath set before us, Acts 16.9f., the fields being white to harvest, Jn. 4.35, Mat. 9.37. and the abounding also of the mystery of iniquity.[195]

The "open door" was a reference to the toleration, and support for Baptists at the highest level of government, which accounts for the success of Particular Baptists in expanding the number of their churches.

Other means of spreading Baptist convictions included the preaching and testifying of Parliamentary soldiers who moved throughout the British countryside during the Civil War. The Church at Chard owes its beginnings to Captain Joseph Wallington who founded the church in these types of circumstances.[196]

---

194. Ibid., 42.
195. *ARPB*, 64.
196. See White, "English Particular Baptists," 21.

Summary

The narrative of the origins of the English Particular Baptists brings to light a number of themes that can be identified as significant for delineating the distinct identity of Baptists within the diversity of religious sects emerging in the first half of the seventeenth century.

First, the origins of Particular Baptists are in the tradition of Puritan separatism. From Puritanism they derived a strict piety, a church comprised of saints, believers who intentionally willed to live under the rule of King Jesus, a convictional Calvinism, and from separatism a commitment to complete the reformation of the English church within their own congregations. This latter conviction is evident in a document from the close of the period considered here, the Churchbook of the Watford Baptist church, dated 1659. In a letter from the London churches granting permission to form as a church the conditions of their establishing were defined as:

> Wholly to disown the Church of England and the ministry of it, first, because we could not own their ordination, and secondly, because we could not own their administration of the ordinances of Baptism and the Lord's Supper . . . thirdly, we disowned their mixed marriages and their service read over the dead, fourthly, we disowned the consecration of their holy places or churches as they call them, fifthly, we disown their surplice and common prayer.[197]

Henry Jacob had formed a congregation of semi-separatists in 1616, but the inclination of the majority of Particular Baptists was rejection of the National Church in pursuit of a church formed according to the primitive pattern of the New Testament. The Particular Baptists considered themselves to be true Puritans, advanced Puritans, by virtue of their separatism.

Second, they were Biblicist in their approach to religion, seeking to measure their doctrine, sacraments, ecclesiology by the canon of scripture. Most significantly, this devotion to the literal reading of the Bible led them first to reject infant baptism, then to adopt believer's baptism, and finally to practice believer's baptism by immersion. Biblicism, it should be noted, is evident in all features of their ecclesiology.

Third, early Calvinistic Baptists were evangelical and propagationist, keen to expand their teaching and increase their numbers. They counted among their members gifted preachers and evangelists such as Thomas Collier, Paul Hobson, John Myles who pioneered new churches, and planted new congregations in the West Country, Wales and the North East of

---

197. White, "Baptist Beginnings in Watford," 205.

England. As a consequence of their conversionist theology, their devotion to Christ, and willingness to live under the Rule of Christ, was paramount in the exercise of their religion, privately and corporately. They believed the Kingship of Christ over the church was unmediated, because their experience of salvation was unmediated.

Fourth, although separatist in ecclesiology, early Baptists were not isolationist, but anxious to be recognized as full participants in the mainstream of orthodox Christian tradition. To this extent, they published Confessions and sermons, devotional literature and works of apologetics.[198] Their ambition was to be regarded, not as schismatic and sectarian, but a reforming, purifying influence in the religious affairs of the nation.

---

198. Whitley, *Baptist Bibliography*, 1:17–65.

2

"A True Visible Church of Christ"

The Contours of Calvinistic Baptist Ecclesiology

"A True visible Church of Christ consisteth both of Matter and Form, or of Subjects and Order, for it is Christs Kingdom; and those Subjects must be such visibly as Christ owns, and that Form and Order according to Christs rule, or else it cannot be his church."[1]

2.1 The Rule of Christ[2]

THE EMERGENCE OF PARTICULAR Baptist congregations in the 1640s caused many loyal church people to ask by what right lay people might form a conventicle and call it a true church. Robert Poole, for example, in his correspondence with William Kiffin, repeatedly pressed the question, what *warrant* have you to separate from the national church?, and, what *warrant* have you to form congregations? What *warrant* have you to be a minister of a Separate Congregation? How can you *vindicate* your schism and defection from the reformed Churches?[3] Although the question of "warrant" had political implications, Kiffin's defense was based on bibli-

---

1. Collier, *Right Constitution*, 1.

2. For the development of this conviction amongst wider Independents see Tolmie, *Saints*, 85–86.

3. Kiffen, *A Briefe Remonstrance*, 3. My italics. A similar style of argument concerning the authority by which independent churches might be set up under the authority of King Jesus is seen in Goodwin, *Works*, 11, 302.

cal and theological convictions, stressing that Baptist congregations were "erected and formed . . . according to the Rule of Christ."[4] In response to Poole's third question about his own ministry, he responded,

> but *JESUS CHRIST* is of the Father anointed to be the head of the Church, which is his body . . . and that we are commanded onely to heare him; and that whosoever will not heare and obey him, the Lord will require it at his hands, and hereby wee know wee love God, and hee loves us, when we keep his Commandments. Now then, if wee cannot keep faith and a good Conscience, in obeying all the commands of Christ, so long as we assemble ourselves with you, then are wee necessitated to separate our selves from you.[5]

Having asserted the primacy of the Christological imperative as the major premise in all matters of faith and conscience, Kiffin believed that the Baptists' separation from the National Church was necessitated by the impossibility of maintaining faith and good conscience while in fellowship with them. The Christological imperative was the fundamental theological principle that separated Baptists from a National Church of whatever polity, whether episcopal or presbyterian. Kiffin stressed this point repeatedly to Poole:

> so long as you denie to follow the rule of Jesus Christ, and are not obedient to his commands, but reject the Word of God, which is given by Christ for the purging of the wicked from the godly, and the separating of the precious from the vile . . . we are bound in obedience to JESUS CHRIST, to leave you, while you remaine obstinate to him, and joyne together, and continue faithfull in the order of the Gospel.[6]

The State Church, according to Kiffin, was corrupted by its impure members. It's policy of taking in all without the power "to voide the excrements" meant it "must needs become a rotten, filthie and unclean body."[7] Other corruptions included lack of discipline, compulsion in worship, "tythes and offerings by which a few clergy become rich at the expense of the poor," refusing burial in consecrated ground to the poor, all of which have forced those who listen to the voice of Christ Jesus to make separation.[8]

---

4. Ibid., 6.
5. Ibid., 8. Irregular spelling and emphasis as original.
6. Ibid., 8.
7. Ibid., 9.
8. Ibid., 10.

Among Particular Baptists the conviction that "Christ is both Lord and King of the Churches" was developed as part of their critique of the power and authority civil magistrates claimed to possess in establishing Church government.[9] In response to the question of his invisible interlocutor: "What power the Civill Magistrate has in establishing Church Government?" Thomas Collier's bold answer was, "They [magistrates] have none at all" because Christ is King of saints, of Sion, that is, the church. Collier regarded human power in spiritual matters as a usurpation of the prerogative of King Jesus. Any attempt by the State either to establish, or compel citizens, to conform to true religion was a violation of the rule of Christ, who himself compelled no one.

> Christ overpowers the soule by his Spirit, and then men are willing, and till then, man is not to meddle with them in Spirituall things.[10]

The counter to the Baptist position was twofold, first by precept of scripture and second political. The biblical case was based on Luke 14.23 *"The Lord said unto his servants, Goe out into the high-ways, and hedges, and compel them to come in."* Collier denied that this text had any bearing on the responsibility and power of the magistrate in religious affairs or the religious habits of individuals. In the first place it was descriptive of the ministry of Jesus, and derivatively it applied to Gospel preachers who try to persuade by the preaching of the Gospel.[11] The Presbyterian riposte was to warn of the religious anarchy that would result from such a policy:

> But if the Magistrate should not set up Religion by Authority, but leave it to the liberties of men, there would be so many Religions and Opinions in the World, that a man should not know which to follow.[12]

This statement captured precisely the fears of clergymen like Thomas Edwards, whose extreme antipathy towards sectaries was energized by the threat they posed to the unity and uniformity of religion in the nation.[13] Collier addressed directly the possibility of the multiplication of opinions, arguing that the Truth would draw saints together, and in any case it was beyond the power of any human to suppress opinions. His was an argument for broad toleration of religious convictions, a policy that Presbyterians in the

---

9. Collier, *Certaine Queries*, 24.
10. Ibid., 24.
11. Ibid., 25.
12. Ibid.
13. Edwards, *Gangraena*; Edwards, *Reasons Against Toleration*, 23.

Assembly and Parliament would not countenance. So does the Magistrate have any role in religion at all?, asks Collier. Somewhat provocatively he suggests that if they do they should use their power,

> To dismiss that Assembly of learned men who are now called together for to consult about matters of Religion.[14]

His primary objection to the Westminster Assembly was that he knew of no scriptural precedent for such a gathering, and among the divines were some who had imprisoned saints for holding opinions contrary to their own. The very concept of a national religious settlement, sponsored by Parliament, devised by an Assembly, and imposed by the magistrate was as far from the Baptist way of organizing, and being the church, under the rule of King Jesus, as was possible to imagine.

The practical outworking of the commitment to King Jesus as Lord of the church is seen in Collier's scheme of ten ordinances by which a church is to be rightly constituted. What were to others called sacraments Collier insisted be known as "ordinances," because they were "ordained by Christ to be practiced by his people."[15] These were "*Baptism*," which was "not only a constituting but an initiating ordinance into the Church of Christ." Second, "*Prayer*," by which every member of the body of Christ has free access to the throne of grace, "at all times and, and upon all occasions." Third, "*Praise*, flowing from the souls interested [sic] in his love." The fourth ordinance of Christ was "*Preaching* and prophesying, for the building up of the Church in the faith and knowledge of the Lord." Fifth, "*Breaking of bread*, or communicating together in the Lord's Supper." Collier does not expand on the Baptist theology of communion, beyond saying it is precious as a sign of Christ's love, our interest in him, and our union with him. The sixth ordinance, is to "*assemble together*," to admonish, exhort, consider one another, provoke one another to love and good works, that all things may be done to edifying. Seventh is discipline: "that if any *fall through weakness, to restore such a one by the spirit of meekness, considering thyself, and Gal 6.1, 2. and to bear one anothers burdens, and so fulfil the Law of Christ.*" The eighth ordinance of Christ is disfellowshipping a fallen brother who resists the Church's admonition:

> This power hath Christ left with his Church, which oftentimes through the blessing of God proves an effectuall means for the recovering of souls out of the snare of the devil.

---

14. Collier, *Certaine Queries*, 27.
15. Collier, *Right Constitution*, 9.

Ninth, Christ has ordained that the Church should provide for the poor of the congregation. Tenth, "God hath ordained his people *to walk in every good work*, both of piety and charity."[16]

Collier's blueprint for the church, what might be called the Particular Baptists' *notae ecclesia*, was thoroughly Christological. Every ordinance, it was emphasized, was the word of Christ for his people. Christ made complete provision for the organization and business of the church, and the Baptist ecclesiological project was to conform their congregations to the ordinances of King Jesus.

In the wider literature of the Particular Baptists the principles of a true Church incorporated these features of Collier's *notae* resulting in a series of convictions about the essence of the Church as Christ would have it established.

2.2 A Believer's Church

Of first importance, Particular Baptists demanded a definite type of religious experience as a pre-requisite for membership, namely confession of faith in Jesus Christ.[17] Michael Watts suggests the emphasis on conversion as essential for church membership emerged in the seventeenth century largely as a result of the teaching and influence of William Perkins,[18] but Baptist leaders recognized this as a scriptural principal, a gospel imperative that should be experienced as a contemporary reality. The stress on the primacy of conversion is seen in Hanserd Knollys' account of the manner in which churches were being gathered in London in the mid-1640s:[19]

> Some godly and learned men of approved guifts and abilities for the Ministerie, being driven out of the Countries, where they lived by the persecution of the Prelates, came to sojourn in this great City, and preached the Word of God both publikely, and from house to house, and daily in the Temples and in every house they ceased not to teach and preach Jesus Christ.... And when many sinners were converted by their preaching of the Gospell, some of them that believed, consorted with them, and of professors a great many, and of the chief women not a few.

16. Ibid., 9–18.

17. Niebuhr, *Social Sources*, 17–18.

18. Watts, *Dissenters* I, 171–73. On Perkins see Long, "William Perkins," 53–59. See also Troeltsch, *Social Teaching*, 55, 57 and 993.

19. The theology of Knollys is the subject of Howson, *Erroneous and Schismatical Opinions*. Ecclesiology is treated 221–29.

> And the condition which those Preachers both publikely and privately propounded to the people, unto who they preached, upon which they were to be admitted into the Church was Faith, Repentance, and Baptisme; and none other. And whosoever (poor as well as rich, bond as well as free, servants as well as Masters) did make a profession of their Faith in Christ Jesus, and would be baptized with water into the Name of the Father, Sonne, and Holy Spirit, were admitted Members of the Church.[20]

In Knollys' report we see the importance of Gospel preaching, the conversion of sinners, and baptism of those who repented of their sins in the formation of early Calvinistic Baptist congregations. Latent within this statement is a theology of the church comprised of professing believers in Christ, baptized, gathered, visible, and separatist.

The significance of a believer's church was its contrariness to the concept of a national, or parochial church, into which members are born, and in which membership is considered obligatory, and by virtue of one's national identity.[21] To the Baptists this arrangement had become anathema, and the priority of faith in "the right constitution of a church" was asserted by Thomas Collier under the heading of, "The Materials or Subjects of a true visible Church of Christ," where he stated, "A True visible Church of Christ consisteth of believers gathered out of the World by the preaching of the Gospel, by the powerful ministry of the Spirit."[22] Whatever such people are called, since the New Testament offers a variety of options, what mattered was the reality of their spiritual experience:

> [they are] frequently called Saints, and holy Brethren, partakers of the heavenly calling, the house of God, his Temple, the household of Faith, born from above of the Spirit, that they might worship in Spirit and Truth, all of which discovers the spiritualnesse of the Church of Christ, that they are or should be spiritual Believers.[23]

When it came to explaining what was meant by a "believer's church," Collier described the common practice of Baptist congregations in dealing

---

20. Knollys, *Moderate Answer*, 19–20.

21. Early Baptist objection to the parochial church system is evident in the tract about Baptism published in the wake of a failed disputation between Baptist ministers and Edmund Calamy the elder, curate of St Mary Aldermanbury. See Coxe, Knollys, Kiffen, *Declaration Concerning the Publike Dispute*, 9.

22. Collier, *Right Constitution*, 2.

23. Ibid.

with those who sought membership among them. Two things were required according to the precedent of the primitive New Testament church. First, evidence of faith and repentance, because "repentance or turning from sin to God" was the essence of Apostolic preaching in Acts 2.38, and therefore, "must needs be manifested before admission into the Church."[24] Second, they must have received believers' baptism:

> "none are to be admitted [to the church] before Baptisme," and, "none are to be baptized, but those that are able to manifest faith and turning to God."[25]

To stress the point Collier added, "so that wee have no Rule to Baptize any, till they are Disciples, that is, Beleevers."[26] Only those who conformed to this twofold pattern of conversion and baptism, Collier insisted, may be "looked upon as members of the church." Coxe, Kiffen and Knollys likewise affirmed, "The subject matter of Baptisme, according to the doctrine of the Disciples and Apostles of Christ . . . are such men and women as actually repent and believe."[27] The same was asserted by Hanserd Knollys who argued on the basis of primitive precedent, "the Apostles propounded no other condition or termes for the making all and every one of them members of the Church, but Repentance and Baptisme."[28]

At a meeting of the West Country Baptist Association in 1654, overseen by Collier, it was asked, "whether any are to be received into the church of Christ only upon a bare confession of Christ being come in the flesh?" Even though there was scriptural warrant for such confession, Collier replied with a decisive No!, and continued to explain,

> they may not be admitted on such terms without a declaration of an experimental work of the Spirit upon the heart, through the word of the Gospel and suitable to it, being attended with evident token of conversion, to the satisfaction of the administrator and brethren or church concerned in it.[29]

Collier's response may reflect something of an anti-intellectual approach to religion, down-grading *mere* intellectual conformity to creedal

---

24. Collier, *Certaine Queries*, 10.

25. Ibid., 10, also 11. Many proof texts are appended to these statements demonstrating that this is the biblical pattern of the church.

26. Ibid., 11.

27. Coxe, et al., *Declaration Concerning the Publike Dispute*, 9.

28. Knollys, *Moderate Answer*, 15, 18. The controversy continued in Bastwick's riposte, *The Utter Routing of the Whole Army of all the Independents and Sectaries*.

29. ARPB, 56.

orthodoxy, and prioritizing faith as an existential, measureable, observable experience of Christ evidenced in transformation of character. Whatever the motive, he like others stressed the priority of visible godliness Baptists regarded as essential in a believer's church, because it was essential in the post-Pentecost church.[30]

2.3 Baptism, Infant Baptism, and Church Membership

The Baptist experiment in congregational ecclesiology, consisting of a voluntary church of professing believers, required a safeguard to entry into the church and for this they employed the rite of initiation, namely believer's baptism.[31] Article 39 of the 1644 London Confession stated:

> That Baptisme is an Ordinance of the new Testament, given by Christ, to be dispensed onely upon persons professing faith, or that are Disciples, or taught, who upon a profession of faith, ought to be baptized.[32]

By way of contrast, within English Prayer-Book Protestantism the greater emphasis was on the sacramental, soteriological dimension of baptism.[33] According to the Prayer Book, a child was brought to baptism bearing the burden of sin and guilt inherited from Adam.[34] Baptism, therefore was understood to be an event of regeneration, an engrafting into the body of Christ.[35] In law baptism was to be administered to every child in the parish, indiscriminately, on the basis that they belonged to the national church. This arrangement of baptism, regeneration and *Volkskirche* remained unaltered in the proposals of the Westminster Assembly Directory for Public

---

30. See 2.4 below.

31. See Walker, "Relation of Infants to Church," 242–62. Walker's paper discusses the theology of infant baptism among early General Baptists as well as later Calvinistic Baptists. That the theology and practice of infant baptism was a hotly disputed subject is indicated by the record that between 1642 and 1660 Thomason collected over 125 tracts on this question, and Paul Lim reckons as many as seventy-nine public disputes were conducted. Lim, "Puritans and the Church of England," in Coffey and Lim, *Cambridge Companion to Puritanism*, 233.

32. In Lumpkin, *Baptist Confessions of Faith*, 167.

33. An Anglican defense of paedobaptism published in this period is that of Featley, *The Dippers Dipt*.

34. The Book of Common Prayer (1549), *Publike Baptisme*. See also Featley, *Dippers Dipt*, 20.

35. Featley, *Dippers Dipt*, 21.

Worship.³⁶ The political implication of this position was not lost on Baptist sympathizer, John Tombes, who wrote in 1645,

> When a Nation shall receive the faith, that is, a great eminent part, the Governours and chief Cities, & representative body, shall receive the faith, that Nation shall in like manner have all their little ones capable of Baptisme, and counted visible members of the Church, as the posteritie of the *Jews* were in the time of that Church administration. This I guesse is the businesse that is now upon the anvil.³⁷

What precisely was upon the anvil was the meaning of the great commission in Matt 28.19, "to make disciples of all nations," which could be taken to mean the conversion of nations *en bloc*, after the manner of *cuius regio, eius religio*,³⁸ or could refer to the making of individual converts within all nations. Presbyterians of the time such as Blake and Rutherford argued that this text was the fulfilment of the Abrahamic promise that, "In thee shall Nations be blessed."³⁹ Stephen Marshall used the text to assert that, "*every Nation which should receive the faith, should be to him now as the peculiar Nation of the Jewes had been in the past.*"⁴⁰ Consequently, the text could be used as a justification for baptizing all born within the parish, advocating a "federall or externall holinesse of a believing or chosen nation, giving the right to the infants of that nation to be baptized."⁴¹

Tombes argued against the Presbyterian position that national rulers could determine the faith of its citizens, insisting that disciples were to be made *within* all nations, and he further denied that any nation should be to God a peculiar nation as the Jews had been.⁴² He refuted the interpretation of Matt 28.19 which equated "them" (*autēs*) with "*all Nations*," and instead restricted its reference to those who were taught, and by the means of apostolic teaching were made disciples.⁴³ It was therefore the disciples of all nations who were to be baptized. This was in accordance with apostolic

---

36. A Baptist perspective on the "new-devised-parish-church-worship," especially baptism, was that it remained "as great an observance of the traditions of men, under the Classical Presbytery, as ever they were under the Lordly Episcopacy." See Coxe, et al., *Declaration*, 12.

37. Tombes, *Examen of the Sermon*, 123.

38. Literally, "whose realm, his religion."

39. Tombes, *Examen of the Sermon*, 122.

40. Ibid., 123. Emphasis as original.

41. Ibid., 127.

42. Ibid., 123.

43. See also Coxe, et al., *Declaration*, 19.

precedent, as recorded in Acts, that hearing and believing were prior to, and the recondition for, baptism.[44] Tombes summarizes,

> When Christ saith, Teach all nations, and baptize them, his meaning is, by preaching the Gospel to all nations, make them Disciples, and baptize those that become Disciples of all nations.[45]

This being Christ's clear instruction by which people ought to come to baptism there could be no deviation, according to Tombes. He asserted,

> For the appointment of Christ, is the rule according to which we are to administer holy things, and he that doth otherwise, follows his own invention, and is guilty of will worship.[46]

To those, like Tombes, with Baptist convictions, it was indisputable that Christ appointed one way into his church and it was by repentance, faith and baptism.[47]

The theology of Presbyterians like Stephen Marshall drew from the tradition of Reformed theology which since the time of Zwingli argued for infant baptism on the basis of the covenant of grace.[48] This was clearly affirmed in the Heidelberg Catechism:

> Should infants, too, be baptized? Yes, infants as well as adults belong to God's covenant and congregation. Through Christ's blood the redemption from sin and the Holy Spirit, who works faith, are promised to them no less than to adults. Therefore, by baptism, as sign of the covenant, they must be incorporated into the Christian church.[49]

On this dogmatic foundation Marshall built a defense of infant baptism consisting of a five-fold argument.[50] In the first instance he states,

---

44. Tombes, *Examen of the Sermon*, 126. He cites Acts 2.41; Acts 8.12, 38; Acts 10.48; Acts 16.15, 33.

45. Ibid., 127.

46. Ibid., 132; also Hobson, *Fallacy of Infants Baptism*, 3.

47. See Coxe, et al., *Declaration*, 14. In internal debate John Spilsbury argued against Thomas Kilcop that church foundation was by "covenantal collective" not baptism. This view was based on a desire to preserve the priority of faith in believer's church, and to refute any hint of sacramentalism. See Spilsbury, *Treatise Concerning the Lawfull Subject of Baptisme*, 41. See Wright, *EEB*, 104–9.

48. Zwingli, *Refutation of the Tricks*, in *Selected Works of Huldreich Zwingli*, 219–37, 248–51.

49. Question 74.

50. Marshall, *Sermon of the Baptizing of Infants*. The General Baptists produced

> *The Infants of believing parents are* foederati, *therefore they must bee* signati: *they are within the covenant of grace, belonging to Christs body, kingdome, family; therefore are to partake of the seale of his covenant, or the distinguishing badge between them who are under the covenant of grace, and them who are not.*[51]

Basic to Marshall's defense of infant baptism was continuity between the old covenant and the new, between old Israel and new Israel.[52] In both covenants the one gracious purpose of God is revealed in election and redemption. Since the covenant made with Abraham is still in force, the blessings that were bestowed upon Abraham now "comes on the Gentiles through Jesus Christ."[53] Infants of those in the covenant are therefore to be reckoned covenanters with their parents.[54] Similar sentiments were found in other Puritan divines, including John Owen, Thomas Goodwin and Samuel Petto who, on the analogy of Abraham's institution of the rite of circumcision, saw no grounds for excluding children of believers from the seal of the covenant.[55]

Marshall's argument for infant baptism served not only to define the relationship of infants of believers to the Gospel, but also specified their relationship to the church. To this end he stated,

> Ever since God gathered a distinct, select number out of the world, to bee his Kingdom, City, House-hold, in opposition to the rest of the world, which is the kingdom, city, house-hold of Satan, he would have *The Infants of all who are taken into Covenant with him, to bee accounted his, to belong to him, to his church and Family, and not to the devils.* . . . thus hath the Lord ordained, it shall be in his kingdome and family; the *children*

---

their own response to Marshall. See Denne, *Antichrist Unmasked in Two Treatise*. A summary of the five arguments can be found in Marshall's *Sermon*, 33.

51. Marshall, *Sermon of the Baptizing of Infants*, 8. Emphasis as original.

52. Among Reformed theologians of the time, one notable exception to this view was that of John Owen. See "The Minority Report: John Owen on Sinai," in Beeke and Jones, *A Puritan Theology*, 293–303. It should be noted that Owen's affirmation of the newness of the new covenant did not preclude his continuing commitment to paedobaptism.

53. Marshall, *Sermon of the Baptizing of Infants*, 13.

54. Ibid., 33.

55. Owen, "Of Infant Baptism, and Dipping," in *The Works of John Owen*, ed. Russell. vol. XXI, 547–56; Goodwin, "Of Election," in *The Works of Thomas Goodwin* volume IX, 426ff.; Petto, *Infant Baptism of Christ's* Appointment, 11.

follow the Covenant-condition of their *Parents*, if he take a Father into Covenant, he takes the children in with him.[56]

In speaking about the seal of the covenant Marshall again argued that continuity of the gracious promises of God brings together circumcision and baptism as seals of initiation administered to those who enter the covenant of grace. He reasoned,

> *Circumcision* for the time of that administration which was *before* Christs incarnation, *Baptisme since* the time of his incarnation; both of them the *same* sacrament for the *spirituall* part, though differing in the outward Elements.[57]

The ecclesiological implications of this hermeneutical commitment can now be given full weight as we see in Marshall's assertion,

> both of them [circumcision and baptism] the way and means of solemne entrance and admission into the Church; *both* of them to be administered but *once*, and none might be received into the *communion* of the Church of the *Jewes* until they were *circumcised*, nor into the *communion* of the Church of the Christians until they be *Baptized* . . . and this our *Lord himselfe* taught us by his own example, who was *circumcised*, as a professed Member of the Church of the Jews, and when he set up the new Christian Church, he would be initiated into *it*, by the Sacrament of *Baptisme*.[58]

From the perspective of the Particular Baptists, a new conception of the church, comprised of voluntary professing believers demanded a break from the inclusive policy of paedobaptism in the national Church. Paul Hobson argued the Baptist case saying, "That which doth not only present one, but make one a Member of a Church, before being called of God, That is inconvenient."[59] For this reason, Particular Baptist attempts to deal with the subject of infant baptism also began with the question of the covenant. Once again, Paul Hobson made the point clearly on behalf of Baptists:

> I shall unfold to you what I mean by that which was before Christ, and ended by Christ come in the flesh. That which was before Christ, was, That God made a covenant with *Abraham*, which covenant ran in the flesh, and was intail'd to generation;

---

56. Marshall, *Sermon of the Baptizing of Infants*, 14 and 15. Emphasis as original.
57. Ibid., 26.
58. Ibid., 26–27.
59. Hobson, *Fallacy of Infants Baptisme*, 12.

and not upon condition of Regeneration. . . . And this was that Covenant that Circumcision of Children had a reference to; and whosoever was a childe of *Abraham*, considered as a son of the flesh, had a right to it, and might and did plead for priviledges by it. But when Christ came the natural Branches were cut off, *Rom* 11.20, 21. And no man is now considered a son of *Abraham*, or the Seed of *Abraham*, but as he beleeveth.[60]

Two emphases now emerged in Baptist thinking about the nature of baptism, namely the Gospel requirement of spiritual regeneration and faith prior to the ordinance,[61] and second, an ecclesiological emphasis related to initiation into the visible church. Baptism was indeed, as other Reformed writers maintained, a seal of election and grace. Particular Baptists had not abandoned their Calvinist roots, but evidence of election was required in expressions of repentance and transformation of life before baptism could be administered. John Spilsbury argued this point in his tract on baptism, that according to scripture the blessings of the covenant of grace belong only to believers:

> We shall find in the Scriptures of God, all the sweet promises of Grace under the New Testament, holding forth their blessings, and blessed privileges onely to such as believe.[62]

Paul Hobson saw things in the same way:

> Now there is no promise that runs forth to any considered in reference to a carnal generation; but a spiritual Regeneration. Therefore when they came to *John* to be Baptized, He takes them off from pleading their priviledge considered in the flesh, and tells them, *say not in your heart, You have Abraham to your Father,* and so plead for Baptism: But he exhorts them to *Believe and Repent.*[63]

Believing the visible church to be the only warrantable church, comprised of professing believers, it was impossible for Baptists to accommodate infant baptism since they were incapable of displaying observable signs

---

60. Ibid., 7.

61. From the time of the grand immersion led by Richard Blunt, baptismal theology among the Calvinistic Baptists stressed the death and resurrection motif, which symbolized spiritual conversion. See First London Confession, articles XXXIX and XL. In Lumpkin, *Baptist Confessions*, 167. This is restated in Coxe, et al., *Declaration*, 9.

62. Spilsbury, *Treatise Concerning the Lawfull Subject of Baptisme*, 2.

63. Hobson, *Fallacy of Infants Baptisme*, 7.

of faith in Christ.⁶⁴ Tombes argued that since infants are entirely "passive" in the act of baptism, incapable of offering any indication by which they may be designated visible Christians, especially testimony of grace, they cannot be given the "*note*" of a member of the visible church.⁶⁵ Hobson asserted, "Baptism of Infants cannot be a Baptism of Faith and a baptism of Repentance."⁶⁶ It is therefore in vain that infants are baptized.⁶⁷ Furthermore, if infant baptism is vain, then to confer the privileges of the visible church on infants, or to make them members of the visible church, "is but a dream."⁶⁸ John Tombes stressed,

> As for being members of the Church, if you mean the invisible Church, neither I nor you can affirm or deny; its in Gods bosom alone; if you mean the visible, you must make a new definition of the visible Church afore Infants baptized will be proved members.⁶⁹

Again he writes,

> To make them [infants] actually members of the visible Church, is to overthrow the definitions of the visible Church that Protestant writers give . . . who make the *visible Church a number of Christians by profession*.⁷⁰

This step in the argument shows that for Tombes, the question of paedobaptism was not only a soteriological question, indeed most Baptists of the time were agnostic about the salvific status of children of believers,⁷¹ but equally a question of ecclesiology. Holding to the convictions of a believer's church and believer's baptism meant theology and practice were mutually determinative. Since the baptismal experience of children lay outside the sphere of conversion, they could never be reckoned members of the visible church.

As can be seen in the debate between John Tombes and Stephen Marshall the question about the privileges of descent brought into focus the analogy between baptism and circumcision. Particular Baptists denied

---

64. Coxe, et al., *Declaration*, 9.
65. Tombes, *Examen*, 42 and 161.
66. Hobson, *Fallacy of Infants Baptisme*, 11.
67. Tombes, *Examen*, 46.
68. Ibid., 47.
69. Ibid., 167.
70. Ibid., 41.
71. Spilsbury, *Treatise Concerning the Lawfull Subject of Baptisme*, Epistle to the Reader.

there was any "fleshly privilege" for the children of believers. Francis Cornwell stated that the new covenant did not recognize "fleshly seed," and Thomas Collier asserted that the new covenant only included such as are Christ's.[72] The "Scotchman" who debated baptism with Daniel Featley argued that while there was an express command in scripture to circumcise Jewish male infants there was no such express command for the baptizing of infants.[73] That neither precept nor explicit precedent for the baptizing of infants could be found in scripture was also decisive against the practice for John Spilsbury.[74]

Since the biblical perspective on any matter was decisive for Baptists John Tombes set out his exegesis of Col 2.8–12 to demonstrate there was no textual support for Marshall's claim that baptism and circumcision were continuous.[75] The main thrust of the argument centered on the achievement of Christ as the initiator of the new covenant, which lead to the conclusion:

> The Apostle teacheth them that they needed not circumcision, but not because they had Baptisme in lieu of it, but because all was in Christ now, who hath abolished all these rites.[76]

It is not baptism which has replaced circumcision, Tombes stressed, but Christ. All that was offered in Jewish rites and ceremonies finds fulfilment in Christ, not a new ceremony.[77] Close reading of the Colossians text made it clear that, "by putting on Christ, we come to be exempted from the schoolmaster, that is, the Law, and so from circumcision; that being planted into Christ, we walk in newness of life."[78] In his interpretation of Col 2.11, 12, John Spilsbury similarly argued that circumcision sealed its subjects to temporal and carnal things, whereas baptism seals only to faith in Christ.[79]

The Particular Baptist understanding of the covenant of grace thus excluded infants from membership of the visible church. They stressed that believer's baptism initiated saints into the privileges and responsibilities of church membership. To grant baptism to a believer was to grant the right to communion.[80] The oneness which Christ intended between the sacraments

---

72. Cornwell, *New Testament Ratified*, 21; Collier, *Discourse of True Gospel*, 17.
73. Featley, *Dippers Dipt*, 9.
74. Spilsbury, *Treatise Concerning the Lawfull Subject of Baptisme*, A3.
75. Tombes, *Examen*, 91f.
76. Ibid., 92.
77. Ibid., 93.
78. Ibid., 94.
79. Spilsbury, *Treatise Concerning the Lawfull Subject of Baptisme*, 24.
80. Hobson, *Fallacy of Infants Baptisme*, 13.

of baptism and the Lord's Supper ought to be preserved in the church. To deny those who are baptized access to the Lord's Supper, or for those who take the Lord's Supper to be unbaptized, "doth make a separation and distraction in Christ's conjunction."[81]

In the mid-1640s the argument linking baptism, church membership and the Lord's Supper was being made against opponents outside of their circle, a decade later the issue was debated within their own ranks. In the 1650s Baptists were wrestling with an increasing problem of mixed membership in their churches, that is, baptized and non-baptized believers admitted equally into the church. In Wales a hard line was taken against Thomas Proud who was excommunicated from his own church for a period for operating a policy of open membership,

> Having grievously sinned against God by broaching yt [the] destructive opinion maintaining ye mixed communion of ye baptized and unbaptized invisible fellowship, and having endeavoured to draw other[s] to ye same judgement.[82]

According to the records of the seventeenth meeting of the Abingdon Association in 1657, a question was raised about the status of believers who were baptized by "a Gospell preacher practicing and pleading for mixt communion of beleevers baptized and unbaptized in church fellowship." If subsequently, a person baptized by such a minister desired full communion "with a true church" ought they to be re-baptized? The Messengers decreed that no further baptism be administered, even though it had been administered by a minister, and in a church, in "errour in judgement and practice about mixt communion."[83]

This response shows that the early Baptist practice of closed communion, which required believer's baptism as necessary for church membership and the primary evidence of faith, though the majority view, was not universally maintained.[84] Even John Tombes, who defended believer's baptism so strongly, did not press the necessity this far. He questioned "whether a Minister can justify it before God, if he reject such a *Christian* from the Lord's Supper, because not baptized."[85] On the other hand, there were a number of Baptists who clearly believed that churches practicing open com-

---

81. Ibid., 13.

82. Owens, *Ilston Book*, 20. Proud was "disfellowshipped" for approximately three and half months.

83. *ARPB*, 176.

84. See Bunyan, *Differences in Judgement*. Also, Hill, *A Turbulent, Seditious, and Factious People*, chapter 24.

85. Tombes, *Examen*, 85. See also White, "English Particular Baptists," 16–17.

munion were not "true churches."[86] It further demonstrates they thought it desirable for baptized believers to belong to closed communion churches, where no compromise was permitted in regard to "believe and be baptized" as the foundation for a true church.

In summary, we can say that the opposition of early Calvinistic Baptists to infant baptism was based on the conviction that there was neither command nor example in the New Testament for such practice. The strength of their conviction against the practice is indicated by the assertion that to baptize a child was "a high contempt and injury to Christ," the husband of the church, since it forced upon him an unnatural wife, by which was meant a church founded on natural birth, rather than born of the Spirit. Infant baptism, it was argued, "destroys the body of Christ,"

> For in time it [i.e. the church] will come to consist of naturall, and so a nation, and so a nationall Generation, & carnall members, amongst whom if any godly be, they will be brought into bondage, and become subjects of scorn & contempt, and the power of government rest in the hands of the wicked.[87]

The evidence available to us regarding the practice of baptism supports the proposal that Christology was the controlling principle of ecclesiology among the early Calvinistic Baptists, since the link between Christ and a truly constituted church required that the saints be precise in the matter of baptism. John Spilsbury said on their behalf: "for that Church where Baptisme is the true ordinance of God, in the administration thereof, is by the Rules of the Gospel a true Church."[88]

2.4 A Gathered Church

The concept of the gathered church[89] had its importance for early Particular Baptists as a consequence of the emphasis placed on individual conversion, which was maintained in balance with an equal stress on the corporate dimension of faith in Christ. Well aware of the criticism that sectarianism

---

86. Christopher Hill suggests that it was this hardline approach that decided John Bunyan to adopt the name "Independent" rather than Baptist, even though he was baptized in 1655. When the Bedford church took out its license in 1672 it was as "congregational," not Baptist. Hill, *A Turbulent, Seditious, and Factious People*, 293.

87. Spilsbury, *Treatise Concerning the Lawfull Subject of Baptisme*, 25.

88. Ibid., 25.

89. The most comprehensive defense of the concept of the gathered church by a Puritan was Goodwin, *Government of the Churches of Christ*, in *The Works of Thomas Goodwin* vol. XI.

minimized the communal dimension of faith in favor of individual freedom and personal responsibility, Thomas Collier insisted that a church is

> not a company of Saints walking at liberty, not compacted together, as some have thought, but those that are the Church of Christ, are to walke in the order and forme of the Gospel.[90]

Writing as Messenger to the West Country Baptist churches in April 1657 Collier reminded the believers there of the corporate nature of the church,

> through the working of his holy Spirit he hath called very many precious souls out of Babylon's wayes and worships and hath placed them together in families like a flock.[91]

The juxtaposition of the individual and the corporate is seen in another of Collier's writings, where he drew first on the biblical metaphor of, "living stones"[92] to speak of the election of believers called out of the world by the preaching of the Gospel: "By the Ministery of his Word, [God] diggs men, *living stones*, out of the dead quarry of mankind."[93]

This is the material from which the Lord builds his house, and none are to be taken for living stones except those who particularly hold forth faith and repentance, that is, turning to God.[94] Second, he argued that while believers constitute the formal "order" of the church, its true "form" is to be gathered and unified in one body:

> there may be stones and timber all fitted and ready for the building, yet it is not a house till compacted together . . . no more is the spirituall Temple and house of Christ now in the Gospel, till it be brought into forme, and compact together. . . . Thus you see now, that the Church of Christ is a Building, and a Building fitly framed together for an Habitation of God.[95]

Changing the metaphor, but making the same argument Collier says that the Church of Christ is a body, and, "a body is compact together, else no body."[96]

90. Collier, *Certaine Queries*, 8.
91. *ARPB*, 89.
92. 1 Peter 2:5. Collier, *Certaine Queries*, 1.
93. Ibid., 9.
94. Ibid., 3.
95. Ibid., 7.
96. 1 Cor 12:27. Collier, *Certaine Queries*, 8. The image of the Church as a "City compact together" occurs again in Collier, *Right Constitution*, 38.

According to the Messengers of the Midland Association in 1657, twelve or thirteen was the minimum number of disciples required to "sit downe as a church,"[97] presumably, though it is not stated, according to the pattern of the twelve apostles plus Christ. At the Abingdon Association General Meeting in 1653, the issue of baptized believers "who stand not related to any church of Christ," was discussed as a matter of grave concern. Such persons were, "to be instructed and encouraged to joyne themselves to some true church of Christ."[98] This, they stated, was to be the normal practice in all their churches for all members.

What this might mean in practice may be judged from a question raised at the Midland Association gathering in June 1656, where it was asked, "whether a competent number of baptized believers in a troop or regiment may there walke as a church."[99] The answer given stated:

> wee do not discerne that a number of disciples in a troop or regiment canne there walke as and act as a perticular church of Christ as seeing no Scripture to warrant it nor discerning them to be in a capacity to keep close to the rule of the worde in receiving of members, dealing with them in all cases as the matter shall require, and that they are continually liable to be dissolved.[100]

It is not clear what was meant by the lack of "Scriptural warrant" for forming "a church" within the army. It might be interpreted to mean their concern was the composition of this church, since there was no precedent in the New Testament for a church comprised of soldiers.[101] Alternatively, it might have been the location of the church, given that the New Testament has no record of a congregation of believers within the army, though Roman soldiers might have been members of a New Testament church. What is clear is that a group of believers within the army was deemed not competent

---

97. *ARPB*, 33. In the Abingdon Association the church at Watlington was eighteen strong and asked permission of the association to disband. This was refused on grounds that it would foreclose the holding forth of the word and way of Christ in Watlington. *ARPB*, 196.

98. Ibid., 132.

99. White draws attention to a similar situation involving Cromwell's Cambridge Troop, who proposed to make themselves into a church with Richard Baxter as Pastor. See *ARPB*, 41 n. 23. The account is told in *Reliquiae Baxterianae*, I.51.

100. *ARPB*, 27-8.

101. That Baptists were concerned about the spiritual status of soldiers is evident from a question about soldiers receiving communion discussed in the West Country Association. The issue was not their participation in militarism and bloodshed, but being subject to state power. See ibid., 102.

to regulate their membership in order to maintain a believer's church, that is, "keep[ing] close to the rule of the worde in receiving of members." Why it should be more difficult for a group of believers in the army to assess the spiritual condition of another man is not elaborated. The Messengers did, however, make it clear that the threat of dissolution of the army undermined the "compactness," or gatheredness, of a church, making impossible longevity of any church comprised of soldiers, an essential element in emerging Baptist ecclesiology.

The priority of the local gathered congregation in Baptist ecclesiology is evident when Collier discusses the form of government and discipline in a true Church which was in his view,

> Not an Episcopall Government by Lord Bishops, not a Presbyterian Government of many, to rule over one.
> But every Assembly of Saints thus gathered, . . . are to elect and Ordaine Officers, and to them Christ hath given full power to perform every duty of a Church, that is, to watch over one the other, to admonish one the other, to Censure such as are disorderly, in a word, to receive in such as they conceive the Lord hath added; to cast forth such as walke disorderly.[102]

In contrast to the hierarchical structure of Presbyterianism, and the presbyterial oversight of Independency, Baptist ecclesiology asserted the authority of each gathered congregation of believers, under the Kingship of Jesus, to appoint its own officers and expel disorderly members.[103] With a hint of polemical tone Collier says,

> You never read of any one Church in Scripture, exercising power over each other; you never find the Lord JESUS in Scripture, to charge any one Church to look to others, but to themselves.[104]

While this vision of the church emphasized the status and responsibilities accorded to each church in the New Testament, there was the potential to develop an unhealthy isolation, one church from another. Particular Baptists, in reality, over the next decade, rejected an extreme form of independent congregationalism by cultivating associations of churches which might assist and help one another.[105]

---

102. Collier, *Certaine Queries*, 22–23.

103. On the authority of Baptist congregations to try, elect and ordain their own minister see *ARPB*, 171.

104. Collier, *Certaine Queries*, 23.

105. For example, see *ARPB*, 129. Baptist associationalism is the subject of ch.5.

The primacy of the gathered congregation also determined Collier's understanding of the circumference of jurisdiction for Ruling Elders and the wider Eldership. Writing against the background of the Westminster Assembly, it cannot be coincidence that in his major defense of Baptist ecclesiology Collier asks, "What is meant by the Presbytery[?],"[106] in other words what is the nature of eldership in the church. In defining the word, he had nothing remarkable or particularly new to say, explaining that "*Presbyteros*, or Presbyterian is a Greek word meaning Eldership, or the Ruling Elders." His understanding of the domain of the Elder, however, is entirely congregational. He interpreted 1 Tim 5:17 to mean that Elders, or an Eldership, function in only one and the same Church, "not that one Eldership should have power over another, but all for the good of the same body."[107] The gathered congregation is the proper context and the boundary for the ministry of elders.

This understanding of eldership had a Christological perspective and derived from the core conviction that churches made ministers, not ministers churches, that the pastoral office was derived from the congregation, gathered in Christ's name, which chose and ordained them.[108] This pattern of congregational ministry was affirmed by the sixteenth meeting of the Abingdon Association of Baptists in 1656 which discussed the question, to whom were given the ministry gifts bestowed on the *church* by the ascended Lord, according to Eph 4.8–14. While it was acknowledged that Christ's ministry gifts had been given to the universal church, nevertheless, they noted verses 14–16 of this text were addressed specifically to the Ephesians, and so they concluded,

> some of the gifts here, viz., pastours and teachers, which we conceive to be one office variously named, as elders, bishops, overseers and pastours, and with respect to the severall parts of the worke assigned to the office are such whose ministration is appropriated to the body of Christ considered in particular congregations.[109]

---

106. Collier, *Certaine Queries*, 23. In the following paragraph italics and capitals follow the original.

107. Ibid., 24.

108. Tolmie, *Saints*, 97. Thomas Collier's statement about ordination in a Baptist congregation lists 1. election by the church, 2. approbation by the church, 3. laying on of hands by representatives of the congregation. See Collier, *The Right Constitution*, 31–33.

109. ARPB, 170.

Although Ephesians 4 describes ministry gifts distributed universally to God's people, ministers function only in particular congregations, in early Baptist polity, because Christ's authority is mediated congregationally. The gifts of ministry are common to all churches, but exercised locally.

The experience of community in the gathered church is further treated in Collier's essay *The Right Constitution*, where chapter six is devoted to the duties of members of the church to the Lord, to each other, and to all men.[110] The principal duty of church members is to "walk in love," to cultivate relationships of mutual edification and help. In this vision of the congregation the strong are to bear with the infirmities of the weak, to restore one another, to seek to please one another, to exhort, admonish, reprove, and do every duty of love to each other. When members of a congregation in the Midlands asked permission of their Messengers to absent themselves from the breaking of bread in their own church, in order to attend another church where there may be "more eminent brethren to minister," their request was denied, "because the greater ende of church fellowship is not answered in so doing."[111] This was the strength and appeal of the gathered church, according to the Baptists, that members were taught to care one for one another, and each experienced support in the fellowship of believers.

For those outside of Baptist circles the congregationalist concept of the gathered church was not without dangers and therefore not a practice universally approved or welcomed even by Advanced Believers in the 1640s. Concerns about the Baptist insistence on prioritizing the local, particular, expression of church focused on the potential compromise of the principles of universality, uniformity and unity which had characterized the English church both pre- and post-English Reformation, and was prized by Episcopalians and Presbyterians alike.[112] Baptist polity, it was believed, inevitably resulted in ecclesiastical plurality, in which there was little regard for a national church. Indeed, this was true, and Particular Baptists directed their energies to forming congregations on the basis that where two or three were gathered in the name of Christ, he was present among them, confirming their competence to be fully a church.

---

110. Collier, *Right Constitution*, 38ff.

111. *ARPB*, 35.

112. Thomas Goodwin describes Presbyterianism as holding to the universality, uniformity and unity of the church, "even as every part of water hath the nature of the whole." Goodwin, *Works* XI, 4.

2.5 A Visible Church

According to the First London Confession, Calvinistic Baptist ecclesiology focused on the church, "as it is *visible* to us," a company of "*visible* saints," to the "*visible* profession of the faith."[113] A significant point about this emphasis on the "visible" church was its distinctiveness in relation to the majority of other Reformed theologies of the 1640s.[114] In contrast to mainstream Congregationalism which admitted a visible catholic church, "comprehensive of all who throughout the world outwardly own the gospel,"[115] Baptists in the 1640s focused narrowly on the local, congregational manifestation of the visible church. In contrast to Presbyterianism, they entirely ignored the notion of an "invisible church."[116]

Traditional Calvinism employed the concept of the invisible, universal church, as a necessary construct in the doctrine of election to account for the salvation of pre-Christian saints, and the elect who never heard the gospel.[117] The concept of the "visible church" was applied to a parochial church structure as a means to distinguish between true and false believers. All true and genuine believers are members of the invisible church, whether alive or dead, in heaven or on earth, though not all true believers are members of the visible church. The visible Church is comprised of the elect and non-elect, and as such is not perfect, but always *in via*, in a state of becoming. In the 1570s, Beza was cited at length by John Whitgift who had identified four types of members of the visible church. These were, first, the reprobate and vessels of anger appointed to destruction; second, those chosen in Christ by eternal election, who had yet to come to a proper profession of

---

113. Article XXXIII. In Lumpkin, *Baptist Confessions*, 165. My italics.

114. According to Peter Lake, "Disagreement about the visible godliness of the visible church or, stated differently, over the extent and nature of the Christian community was arguably the crucial divide in English Protestant opinion during this period." Lake, "Calvinism and the English Church," 39. See also Avis, *Church in the Theology*. Arminian theology also had mechanisms for breaking down the barrier between the visible and invisible church. Richard Hooker taught that since Christ died for all men, all men were actually or potentially part of Christ's body, the church. In addition, he emphasized the importance of the sacramental elements in public worship, since all who received Christ's body and blood in good faith, were *de facto* incorporated into Christ's mystical body. See Lake, "Calvinism and the English Church," 42.

115. Owen, *Discourse Concerning Evangelical Love*, in *The Works of John Owen*, 32.

116. Rupp, "Luther and the Doctrine," 386. See also Mayer, "Proper Distinction," 177–98.

117. Calvin, *Institutes* 4.1.7. *Westminster Confession of Faith*, chapter XXV "Of the Church." Augustine had first proposed that the Invisible Church was comprised of the elect whom no one knows except God, in his controversy with the Donatists. Mayer, "Proper Distinction," 179.

true belief; third, those who by virtue of election are indeed "sons of God"; fourth, those of the elect who had been called and engrafted into Christ, but who having fallen in something, had been excommunicated or delivered over to Satan, in hope of repentance. Such a clarification was necessary in a civic arrangement where church membership and state citizenship where coterminous, and the *ecclesia* a *corpus permixtum*.[118]

This theology posed no problem for many Puritans, as evidenced in William Perkins, who observed,

> [the visible Church is] a mixed company of men professing the faith, assembled together by the preaching of the word in which there are to be found true believers and hypocrites, elect and reprobate, good and bad.[119]

An important statement of Reformed theology about the nature of the church formulated at the same time as that of Calvinistic Baptists, was codified in the standards of the Westminster Confession chapter 25:[120]

> I. The catholic or universal Church, which is invisible, consists of the whole number of the elect, that have been, are, or shall be gathered into one, under Christ the Head thereof.
>
> II. The visible Church, which is also catholic or universal under the Gospel (not confined to one nation, as before under the law), consists of all those throughout the world that profess the true religion; and of their children, and is the kingdom of the Lord Jesus Christ, the house and family of God, out of which there is no ordinary possibility of salvation.

The primary characteristic of the invisible church in this formula is election,[121] the saints God predetermined to be saved. The essence of the

---

118. In London one defense of the Presbyterian system of church government argued for the non-inclusion of church members in the election of a minister on the grounds that, "There are some Congregations wherein the *major* part are wicked . . . There are some wherein possibly the *major* part may be hereticall." [Provincial Assembly of London], *Jus Divinum*, 132.

119. Cited in Avis, *Church in the Theology of the Reformers*, 47.

120. The dependency of the Westminster Assembly on the Irish *Book of the Articles of Religion* is tabulated by Schaff, in *Creeds of Christendom* I.762–66.

121. Jelle Faber criticizes the invisible-visible distinction in the Westminster Confession for pushing the Church in the direction of a Platonic Republic. This was a charge made against Luther's doctrine of the Invisible Church which was robustly answered by Melanchthon. See Faber, "Doctrine of the Church" 112–15. Melanchthon, "Apology to the Augsburg Confession," in *The Book of Concord*, 169. Also, Pelikan, *Christian Tradition* 4:174.

visible church is profession of faith,[122] as also affirmed in Baptist statements, and, in addition, those who are the offspring of believing parents, which had no parallel in Baptist ecclesiology.[123] Article 25.II says the visible church is like a "house" or family into which every member of society is born, and within which every member is to be guided and disciplined throughout the whole of life, to bring them to salvation. Thus the Presbyterian Confession continues:

> Unto this Catholic visible Church Christ hath given the ministry, oracles, and ordinances of God, for the gathering and perfecting of the saints, in this life, to the end of the world.[124]

Following Calvin's thinking, the Westminster Divines stated that the function of the visible Church, through the offices of Teacher, Pastor, Presbyter and Deacon, was to make the visible Church a holy Church, through "enforced sanctification." Thus, according to F. E. Mayer, in Presbyterian churches it is imagined that, "the communion of saints becomes a congregation, not of believers, but obeyers."[125]

Particular Baptist theology of the visible church, however, rejected this inclusivist policy and focused exclusively on the third category in Whitgift's scheme, those who were true, professing, believers. How then did the early Calvinistic Baptists arrive at a very different understanding of the character of the visible church? Here, as elsewhere,[126] it is proposed that in the area of ecclesiology their source was William Ames, particularly in relation to the nature of faith, and the stress on verbal profession of faith. In *The Marrow of Sacred Divinity*, Ames writes,

> 1. The Church as it lives on Earth . . . is visible in its parts, both dividedly in the severall members, and joyntly in companies or Congregations.
>
> 2. The former visibility is by mens personall profession which doth not make a Church simply visible, but in certain members,

---

122. The focus on profession as a mark of visible church membership has been criticized by modern Presbyterians. See Murray, "The Church: Its Definition in Terms of "Visible" and "Invisible" Invalid," *Collected Writings* 1.231–23. The issue is discussed in Jones, "The Invisible Church of the Westminster Confession of Faith," 71–85.

123. Baptists explicitly rejected the notion of proxy faith in the children of believing parents. Collier, *Certaine Queries*, 16–17. See section 2.2 above.

124. *Westminster Confession of Faith*, chapter 25.3.

125. Mayer, "Proper Distinction," 183.

126. See chapter 3.

or visible members of the Church, although the Church in it selfe or in its integrall state is not visible in the same place.

3. That visibility, which is in distinct companies or congregations, doth not only make a visible Church, but touching the outward forme doth make so many visible Churches as there are different congregations.[127]

The emphasis which Ames places on individual, personal faith in Christ, made visible by profession, as the foundation of visible churches or congregations, is precisely reproduced in the theology of early Particular Baptists like Thomas Collier. Faith was the inward reality of spiritual union with Christ, and the *sine qua non* of a believer's church, gathered under the rule of King Jesus. Ames emphasized this point in his definition of the church:

> The forme or constituting cause of the Church must needs be such a thing which is found alike in all the called: but this can be nothing else then a relation, neither hath any relation that force besides that that consists in a chiefe and intimate affection to Christ: but there is no such in man besides Faith: Faith therefore is the forme of the Church.[128]
>
> [The Church] is a society of believers: because that same thing in profession doth make a Church visible, which by its inward and reall nature doth make a mysticall Church, that is, Faith.[129]

By "faith" Ames meant something that was visible, manifested in action, both by declaration and good works.[130] He writes,

> Hence none is rightly admitted into the Church, but by confession of Faith and promise of obedience.[131]

Granting that obedience included being baptized as a believer, this statement could have been affirmed by Baptists, and would have legitimated their strict policy of guarding admittance to church membership.[132]

127. Ames, *Marrow*, 22.1–3.
128. Ibid., 21.11.
129. Ibid., 22.7.
130. See Brachlow, *Communion of Saints*, 126.
131. Ames, *Marrow*, 22.17.
132. The strictness of the policy can be measured by the condemnation of Thomas Proud in Illston, South Wales, who was adjudged to have "grievously sinned against God" for allowing "mixed communion" of baptized and unbaptized in visible church fellowship. *ARPB*, 5, also, 8.

Thomas Collier clarified the Baptist understanding of the character of the visible church in his 1654 work *The Right Constitution and True Subjects*:

> the visible Church of Christ in the right constitution of it, is a company of people gathered out of the world by the Spirit of Christ in the Ministery of the Gospel, to believe in him, and love his name, and to yield up themselves in a professed obedience to the whole will of Christ, as the effects and fruits of the work of the Spirit in faith and love.[133]

The Christological alignment of the visible church is prominent here, and for Collier, the defining characteristic of the visible church was the ability of its members to make a profession of faith in Christ in an audible and visible manner.[134] The act of "profession" could refer to two public evidences of the work of Christ in a believer, namely testimony,[135] that is, a declaration of the experimental work of Christ, and public baptism by immersion. At the general meeting of the Western Baptist Association in 1656 Collier declared,

> it's the duty of those that believe in Christ to put on Christ in a visible way of profession by which they are distinguished from the world which profession or putting on is entred into by one baptism.[136]

While Presbyterians baptized infants on the basis that they belonged to the invisible church on account of the covenant of grace,[137] Collier asserted, "We are not to Administer Ordinances from God's election, but from faith's manifestation."[138]

The same scheme of thought can be found in the writing of fellow leader among London Baptists, Hanserd Knollys. Knollys, in response to

---

133. Collier, *Right Constitution*, 8.

134. In the Reformed tradition the doctrine of the invisible church made provision for the secret, hidden work of divine election, and spiritual union with Christ, which were not made manifest in this way. See Vos, "Visible Church," 147.

135. *ARPB*, 19, "all those that professe faith in Christ and make the same apeare by their fruites ar the proper subjects of baptisme." Irregular spelling as in the original.

136. Ibid., 64.

137. For example, *Westminster Confession of Faith*, chapter 28.1 says, "Baptism is a sacrament of the new testament, ordained by Jesus Christ, not only for the solemn admission of the party baptized into the visible church; but also, to be unto him a sign and seal of the covenant of grace, of his ingrafting into Christ, of regeneration, of remission of sins." Applied to baptized infants this theology of baptism, as belonging to the covenant of grace, implies election to salvation. See 2.2 above.

138. Collier, *Certaine Queries*, 17.

the Presbyterian John Bastwick,[139] argued that the New Testament model of the church was decidedly visible and congregational:

> Faith, Repentence and Baptisme; and none other. And whosoever (poor as well as rich, bond as well as free, servants as well as Masters) did make a profession of their Faith in Christ Jesus, and would be baptized with water into the Name of the Father, Sonne, and Holy Spirit, were admitted members of the Church; but such as did not believe, and would not be baptized they would not admit into Church communion. This hath been the practice of some Churches of God in this City.[140]

Knollys's ideology was born of his own conversion experience and subsequent study of scripture,[141] and his convictions were little changed at the end of his life, when he wrote:

> A true visible Constituted Church of Christ under the Gospel is a Congregation of Saints, Called out of the World, Separated from Idolaters and Idol Temples, from the unbelieving Jews and their Synagogues and all legal observances of holy days, and Mosaical Rites, Ceremonies and shadows, and assembled together in one place.[142]

According to the records of the Abingdon Association in 1656, the Baptist commitment to the visible faith of the visible church remained undiminished, however, a recognition of the possibility of a wider, catholic expression of the visible church, signalled a maturing of their theology. At the assembly the Reading church asked, by what meanes and rules of Scripture, may any person be justly judged a visible believer?" The answer reaffirmed the commitment to a "profession or confession of Christ," since a visible believer will be able to make an

> experimentall declaration of the worke of regeneration and of the work of faith with power.[143]

The second part of visible faith was a believer's "practice or conversation." This consisted of:

---

139. See Bastwick, *Independency not God's Ordinance*.
140. Knollys, *Moderate Answer*, 20.
141. On the conversion of Knollys and his separation from the Church of England see Kiffin, *Life and Death of Mr. Hanserd Knollys*, 9–14.
142. Knollys, *Parable of the Kingdom of Heaven Expounded*, 4 and 5.
143. *ARPB*, 146.

> His love to all saints ... His universall obedience to God's commands according to the measure of light received ... His readinesse to lay downe all that he hath for Jesus Christ, rather than to sin against him.[144]

The fruits of the Spirit, love, obedience and self-sacrifice, evident in Christian character were regarded as the distinguishing marks of true believers, a sign of their election.

The essence of the visible church among the Particular Baptists was not the sociological reality of the Reformed tradition, but spiritual affection for Christ, and professed obedience to Christ evidenced in baptism, which are dependent upon and evidence of the work of the Spirit.[145] These twin Baptist *notae* of "affection" and "profession," were aligned with the theology of Independent Congregationalists, but distinct from the theology of the Reformers as preserved by Presbyterians. The Reformers would have considered Baptist statements about the visible church idealistic and unrealizable.[146]

2.6 A Separate Church

The Baptist practice of forming separate congregations apart from the National Church in the mid-1640s was a policy that required to be defended against the charge of schism from those who believed the Church could be reformed and purified from within.[147] In his principal work in defense of Baptist ecclesiology, Thomas Collier argued that it was not the task of saints to reform the Church of England, but rather to begin again, laying a new foundation for the church. This posture was typical of the perspective of moderate Puritans regarding the corruptions lately visited upon the National Church under the Laudian regime.[148] Collier's conviction was that the

---

144. Ibid., 146. I have omitted the many biblical texts inserted between each of the practices.

145. Collier, *Certaine Queries*, 10–11.

146. Vos, "Visible Church," 147.

147. See Edwards, *Gangraena* I.i., 61–62; Baillie, *Anabaptism*, Dedicatory Epistle & Preface; Poole, whose accusations we know via Kiffen, *A Briefe Remonstrance of the Reasons and Grounds of those People commonly called Anabaptists, for their Separation*, see below. The charge of schism was rebutted in the *First London Confession*, "To All that Desire . . .," and article XLVI, Lumpkin, *Baptist Confessions*, 154 and 168. Baptist sensitivity about schism is reflected in the Midland Association debate about the lawful conditions under which a member may leave a parochial church. *ARPB*, 36.

148. See for example, Tyacke, "Archbishop Laud," in Fincham, *Early Stuart Church, 1603–1642*, 51–70; Lake, "Laudian Style," in Fincham, *Early Stuart Church*, 161–85.

fundamental ideology of a National Church was erroneous and therefore the saints were under no obligation to seek its reformation.

> For I deny the whole Nation of England, that is, the people of the Nation, ever to be the true Church of Christ.[149]

Collier's separatist ecclesiology was based on the proposition that compulsion in religion is evidence of false religion.[150] He blamed the advent of "Popery" into England for the creation of a state church into which all citizens are compelled to come, a mixture of the faithful and the faithless.[151] Such a church was not built on Gospel preaching, but upon the power of the magistrate, before which all must submit, and by which all citizens were made Christians.[152] Far from being the Church, such an institution was "the beast" and usurped the authority of God to create the church, because Christ ordained that by means of preaching the Gospel that "stones were hewn," and the church built. Collier further argued that the prestige of succession in ecclesiology, greatly prized among Episcopalians, was worthless if the church was founded by Antichrist.[153] Thus, in his view, the Church of England was incapable of being reformed, nor should it be, because its foundation was false.

William Kiffin's defense of separate congregations was presented in a public correspondence with Robert Poole.[154] Poole believed Baptists were schismatics and asked of Kiffin,

> *How can you vindicate by the Word of God your Anabaptisticall way, from the sinfull guile of notorious Schisme, and defection from the Reformed Churches.*

Sharpe, "Archbishop Laud," in Todd, *Reformation to Revolution*, 71–77.

149. Colyer [Collier], *Certaine Queries*, 5. I will employ the usual spelling of Collier for the sake of consistency.

150. Brown argues, "The salient feature of [Baptist] faith was the principle that a church, according to Scripture, is a voluntary association of believers, with whose organization and support the state has nothing to do, and over whose belief and worship no civil power has jurisdiction." Brown, *Political Activities*, 2.

151. Collier, *Right Constitution*, 7. Such a view was common among Puritans and can be seen for example in Henry Barrowe, *Brief Discoverie*, 9–10.

152. Collier, *Certaine Queries*, 5.

153. Ibid., 6.

154. Robert Poole left no indelible mark on the seventeenth century but was almost certainly the father of Elizabeth Poole who has her own entry in ODNB. Elizabeth came under the influence of Kiffin at about sixteen years old and joined his church. Some time prior to 1648 she was expelled from the congregation for heresy and immorality. She later gained notoriety as a prophetess in politics. "Poole, Elizabeth (*bap*. 1622?, *d*. in or after 1668)," Brod in *ODNB*, eee online ed.

> By what warrant of the Word of God, doe you separate from our Congregations, where the Word and Sacraments are purely dispensed?[155]

In reply, Kiffen took issue precisely with the manner in which the Word and Sacraments were dispensed in the National Church. First, the Word was compromised by permitting the ungodly to participate in worship, their sins being unchallenged.[156] The National Church had become like apostate Israel as described in Jer 7.8, 9, 10

> Behold, ye steal, murder, and commit adultery, and swear falsely, and burn Incense unto Baal, and walk after other gods whom ye know not; and come and stand before mee, &c.[157]

Kiffen deplored the policy of mixed church membership. He opined that some congregants were found in church who "leaven the whole lumpe, 1 Cor 5.6."[158] The remedy to this situation was provided by God's Word, which, if purely dispensed, might heal the sinner, but the Word was preached without efficacy. Second, turning to baptism, Kiffen challenged Poole,

> shew me what Gospel Institution have you for the Baptizing of Children . . . what can you finde for your practise therein, more then the durty puddle of mens Inventions.[159]

Baptism was no longer administered "according to the pure institutions of the Lord Jesus,"[160] the fundamental criteria of a true church for Particular Baptists. Baptists, therefore, could hardly be judged schismatic, Kiffen argued, by a church that corrupted the sacraments, failed to discipline sinners, and preached not the word. Unlike Thomas Collier, however, who regarded a National Church as inherently flawed on account of the essential link between Church and State, Kiffen, like Henry Jessey, could imagine worshipping in the National Church, if it could be purified and disciplined.[161] If the Church were

---

155. Kiffen, *Briefe Remonstrance*, 3 and 4. Italics as original.
156. Ibid., 5.
157. Ibid.
158. Ibid.
159. Ibid.
160. Ibid.
161. Collier's uncompromising stance on the question of separation is evidenced in *ARPB*, 61 where he forbids baptized believers even to listen to the preaching of parochial ministers.

a pure lumpe of Beleevers, gathered and united according to the Institution of Christ, wee (I hope,) shall joyne with you, in the same Congregation and Fellowship, and nothing shall seperate us by death.[162]

But since this was not the case separation was not merely justified, it was necessary, Kiffen asserted. The two fundamental *notae ecclesia*, which had been central to the Reformation project to establish a true church, namely Word and Sacrament, were corrupted and powerless.[163] Until such time as the Church of England be reformed, therefore, the gathering of Calvinistic Baptist believers in congregations wholly separate from the National Church would continue.[164] Poole stated to Kiffen that the great work of reformation in the Church was taking place, and asked why Baptists, by pursuing a policy of separatism, were placing this in jeopardy. Kiffen responded saying he placed no confidence in the Westminster Assembly to bring reform to the Church, and in any case the proposals for change were bringing the National Church closer to the religion practiced and enjoyed already by Baptists. How could Poole, therefore, regard Baptists as a disturbance, since they were in fact contributing to the furtherance of reformation, by pursuing the same ends?[165]

That the policy of separatism was of the essence of Baptist ecclesiology is evidenced by the decision of the Abingdon Association in 1656 to buy a burying place for their own church members, so that there might be no "unnecessary mingling" with false worshippers, or those with corrupt customs, even in death.[166]

Summary

In this chapter we have outlined the primary contours of emerging Baptist ecclesiology in the historical and theological context of the mid-1640s. Whilst working within a Calvinistic framework of theology, the Particular

162. Kiffen, *Briefe Remonstrance*, 6.

163. On the importance of Word and Sacrament in Luther and Calvin, see for example, Avis, *The Church in the Theology of the Reformers*, 13–50. At the General meeting of the Midland Baptist Association in 1656, the ministry of national church ministers was declared "Babilonish." *ARPB*, 25.

164. Kiffen, *Briefe Remonstrance*, 6 and 13.

165. Ibid., 7.

166. *ARPB*, 152–53, also 158. Randall Bate commented on the refusal of separatists to be buried in churchyards in the Elizabethan era. See Collinson, *From Cranmer to Sancroft*, 137. Abingdon also had a strict policy forbidding Baptist members to listen to parish minister's preaching. See *ARPB*, 159, 169.

Baptists emphasized the human response to the Gospel, the voluntarist element in the act of faith in Christ. For this reason, Knollys reported that congregations were being formed as sinners were being converted and people admitted to the church on the basis of "Faith, Repentance and Baptism." No reference was made to election, though Particular Baptists were committed to the doctrine of predestination.[167] Rather, they stressed the experimental nature of faith, looking to the paradigm of the New Testament church, especially the accounts of Apostolic preaching in Acts.

Particular Baptist ecclesiology sought to restore the church to its primitive state in which preaching awakened the conscience, leading to repentance, followed by baptism. A conversion event separated saints from sinners, the godly from the profane. Rejecting the Reformed model of a mixed church of the regenerate and the reprobate, they believed the church was to be separate and distinct from the "world," neither could it be defined or controlled by the State. Orthodox doctrine was not sufficient for entry into the church, neither was infant baptism. Evidence of a vital relationship to God, a profession of faith in Jesus as Savior and Lord, was essential for church membership.[168]

Although the emphasis on personal conversion suggested a strongly individualist approach to church membership, Baptists sought to balance this priority with an equal stress on the gathered nature of the church. No believer should remain alone, but as a "living stone" be built into the church, the body of Christ. This was the concrete reality of the church, the visible church, the only expression of *ecclesia* which concerned Calvinistic Baptists. The invisible church, which answered to the mystery of God's eternal decrees, held little interest for them. The visible church, comprised of saints separated from the world, was a compact, committed, congregation of believers, covenanted to live under the rule of King Jesus, the implications of which are further explored in the next chapter.

---

167. The situation appears to have been opposite to this in the sixteenth century among the early Separatists. Michael Watts notes that the notion of conversion was absent from the writings of Robert Browne, Henry Barrow and John Greenwood. Watts, *Dissenters* 1, 171.

168. An illuminating example of a "Particular Baptist" conversion to Jesus Christ is that of William Kiffin. See Orme, *Remarkable Passages*, 10–11.

3

"To follow the Lambe wheresoever he goeth"[1]

The Church of King Jesus

Introduction

IN THIS CHAPTER WE come to the central argument of this book, namely that the controlling dynamic of Baptist ecclesiology in the 1640s and 1650s was the express intention to organize a church according to the rule of Christ, Priest, Prophet, and King.[2] The commitment to organizing the church within this "Christological"[3] framework was stated in a letter distributed by Baptist messengers to the Abingdon Association by on 16 October 1657:

> It is likewise our earnest request unto the Lord that you may rightly understand not only the propheticall and priestly office

---

1. Preface to the 1644 Confession. In Lumpkin, *Baptist Confessions*, 155. The phrase was earlier used by Goodwin in, *A Glimpse of Sions Glory*, 26. Kiffin, who wrote the preface for Goodwin's tract, may have borrowed it for the Baptist document.

2. See, for example, the Irish correspondence of 1653 in *ARPB*, 115, where Baptists are described as, "the flock of our Lord Jesus that are, or have given upp their names to bee, under his rule and government." The common greeting in Baptist correspondence of the 1650s invokes the threefold office, indicating its fundamental importance. See *ARPB, passim*. Knollys includes the threefold formula in a list of titles attributed to Christ in his preaching. See Knollys, *Christ Exalted*, 4.

3. Throughout this chapter I am using "Christology" in a functional sense, referring to the Baptist inclination to defer to the mind, will and purpose of Christ for his church in all matters ecclesiological.

of Christ but his kingly office also: that he is over all and Lord of all, Ro. 9.5, Acts 10.36. That the Father hath put all things under his feet and given him to be head over all things to the church, and hath committed all judgement unto him having given him all power both in heaven and in earth. And that you, knowing this, may be allwayes carefull to obey all the commands of this your Lord and King Christ Jesus.[4]

The idea of the church submitted to King Jesus was neither new, nor unique,[5] but Baptist ecclesiology of the period was distinctive in its thoroughgoing application of this Christological paradigm to all aspects of the local congregation.[6] The rule of Christ was determinative in their practice of entrance by believer's baptism,[7] the organization of ministry,[8] and the expulsion and excommunication of gross sinners.

The development of "Christology" as the ideological catalyst for ecclesiological reform was present in the theology of the congregationalist Henry Jacob and his thinking must be explored because it provides a necessary basis for considering the "Christology" of the Particular Baptists in their first major doctrinal statement as a group, the First London Confession. Subsequently, Thomas Collier put "Christology" at the heart of the Baptist ecclesiological project and some consideration of his work will enable us to see how the link between the two theological themes made church polity a non-negotiable conviction for Baptists. Collier was among the prominent leaders of the Baptist movement in the late 1640s, and his theology both reflects wider Baptist commitments and, as an evangelist and Messenger of a Baptist Association, exerted influence on the emerging constituency. In addition, Collier provides us with an extended essay on the person and

---

4. *ARPB*, 179. A threefold office of Christ can be found in Justin Martyr, Tertullian, Cyprian, Eusebius, and Thomas Aquinas speaks of Christ as *legislator, sacerdos*, and *rex*. In the *Westminster Confession* it was included in Chapter VIII. Calvin's treatment of the doctrine in the *Institutes* II.XV.1–6 became the basis for its development in Puritan religion. See Jansen, *Calvin's Doctrine of the Work of Christ*; McCulloh, *Christ's Person and Life-Work in the Theology of Albrecht Ritschl*. Calvin's doctrine of the threefold office is contextualized within his larger doctrine of atonement in Partee, *Theology of John Calvin*, 158–67.

5. On the Kingship of Christ in emerging Presbyterianism, see Paul, *The Assembly of the Lord*, 513–14; also Westminster Confession, Article XXX.

6. See for example the frequent reference to "Our Lord Jesus Christ, who is head of the Church," in the *ARPB*.

7. In the West Country Association the general meeting of 1656 debated the question, "whether baptism be absolutely necessary to an orderly church communion?" The answer given was, "we judge it so to be, because it's suitable to the declared will and ordinance of Jesus Christ." Ibid., 63.

8. See ibid., 168–69, 171.

work of Christ running to over two hundred and fifty pages, one of the most substantial theological works to emerge from the Particular Baptists in the period, and the only one of such length on the threefold offices of Christ.

3.1. The Forerunner, Henry Jacob

By 1604–5 Henry Jacob[9] had come to clear convictions about the congregational nature of a true church, a principle he regarded among the *fundamenta* in religion.[10] In a catechism entitled *Principles and Foundations of Christian Religion* he stated:

> Question. What is a true Visible or Ministeriall Church of Christ?
>
> Answer. A true Visible or Ministeriall Church of Christ is a particular Congregation being a spirituall perfect Corporation of Believers, & having power in it selfe immediately from Christ to administer all Religious meanes of faith to the members thereof.[11]

This statement occurs in a section of the catechism dealing with the instrumental outward means that Christ, "our Prophet and King," has provided for the sanctification of the saints. Jacob was committed to the Puritan view, formerly seen in Henry Barrowe, that true faith depended upon true order, that ecclesiology could not be separated from soteriology, because church polity was the substance of the second commandment.[12] This explains Jacob's total commitment to the formation of a church reflecting the will of Christ as King, and his citation of Cyprian's dictum, *extra ecclesiam non est salus* in 1611, in reference to congregationally organized and governed churches.[13]

By 1610, exiled in Middelburg, writing *The Divine Beginning and Institution of Christ's true Visible and Ministeriall Church*, Jacob elaborated further his understanding of a non-parochial, gathered church as a true,

---

9. Background to the emergence of the Jacob Church is found in Tolmie, *Saints*, chapter 1.

10. His previous equivocal opinions are recorded in, Jacob, *A Defence of the Churches and Ministery of Englande*.

11. In Burrage, *EED* 2, 157.

12. Rohr, "*Extra Ecclesiam Nulla Salus*," 116. Also Brachlow, *Communion of Saints*, 26, 52 and *passim*. Brachlow, "Elizabethan Roots," *passim*.

13. Jacob, *Declaration and Plainer Opening*, 40.

visible church in its own right.[14] Such a church, he argued, must be free from episcopal jurisdiction, though he did not deny the right of magistrates to oversee the ordinary affairs of Christians. In this work Jacob contrasts two types of Christian, those who believe church order and government to be *adiaphora*, that is, a matter of indifference, since Christ did not establish one certain pattern of Church government in the New Testament. With moderate English Puritans clearly in view, he states that such who take this view, "hold and professe that Christ in respect of his Church . . . is not King, Lord and Lawgiver."[15] The second sort hold the contrary view, namely, they "do plainly and cleerely acknowledge that Christ is King, Lord and Lawgiver of his Church as it is Visible and outward,"[16] and that in the New Testament Christ has instituted a universal and eternal Church order and polity, "for us everywhere & for ever, not to be altered or changed by any man or men whatsoever they be."[17] This said, Jacob expressed his frustration that the "second sort," while acknowledging Christ had ordained a clear form of Church government, failed, or refused, to implement the vision, and some were still submitting to bishops.[18] In such a Church, which in England remained dominant, Christ was not King.

The Christological form of a church was a concept not without ambiguity, as Jacob was willing to concede. In *The Divine Beginning* of 1610, he distinguished between those elements of ecclesiology which were "accidental and mutable," and those which belonged to the "essence, nature and constitution" of the church, which determine the "matter and forme of the same."[19] It was only in relation to the latter elements that Christ's rule must be maintained. "Our purpose," he writes, "is not to intitle Christ to be the special Author & institutor allways & necessarily of things Accidentall and mutable in the Church."[20] This explains why, in 1616, Jacob and his congregation partook of communion in parish churches, "where neyther our assent, nor silent presence is given to any mere human tradition." To listen to godly ministers preaching the word was also permissible because

---

14. Jacob held these views at least as early as 1605 according to *Principles and Foundations of Christian Religion*. Yarbrough, "Ecclesiastical Development," 183–97. Jacob met John Robinson in Leyden in 1610, and this, at least, must have given impetus to Jacob's Congregationalist convictions. See Brachlow, "The Elizabethan Roots of Henry Jacob's Churchmanship," 228–54; Paul, "Henry Jacob," 105–13.

15. Jacob, *Divine Beginning*, 2, 7.

16. Ibid., 2.

17. Ibid., 3.

18. Ibid.

19. Ibid., A5.

20. Ibid., A4.

it was ordained by Christ. Members, however, were not permitted to attend any parish "where cope and surplice were worn, the sign of the cross or kneeling was observed, or a homily read,"[21] since Christ had commanded none of these for true worship.

Jacob's ecclesiastical vision of the church included freedom from episcopal jurisdiction, though under the oversight of the king's "subordinate civil magistrates," in order to be subject solely to the "kingly office of Christ . . . the immediate head of each individual congregation."[22] To those Puritan leaders who could not follow the logical progression of Jacob's theology into semi-separatism,[23] he wrote,

> To say that he [Christ] hath now no Visible Kingdō or administration on earth, or that he instituted not any for us, but hath left it to mens discretion both to institute & to order: this truly doth very much impayre his Honor, & diminish his Glory, & lessen his majestie amōg mē.[24]

In *A Confession and Protestation* of 1616, written under pressure to justify his ecclesiological experiment, Jacob argued that all outward matters used in the exercise of religion are inherently spiritual, and therefore only that is lawful which has been appointed by Christ. That certain outward practices of religion, of men's institution, are discretionary, merely voluntary matters of convenience, for example the Prayer Book, and not inherently spiritual, Jacob could not countenance.[25] In Jacob's thinking, everything used in the exercise of religion is spiritual, and being spiritual, every element in true worship has been ordained by Christ, since "Christs Prophetical, and Kingly Offices even in outward spirituall matters [are] absolute and perfect."[26] To employ ordinances from men would be to compromise the perfection and all-sufficiency of Christ's governance of the Church. So he argues,

> we are contradicted by some, who say plainely that Christ in the Gospell though he bee the Prophet, King and Priest to his

---

21. Brachlow, "Elizabethan Roots," 238. Also, Jacob, *Confession and Protestation*, A3.

22. See Tolmie, *Saints*, 8.

23. Two prominent puritans who accused Jacob of Brownism were Richard Maunsell and Arthur Hildersham. See Brachlow, "Elizabethan Roots," 238.

24. Jacob, *Divine Beginning*, 5.

25. Jacob shared fully in the Puritan complaint concerning Anglican liturgy. Henry Barrowe described the Prayer Book as containing "old written rotten stuffe." Barrowe, *Brief Discoverie*, 65. See Rohr, "*Extra Ecclesiam Nulla Salus*," 114.

26. Jacob, *A Confession and Protestation*, A5.

> Church, yet he is not the onely, or absolute Teacher, Institutor, King, and Lawgiver, of his outward Church, nor of the visible administration thereof . . . And likewise that Christians now have libertie and free choice for the saide outward things in the exercise of Religion, till mans Authority do determine them . . . This we cannot consent to: but we renounce it, as highly derogating from the true, and due offices, and honour of Christ.[27]

For Jacob there was no room for compromise on this point. He opined,

> Yea we are perswaded, if we should believe otherwise, we should rob Christ of his honour and give his glorie to others; which is a part of the highest sacriledge that can be.[28]

In 1616 Jacob was convinced of the need to form his own congregation in order to fulfil his vision of true church, a decision which rested upon Christological convictions. To the puritan leaders who were not ready to make the break, Jacob stated his case:

> We believe that Christ in these things (no lesse then in matters inward concerning religion) is the foundation to the whole building even of his visible and politicall Church now under the Gospell, as well and as thoroughly as he was under the Law, appointed by God over all things as head to his sayd Church which is the fulnesse of him that filleth all in all things.[29]

As a puritan Jacob believed Christ must reign in the life of the believer, and as a non-conformist he asserted Christ's reign to be as necessary, complete and universal in the Church, as a matter pertaining to salvation.[30] Only in such a church are the promises of God given and received, therefore, "we are all bound with all care to hearken to the expresse precept of the Holy Ghost concerning even this point, saying *This is the way walke yee in it.*"[31]

The Christological convictions which led Jacob to gather a new church, organized under the rule of Christ, were to remain fundamental to this congregation, the mother of later Calvinistic Baptist churches.

---

27. Ibid., A6.

28. Ibid.

29. Ibid. On this point see Duesing, "Henry Jacob (1563–1624) Pastoral Theology and Congregational Ecclesiology," 297.

30. See Jacob, *Confession and Protestation*, A8. Also Brachlow, "Elizabethan Roots," 240–44.

31. Jacob, *Confession and Protestation*, D4.

3.2. "Christology" in Early Particular Baptist Confessions

In the introductory letter to the First London Confession of 1644, the seven signatory Calvinistic Baptist congregations affirmed their common commitment to Christ as sovereign over the church. Demonstrating a sense of unity in Christ they stated:

> *Yet are all one in Communion, holding Jesus Christ to be our head and Lord; under whose government wee desire alone to walke, in following the Lambe wheresoever he goeth.*[32]

They also stated their intention to,

> *more studie to lift up the Name of the Lord Jesus, and stand for his appointments and Lawes; which is the desires and prayers of the contemned Churches of Christ in* London *for all Saints.*[33]

This declaration of intent continued the tradition of Henry Jacob, and served notice of the Baptist program of forming churches according to the New Testament pattern given by King Jesus, the Lord of the church. The statements made in the Confession about the nature and form of the church cannot be understood apart from their Christological foundation.

It is now recognized that Baptist confessional "Christology" both followed the model within, and borrowed content from, the Separatist *True Confession* of 1596.[34] In addition, material was derived from William Ames' *The Marrow of Sacred Divinity*,[35] particularly in development of the threefold offices of Christ. This served to position Baptist theology within the mainstream of English Puritan, Separatist, and Calvinist traditions, and

---

32. Preface to the 1644 Confession, in Lumpkin, *Baptist Confessions*, 155. Italics as original.

33. Ibid., 155–56. Italics as original.

34. Almost half of the fifty-three articles in the 1644 London Confession are derived from *A True Confession*, at some points almost word for word, though no article was taken over from the Separatist statement without alteration. This observation appears to have been made first by Whitley, *HBB*, 94, followed by White, *English Baptists*, 62; also, Nelson, "Reflecting on Baptist Origins," 34. Analysis of the socio-political perspectives of both confessions is found in Thompson, "Seventeenth-Century Baptist Confessions in Context," 335–48.

35. It appears that Glen Stassen was the first scholar in recent times to note the connection between the Baptist Confession and the work of Ames. See Stassen, "Anabaptist Influence in the Origin of the Particular Baptists," 332. The link between Ames and the Baptists was given further examination in Nelson, "Reflecting on Baptist Origins," 34-5; White notes the linkage but does not pursue the influence in his exposition of the London Confession. See White, "Doctrine of the Church," 575 n. 3; 576 n. 3. See also Sprunger, "William Ames," 72–74.

demonstrated non-reliance on Continental Anabaptists, as was made plain on the title page of the Confession.[36]

The "Christology" of early Calvinistic Baptists was constructed from biblical texts taken from both Old and New Testaments. Article 8 in the 1644 Confession states that in scripture, "God hath plainly revealed whatsoever he hath thought needfull for us to know, believe, and acknowledge, touching the Nature and Office of Christ."[37] Many subsequent Christological statements drew on biblical language and imagery,[38] rather than the language of the creeds.[39] Although the early Baptists were not hostile to historic creeds,[40] and did not deny anything they taught, reverting to scripture reflected their preference for primitive Christianity over later constructs of doctrine.

In order to affirm their theological orthodoxy in regard to the divinity of Christ,[41] the compilers of the Confession drew images and metaphors from the books of Proverbs, John's Gospel and Colossians, from which they formulated the statement,

> The Lord Jesus is the Sonne of God the Father, the brightnesse of his glory, the ingraven forme of his being, God with him and

---

36. Lumpkin, *Baptist Confessions*, 153.

37. Ibid., 158.

38. See Lumpkin, "Bible in Early Baptist Confessions," 33–41.

39. Confessions, as distinct from creeds, have traditionally been regarded as non-binding statements around which congregations covenanted to walk together. The Southern Baptist Convention document *Baptist Faith and Message* (2000), rejects credalism because creeds are imposed as "instruments of doctrinal accountability." See *Preamble*. Estep defended the thesis, "Baptists are not a creedal but a confessional people," in Estep, "Nature and Use of Biblical Authority," 3–4. Philip Thompson has argued that Baptists only collected their confessions for historical interest, "not to provide an authoritative manual of doctrine." Thompson, "Seventeenth-Century Baptist Confessions in Context," 335. More recently, Paul Fiddes understands Baptist suspicion of the creeds in linguistic terms, highlighting the danger of confusing the signifier with the thing signified, stating, "[Baptists] have thus refused to be bound by the words of the creeds." Fiddes, *Tracks and Traces*, 2.

40. Steven Harmon traces echoes of *Nicaeno-Constantinopolitan Trinitarianism and Chalcedonian "Christology"* in early Baptist confessions in, "Baptist Confessions of Faith," 349–58.

41. The later *Somerset Confession* is more creedal in its theology: "We believe that Jesus Christ is truly God and truly man, of the seed of David." Article XIII, in Lumpkin, *Baptist Confessions*, 206. Harmon finds echoes of the Chalcedonian Definition that Christ is "one person in two distinct natures, true God and true Man." See Harmon, "Baptist Confessions of Faith," 351.

with his holy Spirit, by whom he made the world, by whom he upholds and governes all the works hee hath made.[42]

In affirming the humanity Christ they drew on Pauline language,

When the fulnesse of time was come, [Christ] was made man of a woman, of the Tribe of Judah, of the seed of Abraham and David . . .[43]

The Virgin Birth, and sinlessness of Jesus, similarly employs Lucan language:

. . . to wit, of Mary that blessed Virgin, by the Holy Spirit coming upon her, and the power of the most High overshadowing her, and was also in all things like unto us, sinne only excepted.[44]

Article 10 affirms the role of Christ as mediator of the new covenant of grace, and regarding the *munus triplex* states that Christ is, perfectly and fully the Prophet, Priest and King of the Church of God for evermore."[45] To this office of mediator Christ was appointed from his birth, anointed by the Spirit, and endued with all necessary gifts for salvation.[46]

Article 13 asserts that the threefold office of Christ belongs to him alone, a statement with implications for Baptist views concerning ministry. There is no priest in the church other than Christ, and the primary ministry in the church is that of Christ, all human ministry being secondary and derivative. Article 14 states that the threefold office of Christ corresponds to the threefold need of sinful humanity, namely ignorance, alienation and powerlessness. As prophet, Christ reveals the whole will of God that is needful for his servants to know, believe and obey.[47] As Priest, Christ, by the sacrifice of himself put away sin and effected the reconciliation of the elect, and

---

42. Article IX, in Lumpkin, *Baptist Confessions*, 158.

43. Article IX. Lumpkin, *Baptist Confessions*, 158. The second edition of the First London Confession added many more proof texts affirming Christ's deity and humanity. In Underhill, *Confessions of Faith*, 33. The Particular Baptist *Midland Association Confession* of 1655 repeated this statement, showing these statements were true of Particular Baptists generally, and not merely the beliefs of one regional constituency. In Lumpkin, *Baptist Confessions*, 199.

44. Article IX. Lumpkin, *Baptist Confessions*, 159.

45. Lumpkin, *Baptist Confessions*, 159. Once again, this is repeated in *The Midland Confession*. Op. cit.

46. Article XI, in Lumpkin, *Baptist Confessions*, 159.

47. See also the pastoral letter to the Somerset churches of Thomas Collier in 1657: "Our Prophet hath taken away the vail from off his people's faces in giving the knowledge of his will in the practical part of the Gospell, in his ordinances and matters of worship." *ARPB*, 89.

lives now in the heavens where he makes intercession for the saints. From the Priesthood of Christ is derived the priesthood of believers.[48] Article 19 concerns the Kingship of Christ:

> Christ being risen from the dead ascended into heaven, sat on the right hand of God the Father, having all power in heaven and earth, given unto him, he doth spiritually govern his Church, exercising his power over all Angels and Men, good and bad, to the preservation of the elect.[49]

Corresponding to the Kingship of Christ, the Confession defines the church as a,

> spiritual kingdom . . . joined to the Lord . . . in the practical injoyment of the Ordinances, commanded by Christ their head and King.[50]

In this statement the doctrine of the church is brought into explicit relation to "Christology," in as much as the church defines its essence as Christ's spiritual kingdom, comprised of those "he hath purchased and redeemed to himself."

In a series of five articles[51] interpolated between three statements taken from *A True Confession* regarding the threefold office of Christ, material derived from William Ames was inserted verbatim into the London Confession.[52] Article 12 is an elaboration of Christ's role as Mediator of the New Covenant.[53] The Article emphasizes that Christ was divinely appointed and called to this office, as taught in Heb 5:4–6, a calling which contains three elements, or moments in salvation history, initiated by God, namely, "chusing, fore-ordaining, and sending." Article 14, as stated previously, correlates the three offices of Christ's ministry to humanity's threefold problem.[54] Article 16 elaborates the prophetic office of Christ, stressing the revelatory necessity of his being both God and man in order to make each known to the other.[55] Article 18 follows the usual pattern, supplementing the teaching of the *True Confession*[56] by emphasizing that Christ's priesthood is "perpetual

---

48. Article XVII. Lumpkin, *Baptist Confessions*, 160–61.
49. Ibid., 161.
50. Article XXXIII. Ibid., 165.
51. Numbers 12, 14, 16, 18 and 19.
52. Ames, *Marrow of Sacred Divinity*, 74–76.
53. Ibid., 19.3–7, 74.
54. Ibid., 19.10–11, 74.
55. Ibid., 19.16. 75
56. True Confession, Article 14. Lumpkin, *Baptist Confessions*, 85.

and proper to Christ,"⁵⁷ and therefore does not give rise to an equivalent human priesthood to be handed on by succession. Article 19 of the London Confession inserts into the material derived from the *True Confession*, article 15, the additional words, "He doth spiritually govern His Church." This makes explicit the ecclesiological implications of the Kingly office of Christ for the Baptists, the subject under discussion in this statement.

It can be argued that the additions to the London Confession, supplementing the basic "Christology" of the *True Confession*, evidence a developed interest in the person and work of Christ among Baptists, which had in turn a number of implications for ecclesiology. In the Baptist vision of the church the only true and valid ministry is that of the living Christ, eternally present to his people gathered in his name, as stated in Article 13 in the 1644 Confession:

> This office to be Mediator . . . is so proper to Christ, as neither in the whole, nor in any part there-of, it can be transferred from him to any other.

In a pastoral letter to the West Country Churches in April 1657 Thomas Collier bewailed his inadequacy for the demands of ministry, adding: "Oh, who is sufficient for these things, none but the Lion of the tribe of Judah, the great Shepherd and Bishop of our souls."⁵⁸ Whatever ministry the church possesses, and however it is understood, it cannot in any fashion usurp or challenge the unique and essential role Christ occupies among his people.

In his analysis of the First London Confession, Mennonite scholar Glen Stassen has so stressed the importance of the Christological motif to the early Particular Baptists that he is prepared to argue,

> All the major innovations [in the theology of the London Confession] are readily understandable as the consistent carrying out of the implications of that new centre.⁵⁹

This argument serves Stassen's purpose of accentuating possible links between the London Baptists and continental Anabaptists, via Richard Blunt. However, it can be argued that the Christological priority evident in the First London Confession was rooted in conversionist faith, and does not represent the discovery of a "new motif" of Christology in Mennonite theology, as Stassen suggests.⁶⁰

57. See Ames, *Marrow*, 19.18–19, 76.
58. *ARPB*, 88.
59. Stassen, "Anabaptist Influences," 334.
60. Stassen asserts that the Baptists did not merely make modifications to Congregationalist theology but introduced a "basic new motif." The new motif is centered in

My argument on this point derives support from close analysis of articles 21 to 32 which are creedal in style[61] and follow a traditional Calvinist scheme of Covenant Theology, such as that reflected in the near contemporary *Westminster Confession*.[62] In numerical order, these articles teach: Christ the only Savior died only for the elect; salvation is by faith alone wrought by God in the hearts of the elect by the Spirit of God; the elect will be kept always in the way of salvation by God's power since they are engraven on the palms of God's hands; faith comes by hearing the preached word of the Gospel; the power of the Gospel alone is sufficient to convert sinners and requires no preparatory work of the law; the power which saves sinners is the same power which keeps sinners through duties, temptations, conflicts and sufferings; salvation as adoption into union with the triune God; union with Christ means justification; salvation brings sanctification; salvation means reconciliation with God through Jesus Christ; spiritual warfare as an enduring reality for believers; triumph over temptation and opposition in the Christian life is through the strength of Christ alone. In each of these articles Christ is prominent, naturally, since the agenda is the scheme of salvation, but what the London Baptists constructed was not a dogmatic Christological statement, as Stassen implies, but a *kerygmatic* statement, reflecting a primary concern for what Christ means for the saints.[63]

That the Christocentric view of the church remained fundamental to Baptists can be seen in the Association Records of the Particular Baptists of the 1650s. In the West Country Association, the threefold office was often used in epistolary greetings, as was also the practice of the Abingdon Association.[64] In the Midland Association "Confession,"[65] article 9 stated: "That Christ is the onely true king, priest and prophet of Church."[66] In the Abingdon Association letter of 13 October 1657 the Messengers stated,

---

the death, burial, and resurrection of Christ and its manifestation in the believer. See Stassen, "Anabaptist Influences," 334.

61. Nelson describes them as catechetical, and offers a reconstruction of a "Q" form of the articles, but the reconstruction is unnecessary and unconvincing. See Nelson, "Reflecting on Baptist Origins," 36–38.

62. See *Westminster Confession*, chapter 7.

63. See also Knollys, *Christ Exalted*, 7. There he writes, "[Christ] is our Father, our Husband, our Brother, our Friend, our King, Priest, and Prophet; He is our Justification, Sanctification, and Redemption; He is our Peace, our all."

64. *ARPB*, 103 and 166.

65. This document was preserved in the Tewkesbury Church book, and was signed by the founding churches of the Midland Association on 2 May 1655. Ibid., 18–20 and 39.

66. Ibid., 19.

> It is . . . our earnest request unto the Lord that you may rightly understand not only the propheticall and priestly office of Christ but his kingly office also: that he is over all and Lord of all. . . . And that you, knowing this, may be allwayes carefull to obey all the commands of this your Lord and King Christ Jesus.[67]

The evidence of earliest Baptist Confession, the First London of 1644, and continuing thereafter in other Confessions and other formal documents,[68] shows that the theory and practice of Baptist ecclesiology was developed within a Christological framework.

3.3 *Munus Triplex Christi* and Ecclesiology in Thomas Collier[69]

One particular example of attempts by Baptists to provide a theological rationale for their ecclesiology via "Christology" can be seen in the work of Thomas Collier, primarily *The Exaltation of Christ*,[70] but also in other writings.[71] Collier's tract, *The Exaltation*, expounds the text of John 3.14 "And as Moses lift up the serpent in the wildernesse, so it behoves the sonne of man to be lifted up, &c,"[72] hence the title of the work.

In this work, Collier structured his Christology according to the three offices in such a way as to provide an expansion of the theology found in the

---

67. Ibid., 179.

68. See the Catechism of Benjamin Keach, questions 28–30, produced in 1693.

69. For biographical and theological background to Thomas Collier see Land, "Doctrinal Controversies of English Particular Baptists (1644–1691) as Illustrated by the Career and Writings of Thomas Collier."

70. Full title, Thomas Collier, *The Exaltation of Christ in the Dayes of the Gospel: As the alone High Priest, Prophet, and King, of Saints* (London: 1647). This is the second, corrected edition, the original was published on 26 April 1646.

71. In the later phase of his career Collier was accused of Christological heresy by Nehemiah Coxe, and not without cause. Collier demonstrated a lack of theological skill when explaining the nature of God and lapsed into modalist language. If one compares Collier's *First General Epistle to the Saints* (London: 1648), chapter II, IV-VI and the Racovian Catechism, section III.1, there are alarming similarities regarding the essential unity of God. Collier asserted that God is in the Son, not in terms of essential union, but in the same way he is in things which are not himself, as he is in the saints for example. See *First General Epistle*, chs. V-VI. When speaking about the work of Christ, as opposed to the nature of Christ, Collier was entirely orthodox, and there is no hint of doctrinal deviancy in *The Exaltation of Christ*. Collier was accused of heresy and opposed by Nehemiah Coxe in *Vindiciae Veritatis*. Collier responded in *A Sober and Moderate Answer to Nehemiah Coxe's Invective*. See Land, *Doctrinal Controversies*, 265–81, 302–6.

72. Collier, *Exaltation of Christ*, 1.

1644 London Confession. One example of the importance of this concept to Collier's theology is evidenced by his saying, "Christ [as Prophet] teacheth us to own him as our Priest, as our King."[73] Collier organized his teaching according to the pattern of his kerygma, employing a redemptive configuration which viewed Christ as savior, teacher, and ruler. Collier exalts Christ first as our justification according to his priesthood, secondly acknowledges Christ as our teacher according to Prophecy, and thirdly asserts Christ as law-giver to his people according to his Kingship.[74]

Collier's order is notably different from that in Calvin's 1559 edition of the *Institutes* which employs a *Heilsgeschichte* approach to the three offices,[75] Christ being first prophet, then king, and finally priest according to "gospel doctrine."[76] Calvin has prophecy as primary because it was the task of the prophets to hold the church in expectation until the Messiah's coming, and when Christ came he was anointed by the Spirit to be herald and witness of the Father's grace.[77] Kingship is eschatological, because it is spiritual. Calvin asks, "what would it profit us to be gathered under the reign of the Heavenly King, unless beyond this earthly life we were certain of enjoying its benefits?"[78] Elaborating further he says,

> Thus it is that we may patiently pass through this life with its misery, hunger, cold, contempt, reproaches, and other troubles—content with this one thing: that our King will never leave

---

73. Ibid., 198.

74. Ibid., 3.

75. This is not intended to imply that Calvin viewed the offices successively, but that he identifies the three offices with moments of salvation history, namely anticipation, incarnation, and session. On this point see McCulloh, *Christ's Person and Life-Work*, 152. He accuses Ritschl of misinterpreting Calvin as having separated the offices of Christ, a judgment not supported by a careful reading of Calvin.

76. The earliest edition of the *Institutes* (1537) speaks only of a two-fold office, priest and king, since Calvin's atonement theology emphasized priestly sacrifice and kingly conquest. Luther also interpreted the messianic title as a two-fold office. This is the basis of Jansen's critique of Calvin's use of the triple formula, suggesting it was an aberration in his systematic theology, the two offices being more original and authentic. He further asserts that it has little biblical warrant, and that Calvin nowhere has a use for the formula he himself had suggested. He argues that while the doctrine of the three offices derives its popularity from Calvin, it is not an adequate or true expression of his own theology. Jansen, *Doctrine of the Work of Christ*, 40, 33, and 105. In response, it can be shown that Calvin was working with the threefold formula throughout his career, and has an exposition of it in the *Geneva Catechism* in 1545. Jansen appears to protest too much, though his analysis of Calvin has many illuminating points. See also McCulloh, *Christ's Person and Life-Work*, 125–32, and 139 n. 41.

77. *Institutes* II.XV.1–2.

78. Ibid., II.XV.4.

us destitute, but will provide for our needs until, our warfare ended, we are called to triumph.[79]

The kingship of Christ also has eschatological benefits for the church, Calvin states, since as sovereign Christ assures the perpetuity of the church, its final redemption, and the judgment of her enemies.[80] The priestly office of Christ, Calvin explains, pertains to his work as Mediator, by virtue of which he reconciles us to God, and now lives as our everlasting intercessor.[81]

3.3.1. Collier on Christ's Priesthood

Concerning priesthood, Collier states Christ is the "alone Priest," he is the "great High-Priest of his people."[82] Christ is the atonement, and peacemaker between God and his people, since Christ is both priest and sacrifice.[83] Christ made atonement for the sins of his people and reconciliation to God by sacrificing his own body and blood, an expression of love for humanity and an offering to God.[84] He writes,

> What cause have the saints to admire God in Christ, for *his love*? O admirable love! . . . Beloved, this love of God manifested unto men, it is *Free, Full, Everlasting* Love.[85]

In Collier's theology, the enmity between God and humanity is position of hostility pertaining to the human side of the relationship. While sin is, therefore, punished in Christ, and justice is served in his death, nowhere in this work does Collier speak of Christ appeasing God's wrath by his death, as we see in Calvin.[86] For Collier, God desires only peace and reconciliation with his rebellious creation.[87] In his *First General Epistle* of 1648 Collier

---

79. Ibid.

80. Ibid. II.XV.5.

81. Ibid. II.XV.6.

82. Collier, *Exaltation of Christ*, 106.

83. Ibid., 3, 15, 105. See also the Somerset Confession, Article XVIII, where Christ as priest is the source of peace and reconciliation. In Lumpkin, *Baptist Confessions*, 207.

84. Collier, *Exaltation of Christ*, 16–17, 45.

85. Ibid., 45.

86. In his paragraph on Christ's priesthood Calvin says, "An expiation must intervene in order that Christ as priest may obtain God's favour for us and appease his wrath." *Institutes* II.XV.6.

87. This is also his theology in the *Somerset Confession*, Article XV. In Lumpkin, *Baptist Confessions*, 206.

asserted that the death of Christ satisfies the consciences of sinners, and "brings home love to men."[88]

The significance of the doctrine of Christ priesthood is, *inter alia*, the legitimation it gives to the priesthood of all believers. Collier states, "every believer is made a Priest in Christ," and "all the Saints are priests, and the Church a holy Priesthood."[89] No one person, in Baptist ecclesiology, is "the Priest,"[90] but all believers, and every believer,

> is made a spirituall Priest to the Lord, and so the Church, A holy Priesthood, to offer up acceptable Sacrifice to God by Jesus Christ.[91]

The priesthood of believers, which is a corporate reality in Collier's theology, makes congregational worship and prayer an authentic and valid offering to God.

3.3.2. Collier on Christ as Prophet

The prophetic office of Christ means he alone is the Teacher of his people.[92] Prior to the incarnation, Christ as prophet taught the Jews through the Old Testament prophets who were inspired by the Holy Spirit.[93] During his incarnate ministry Christ taught personally, as we read in the Gospels. Christ, furthermore, is still a prophet in the Church since he is present with his people, though now in heaven (Matt 28.20), and has sent the Holy Spirit

---

88. Collier, *First General Epistle*, ch. 5.

89. Collier, *Exaltation of Christ*, 106. Once again, this suggests a tendency in Collier towards Socinianism, as both Collier and the Racovian Catechism argue that the doctrine of propitiation suggests a self-contradiction in God. Collier writes, "By this it seems that there are two Gods, one God offended, another God to satisfie; which is no less then a destruction to the divine being, if it were possible so to do; it is true, God satisfies God, but it is one and the same; not one offended, and another satisfying; but that one God satisfies himself, and so makes known his *love* to sinners." *First General Epistle*, ch. 2. Compare Racovian Catechism Sect.V, Chapt.8. Evidently, Collier was on a theological journey, as we have an entirely orthodox Calvinistic presentation of the atonement in *The Marrow of Christianity*, 17–25, and also in the *Somerset Confession*, article XIII & XV. In Lumpkin, *Baptist Confessions*, 206.

90. See Collier, *Exaltation of Christ*, 105, where he attacks "the Ministers" of the Presbyterian settlement, "who have given themselves the title of Priests, so that the people must seek the Law at their mouths."

91. Ibid., 79.

92. Ibid., 83. William Ames likewise linked the prophetic office of Christ with teaching. Ames, *Marrow*, 132–33.

93. Collier, *Exaltation of Christ*, 84.

to teach his people (John 14.26). The practical implication of this for Collier was that, "Christ is still teaching and leading his people as a Prophet in the way he would have them walke."[94] This statement fittingly expressed the Baptist's core conviction regarding their Christological-ecclesiological project, namely that they were following "the Lambe wheresoever he goeth."

Opponents of the Baptists suspected that Collier's theology of Christ's prophetic office left little room for church ministry since it appeared that each member of the congregation had personal access to the mind of Christ. In response Collier argued that Christ teaches, "1 *ministerially*. 2 *spiritually*. 3 *powerfully*."[95] First, and crucially, the prophetic office of Christ functions *via* the preaching ministry of the word, that is, by exposition of scripture. While Christ could instruct his people directly, by the Spirit, the Apostolic mission of the first disciples evidences the fact that Christ appoints ministers for the edification of the body, as affirmed by reference to Eph 4.11, Rom 10.14 and 17, and 1 Cor 5.19 [sic].[96] Secondly, because Christ teaches spiritually, the word of Christ and the proclamation of godly ministers will be in harmony:

> The Spirit worketh freely in the preaching of the Gospel, the Word is but an instrument in the hand of the Spirit, by which it works.[97]

Since the Spirit is the Spirit of Christ, the Spirit that worketh in the Word, and by the Word, the Spirit inspired proclamation of the word, cannot be differentiated from the prophetic work of Christ.

Thirdly, Christ teaches powerfully because the word effects what it proclaims.[98] Far from undermining the role of ministry, Collier invested a great deal of authority and responsibility in the ministry of preaching the word, for this is the primary means by which, as Prophet, Christ instructs his people.

Against those who were believed to have abandoned scripture, such as the Ranters in the 1640s and Quakers in the 1650s,[99] on the grounds

---

94. Ibid., 86.
95. Ibid., 114.
96. Ibid., 114–15. Collier intended 2 Cor 5.19
97. Ibid., 115.
98. Ibid., 116. This doctrine is found in Calvin, who says, "For these things—forgiveness of sins, the promise of eternal life, the good news of salvation—cannot be in man's power.... For Christ has not given this power actually to men, but to his Word, of which he has made men ministers." *Institutes* IV.XI.1.
99. On Collier's anti-Quaker literature see Land, "Doctrinal Controversies," 188–207.

that there is a direct spiritual conduit between the believer and the mind of Christ, Collier warned about the danger of shipwrecking the church. He argued, "how can a man worke without his compass, his line?"[100] Scripture is the "rule," says Collier, and the church cannot live without the rule of Christ mediated by the word:

> Now the Scripture being *a sure word of truth*, it is that which ought to be the rule of the Saints in all their actions, and believe it, Christ never teacheth contrary to this Scripture ... those that cast of[f] Scripture, and refuse to walke according to it, under a pretence of being lead by the Spirit, and so above Scripture, refusing to receive the Scripture as the rule by which Christ Teacheth, looking upon the Scripture as nothing to them, have fallen into an absurdity and adopted destructive principles.[101]

Collier believed that Christ, as prophet, had not left essential arrangements of ecclesiastical order to chance or uncertainty, therefore it was essential for believes to be thoroughly acquainted with Christ's teaching, because,

> Christ Jesus as a Sonne over his own house, is faithfull in all things, giving exact rules in every particular, for the well ordering and governing of his house, that is, the Church.[102]

The Christological priority in the use of scripture to organize the church applied especially to the practice of baptism. According to Collier's logic, based on John 15.10, Christ commanded love, and love is demonstrated by obedience to Gospel commands, and

> The first command that Christ requires of beleevers, and that next after faith received, is Baptism.[103]

This order was explicitly laid down in the Great Commission, and, according to Collier, this is the pattern the church is required to follow if it is to demonstrate love for Christ. According to this logic, love of Christ and obedience to scripture lead inevitably to a Baptist mode of initiation:

> In a word, this was the first duty that ever the saints performed, the first ordinance that ever they subscribed to after faith received: in the scripture there is neither precept nor president, either to baptize before faith, or else after faith is received, to

---

100. Collier, *Exaltation of Christ*, 88.

101. Ibid., 87.

102. Ibid., 110. See also 143, where Collier attacks disunity among churches, the result of not forming churches according to the will of Christ.

103. Ibid., 161–62.

neglect or slight baptisme, it being a command of CHRIST: love in the saints compelling them to yeelde obedience to every ordinance of Christ for his own sake.[104]

Christ as prophet and teacher in the Church, rules by precept and precedent,[105] guiding and instructing the godly in the ways of holiness as their all-sufficient Teacher.

3.3.3. Collier on Christ's Kingship

Finally, Christ alone is the King of his people, an office which secures the eternal safety of the saints and righteous governance of the church. These are the two realms over which Christ exercises kingly reign, a twofold kingdom both of which are spiritual.[106]

First is the kingdom within the Saints, the rule of Christ *in* the "heart[s]" of his people.

> Christ rules and reignes *in* the saints: the kingdom of God is within you: beloved, Christ hath a Kigdom within you, if ye are his, *Christ is in you except yee bee reprobates.*[107]

In his Putney sermon of 29 September 1647[108] Collier stressed the spiritual priority of the personal nature of Christ's sovereignty for those who had not previously been instructed in this evangelical gospel,

> The kingdome of God is within you; heaven is the kingdome of God, and this kingdome is within the Saints, and this is the new Creation, the new heaven, the Kingdom, of heaven that is in the Saints.[109]

Further expounding what he understood by the kingdom of God within the saints, and evidencing a tendency towards mysticism, he continued in the same sermon,

---

104. Ibid., 162.

105. The same idea is evident in Spilsbury, *Treatise Concerning the Lawfull Subject of Baptisme*, 25. He employs the language of "command" and "example" of Christ to argue both for believer's baptism and against infant baptism.

106. Collier, *Exaltation of Christ*, 203. This is likewise strongly asserted by Calvin who states, "I come now to kingship. It would be pointless to speak of this without first warning my readers that it is spiritual in nature." *Institutes* II.XV.3.

107. Ibid., 203.

108. Collier was an official chaplain to the Army. See Land, "Doctrinal Controversies of English Particular Baptists," 34–43

109. Collier, *Discovery of the New Creation*, 8; see also 32.

> it is union which the divine nature, the Spirit, hath with and in our spirits, by which union it transforms our spirits into its own glory, which will be their eternal perfection, their heaven, their kingdom, their glory.[110]

The implication of this teaching was that each and every believer could experience the fullness of Christ's kingdom here and now, on earth, immediately, by joining with a congregation of gathered believers. Collier thus invested the act of faith with momentous significance, and elevated the importance of ordinary saints to that of equal standing with the highest ecclesiastical officer for the spiritual experience of both church members and ministers, laity of clergy, was identical.

An essential characteristic of the rule of Christ, as Collier expounded it, was that it operated within a relationship of faith and love requiring,

> the free and full consent of the minde of the person in whom he reigns, for this is both the wisdom and power of Christ, that hee makes his people *a willing people*.[111]

Christ's rule manifests itself in personal fealty and devotion to his will:

> The Lord Jesus with the free consent of the gracious soul, sets up his Kingdome in the heart, so that when Christ sayeth, *My sonne, give me thy heart:* Lord, take my heart, sayeth the soule, dwell there, rule there, set up thy Kingdome there.[112]

There were ecclesiological implications to this voluntarist understanding of faith which Collier could see clearly, and he asked those who sought an Erastian[113] form of state church: "doth the Lord Jesus the King of Saints require or accept of any service, but that is free and voluntary,"[114] the implied answer being a robust no. The manner of the rule of the kingdom *within* the saints had to be consistent with the rule of Christ *over* the saints corporately,

---

110. Ibid., 10.

111. Collier, *Exaltation of Christ*, 206. See also Richardson, *Necessity of Toleration*, 5 and 7. Richardson asks, "Whether Christ hath said, He will have an unwilling people compelled to serve him?" This theme was already present in the thought of Jacob, *Divine Beginning*, A1. There he writes, "A true Visible & Ministeriall Church of Christ is a number of faithful people joined by their willing consent in a spirituall outward society..."

112. Collier, *Exaltation of Christ*, 206.

113. Erastianism is so named after the Swiss theologian Thomas Erastus (1524–83). See Coffey, *Politics, Theology and the British Revolutions*, 207–10. The Erastian party in the Westminster Assembly was led by John Lightfoot and Thomas Coleman, John Selden and Bulstrode Whitelock. See Paul, *Assembly of the Lord*, 127–32.

114. Collier, *Exaltation of Christ*, 225.

namely, by a freely given consent.[115] He wrote, "it is his Kingdome *in* them [a saint, singular] that brings them into submission to his Kingdome *without* them [the saints, plural]," and, "so Hee brings over those in whom hee rules, to submit to the outward regiment of his Kingdom."[116] Fellow Baptist leader William Kiffin described this doctrine as, "this great truth, Christ the king of his church."[117]

In Collier's thought, the kingdom of Christ operates by the law of freedom, so the kingdom cannot be forced upon people, and people cannot be compelled to submit to the rule of Christ. The persecutions, stonings, imprisonings Baptists endured in the early years of their existence was eloquent testimony to the reality of their convictionally rooted dissent.[118]

According to Collier, the nature of Christ's kingly rule over the saints, is fourfold. First, Christ's rule is spiritual. Second, it operates by spiritual laws and institutions. Third, it consists of spiritual executions, and fourthly it works towards spiritual ends.[119] He develops each of these themes in turn.

Emphasis on the spiritual nature of Christ's rule in the *ecclesia* was a significant theological affirmation in the context of contemporary widespread and growing millenarian expectation. Millenarianism[120] consisted of belief in an imminent advent of Christ's kingdom on earth, accompanied by the rule of the saints over the nation, and also the world, according to some.[121] That Baptists were influenced by this radical political eschatology is evidenced by Kiffin's contribution to the tract, *A Glimpse of Sions Glory*, in 1641. The first sentence of Samuel Richardson's *Justification by Christ Alone* warned readers, "Dearly beloved brethren, These are the last times wherein iniquity abounds."[122] Henry Jessey also held strong millenarian views and published a fifth monarchy tract in 1645, *A Calculation for this Present Year, 1645*, in which he interpreted the four monarchies of Daniel chapters 2

115. Ibid., 202 and 221. My emphasis.

116. Ibid., 221.

117. Kiffin, "Epistle to the Reader" in Anon., *Glimpse of Sions Glory*. It is now believed this work was written by Thomas Goodwin. The question is extensively examined in Toon, *Puritans, the Millennium and the Future of Israel*, 131–36.

118. By means of a parable Collier describes the experience of being an enemy of the state for conscience sake. Collier, *Exaltation of Christ*, 218–19.

119. Ibid., 221.

120. The rise of millenarianism in the seventeenth century is outlined in Toon, *Puritans, the Millennium and the Future of Israel*; Jue, "Puritan Millenarianism in Old and New England," in Coffey and Lim, *Cambridge Companion*, 259–76; also Capp, *Fifth Monarchy Men*, 23–49; Hill, *English Bible*, chapt. 13; and Liu, *Discord in Zion*, chapt. 1.

121. There is an expression of this hope in Collier, *A New Creation*, 32.

122. Richardson, *Justification by Christ Alone*, A2.

and 7, as the Assyrian, Persian, Greek and Roman empires, and the Fifth Monarchy, "shortly succeeding, and farr surpassing them all," being that of Christ and his Saints, who would take the reins of government and rule on the earth.[123] Against this background Collier was preaching a counsel of quietism,

> some apprehend, that Christ shall come and reign personally, subduing his enemies, and exalting his people, and that this is the new heaven and the new earth, but this is not my apprehension: but that Christ will come in the Spirit, and have a glorious Kingdome in the spirits of his people.[124]

Although Collier insisted that the nature of Christ's kingdom was spiritual, the political implications of his theology for believers were not far beneath the surface, as is clear from his statement:

> Christ rules and reignes *in* the saints . . . And this is a priviledge more than all the Kings in the earth have, they may reigne here over their subjects, but not in them: but Christ first reigns *in* them, and then *over*, them.[125]

The spiritual, internal, personal reign of Christ within true believers meant for Collier that a political alliance of Church and State would be a "carnal arrangement," an "external compacting."[126] Collier proposed a "new church estate" comprised of, "Saints gathered out of the world, by the preaching of the Gospel, into the order and fellowship of the Gospel."[127] This new church estate was brought into being by the Spirit, "a church clothed with Christ."[128] The possibility of an all-inclusive national church, embracing every citizen, was incongruous to Collier, since, "The Church of Christ are Saints chosen out of the World, they are not of the World, they are a people separated, or severed out of the World."[129] This separatist ecclesiology made the converse also true, that the World is not the Church, and

---

123. Jessey, *Calculation for this Present Year*, 32.

124. Collier, *Discovery of the New Creation*, 8 and 32. Land calls Collier's theology in this sermon, "a rather quietistic, spiritualized millennialism," not to be confused with a "proto-Fifth Monarchism." Land is substantially correct on this point, but there are more radical tones in Collier's sermon when he calls upon the army to play its divinely appointed role in restructuring magisterial power in the country. Collier, *New Creation*, 34. See Land, "Doctrinal Controversies of English Particular Baptists," 40.

125. Collier, *Exaltation of Christ*, 203.

126. Collier, *Discovery of the New Creation*, 26.

127. Collier, *Exaltation of Christ*, 226.

128. Collier, *Discovery of the New Creation*, 27.

129. Collier, *Exaltation of Christ*, 227.

"certainly those are no friends to Christ, that would turn the World into a Church, and so make the Kingdome of Christ, not a spirituall, but a carnall Kingdom."[130] Far from advancing the crown rights of King Jesus in his Church, Collier lamented that national leaders, political and ecclesiastical, had taken matters into their own hands, and trespassed into the spiritual jurisdiction of Christ:

> The most great and learned men in the World at this day rage against the Kingdom of Christ, they would set up a Kingdom of their owne, and compell men unto it . . . and to inflict bodily punishments, upon all who refuse it, or cannot joyn with it, [he] doth what in him lyeth absolutely to destroy the Kingdom of Christ.[131]

Later in the sermon he writes:

> it is Christ's birthright to reign over [the Church], and those who take the rule, the Kingdome from Christ, are no lesse then enemies and traitours to the royall crowne and dignity of the Lord Jesus: and hee will take them alive one day, and cast them into the lake of fire : Revelat. 19.20.[132]

This comment may very well reflect the Baptist perspective on the Westminster Assembly, and in contrast to the achievement of the Assembly, Collier asserted the Church of Christ to be comprised of such, "as are in the order and fellowship of the Gospell."[133] In Collier's opinion,

> for men to set up a Law in matter of worship, and compel unto it, and judge and condemne body and soule, for not submitting is to exalt themselves above Christ, and so indeed is Antichristian.[134]

It is the Gospel, he argued, which is the unifying rule of the church of Christ because the Gospel creates a new political reality under the spiritual reign of Christ.[135]

The idea that Christ's reign on earth was a spiritual reality might appear innocent, yet there was a politically subversive dimension to Collier's teaching, suggesting the church was an *imperium in imperio*. Since the church is

---

130. Ibid., 227–28; Collier, *A Discovery of the New Creation*, 28.
131. Collier, *Exaltation of Christ*, 222. The allusion to Psalm 2 is clear.
132. Ibid., 236–37.
133. Ibid., 228.
134. Ibid., 223.
135. Ibid., 228.

the spiritual kingdom of Christ, ruled over spiritually by Christ the king, political and ecclesiastical rulers have no jurisdiction over the saints. The gathered church is the private business of its members.[136]

Along similar lines he later argued:

> If any Church or Magistrate would exercise that power they conceive Christ hath entrusted them in, above spirituall Church affairs, I humbly conceive that they have nothing to doe with those that are not of the same body with them, or the same society.[137]

Evidence that this was a deeply ingrained conviction is found in the Putney sermon Collier preached to the Army, where he aligned himself with the national grievances of the Leveller program, in particular highlighting,

> Spiritual oppressions in matters of conscience. You know that a long time man hath assumed this power to himself, to rule over the consciences of their brethren, a great oppression, and that which cannot be born in souls who live in light, and that from which God will deliver his people and punish all that oppressed them.[138]

In both *A New creation* and *The Exaltation of Christ* Collier was essentially making an argument for religious toleration based on the Crown Rights of the Redeemer to rule over the Church, a plea made against a background of general intolerance of religious diversity and freedom of conscience under which sectarians had long suffered.[139]

Throughout the sitting of the Westminster Assembly, Presbyterians had preached to Parliament the duty to suppress religious disunity, and to abhor toleration.[140] One example must suffice to give a sense of the hostility Baptists were facing. Lazarus Seaman exhorted MPs:

> Besides the many loose, prophane, and scandalous Ministers, there are a new sort arisen among us, who have thrust themselves

---

136. See Tolmie, *Saints*, 97.

137. Collier, *Exaltation of Christ*, 223. See also the First London Confession articles XLVIII to LI.

138. Collier, *New Creation*, 35. On the relation between Baptists and Levellers see Tolmie, *Saints*, 144–50, 181–84.

139. According to the taxonomy of John Coffey, Collier represented the radical tolerationist view of liberty of conscience. See Coffey, "Toleration Controversy," in Durston and Maltby, *Religion in Revolutionary England*, 44.

140. For wider context see Hill, "Fast Sermons and Politics," in *The English Bible*, 79–108.

into the Lords Vineyard. It's no lesse then persecution (so they commonly give out) to desire that their suspicious opinions may be examined according to the Word of God.

> Consider also [Solomon's] failings, and beware of them. 1. He had many wives, even *seven hundred Wives, Princesses, and three hundred concubines (i).* Let us not have as many Religions. There's some anology between one and the other. 2. There was in his dais first a connivance at Idolatry, then open toleration, and withall Apostacy. . . . To prevent the like we have a *Covenant*. God and his Angels are witnesses of it. The publique faith of the Kingdome is engaged in it.[141]

A common theme in the sermons was the fear of national disunity in religion, which would weaken the country at a time of great political danger. The response within the Baptist fold was typified by Thomas Collier who believed unity was consequent upon the fellowship of the Holy Spirit, not magisterial authority.[142]

In their writings, Presbyterians like Thomas Edwards,[143] George Gillespie and Samuel Rutherford asserted that the magistrate was an antitype of Old Testament kings and, as such, had the right to crush heresy and suppress schism.[144] This was captured in the *Westminster Confession* of 1647, where it was asserted that the magistrate was duty bound,

> To take order that unity and peace be preserved in the Church, that the truth of God be kept pure and entire, that all blasphemies and heresies be suppressed, all corruptions and abuses in worship and discipline prevented or reformed, and all the ordinances of God duly settled, administered, and observed.[145]

In 1647, the year of Collier's sermon, the lawyer William Prynne published *The Sword of Christian Magistracy Supported*, subtitled, *A Full Vindication of Christian Kings and Magistrates Authority under the Gospell, To punish Idolatry, Apostacy, Heresie, Blasphemy and obstinate Schism, with Pecuniary, Corporall, and in some Cases with Banishment, and Capitall Punishments*.[146] On behalf of opponents of sectaries, this said it all.

---

141. Seaman, *Solomons Choice*, 41 and 44. See also, Sedgwick, *Arke Against a Deluge*; Spurstowe, *Englands Eminent Judgements*; Calamy, *Indictment Against England*.
142. Collier, *Discovery of the New Creation*, 18.
143. See for e.g. Edwards, *Gangraena*, First Part, Second Division, 86.
144. Coffey, "Toleration Controversy," 47.
145. Chapter XXIII, *Of the Civil Magistrate*.
146. Prynne, *Sword of Christian Magistracy*.

In addition to sermons and tracts against Independents, Presbyterian ministers in the City of London published a number of declarations against toleration which they submitted to the Westminster Divines.[147] In May 1648, Parliament succumbed to their pressure and passed "An Ordinance for the Punishing of Blasphemies and Heresies,"[148] in which Arminians, universalists, Baptists and antinomians were threatened with imprisonment. The commitment of Baptists to establish and maintain the validity of a separatist, congregational ecclesiology, a spiritual kingdom under the rule of Christ, looked like a courageous and politically significant decision in the climate. If Christ is King over the Church, then let him rule, pleaded Collier.

Having established that Christ's rule is spiritual in nature, in contrast to political coercion, a second dimension to the life of the church was the rule of Christ by his spiritual laws. Collier explained it in this way,

> As Christ hath a Kingdome, and that is spirituall, in relation to the matter, so hee sets no Lawes [but] they are spirituall, the Lawes of Christ in his Kingdome is [sic],
>
> 1. The law of love.
>
> 2. The law of edification.[149]

The "law of love" was essential to Collier's understanding of the Church because the impulse of love caused saints to "walke up according to every rule of the Gospell."[150] Collier eulogizes on his theme:

> "Here is love in the King, love in the subjects, love in CHRIST commanding, love in Christians obeying, a kingdome upheld and maintained by the law of love."[151]

This principle served his previous point, in that love, like true worship, cannot be compelled, or imposed by external constraint. It was an inner spiritual virtue, and "[t]his is the great law by which CHRIST rules *in* and *over* his saints, his Churches, his kingdome: and this is spiritual."[152]

Since Christ rules over his saints his spiritual laws must apply equally to the organization of the *ecclesia*, and in particular to the area of ministry

---

147. See Anon., *Letter of the Ministers*, 6. Also, Downame, *Testimony to the Truth*.

148. "May 1648: An Ordinance for the punishing of Blasphemies and Heresies, with the several penalties therein expressed." *Acts and Ordinances of the Interregnum*, 1133–36.

149. Collier, *Exaltation of Christ*, 229.

150. Ibid., 229.

151. Ibid., 230. Emphasis as original.

152. Ibid., 230.

as to any other dimension of the Christian life. This leads Collier to the conclusion,

> Hee manifests his Kingly power in ordaining Officers with their gifts and callings, which the Scripture seems in the strictest and most refined sense to call *Elders* and *Deacons*, or *Bishops* and *Deacons*.[153]

Collier's understanding of ministry as comprised of two offices was based on his understanding of the Pastoral Epistles,[154] and this arrangement would become the dominant pattern in Baptist congregations. What is particularly interesting to note is the role that the congregation comes to play in Baptist churches in the election of their ministers. Christ's kingly power which is primary in the appointment of ministers was understood to be mediated directly through the local congregation, thereby eliminating hierarchical intermediaries.[155] This theology is echoed by William Kiffin in his assertion, "and Christ hath given [his] power to his Church, not to a Hierarchy, neither to a Nationall Presbytery, but to a company of saints in a Congregational way."[156] The authority of Christ in the appointment of officers flows from the Head to the Body unmediated and undiluted.

The third part of Collier's enquiry into the kingly rule of Christ in the Church comes in the form of a question about discipline:

> But what power hath Christ committed to his Church, wherein his kingly office appears?
>
> *Ans.* Hee hath given power to his Church.
>
> 1. To *Judge*,
>
> 2. To *Determine*,
>
> 3. To *Passe sentence*.[157]

No member might be admitted to the church without the judgment of the congregation concerning the true faith of the applicant. This was a weighty matter, and Collier found justification for the work of judgment in Christ's bestowal of the keys:

> There seemes to bee something to this purpose in that Scripture, Mat 16.19. I will give unto thee the keyes of the Kingdom

---

153. Collier, *Exaltation of Christ*, 232.
154. 1 Tim 3.1, 2, 3 &c. See Collier, *Exaltation of Christ*, 232.
155. This is more fully developed in chapter 5. See also Tolmie, *Saints*, 85.
156. Kiffin, "Epistle to the Reader," in Anon., *A Glimpse of Sions Glory*.
157. Collier, *Exaltation of Christ*, 233. Emphasis as original.

> of heaven, and whatsoever thou shalt binde on earth, shall be bound in heaven. . . . Whatsoever the Church of Christ concludes on earth, is approved in heaven.[158]

That Christ had given keys to the Church, that is, power and authority to make spiritual decisions, was not in dispute amongst advanced Puritans.[159] The point of controversy between Puritans, however, made visible during the "Grand Debate" in the last three days of the Westminster Assembly in October 1643, was to whom they were given.[160] Was it Peter, the Apostles, the church, or a combination of the latter two?[161] The question divided conservative Presbyterians who desired to uphold the status of the clergy and affirm ministerial authority over the laity, and Independents who insisted that Christ had bequeathed the power of the keys to Peter considered as a believer, thereby locating power in the body of the congregation.[162] On 31 October 1643, the conservative majority in the Assembly won the argument and it was affirmed that the power of the keys, that is, church governance, had been given by Christ directly to the apostles, and was to be exercised by church officers apart from the church.[163]

In October 1655 Baptists in the West Country, led by Collier, debated the power of the keys in their Associational General Meeting:

> Query 1. Whether the power of the keys spoken of in Mat. 16.19, John 20.23, Mat. 18.18, be given to the church or to the eldership in the church?
>
> Answer: the exercise of the power of Christ in a church having officers, in opening and shutting, in receiving in and casting out, belongs to the church with its eldership.[164]

---

158. Ibid., 233–34.

159. For an overview see Beeke & Jones, *A Puritan Theology*, 623–25, 628–31, 633–39. John Cotton identified four decisions to which the keys applied. The right of a congregation to: 1. choose officers; 2. Send forth one or more of elders as the public service of Christ and the church; 3. Refuse admission to the communion of the church, or its seals; 4. Join with the elders in inquiring, hearing, judging of public scandals, so as either to censure or forgive the repentant. See Cotton, *Keyes of the Kingdom*, 12–13.

160. See Powell, "October 1643," in Haykin and Jones, *Drawn Into Controversie*, 52–82.

161. A summary of the debate is given in Paul, *Assembly of the Lord*, 146–54. On the division of church power between officers and congregation in Presbyterianism, see "[Provincial Assembly of London]," *Jus Divinum*, 131–32. Also Powell, "October 1643," 63.

162. See Powell, "October 1643," 65.

163. Paul, *Assembly of the Lord*, 153; Powell, "October 1643," 78.

164. ARPB, 60.

The Baptists affirmed what Independents in the Assembly had argued, that the keys were given to Peter, not as Apostle, but as confessor, as the one who declared Christ as Lord. Collier would no doubt have agreed entirely with the Independent William Carter when he argued at the Assembly,

> Our confession makes us all peters[.]
>
> In church fellowship we have to doe only with one Another as confessours[.][165]

Thus in Baptist congregations, members and officers together, equally, judged the genuineness of faith of applicants to join the church, and had equal voice in passing sentence on those facing excommunication. The congregation were the gate keepers of the house of the Lord. According to Collier,

> not but that the Churches of Christ have power to judge and determine of things among themselves, about the spirituall affairs of Christ, and to excommunicate a wilfull offender.[166]

The entering of members into the church, and exiting of members out of the church was, for Collier, "the Kingly office of Christ carried along in the Kingdome, in the Church of Christ under the Gospel."[167] Christ as king of saints ruled his spiritual kingdom through all his people equally.

In Collier's sermon *The Exaltation of Christ*, we see that foundational to nascent Baptist ecclesiology in 1646 was Christ's threefold office in, and among, his people. The church is the voluntary, separated, independent, gathered company of believers, devoted in personal allegiance to Christ, experiencing his power in their midst and mediating Christ's power to the world by preaching the word. The power of Christ, according to Collier is not possessed and controlled by the few, but present to the saints equally. The equal distribution of authority among the saints, however, did not diminish the role of ministers, or the honour and respect they should be given, since Christ invested their work with his own authority. The power of ministry, however, does not elevate the minister above the congregation, as Collier makes clear, "for they are the Churches servants,"[168] and the power of ministry is for effective service, not to rule over Christ's people.[169] Thus the saints

---

165. In Paul, *Assembly of the Lord*, 147.
166. Collier, *Exaltation of Christ*, 223, see also 95 and 235.
167. Ibid., 235.
168. Ibid., 232.
169. This was the essence of Ritschl's criticism of Calvin's inclusion of Prophet in the offices. By using it as the foundation of the ministry Calvin denies the transference

are not merely ministered unto, but may also minister to one another,[170] are subject to one another, and watch over one another. It is no surprise that Presbyterians in parliament regarded Baptists and other sectarians with great alarm, if not outright fear, since congregationalist spirituality was subversive of all external human authority, which applied to the body politic might have rendered the country ungovernable.

Summary

If it were true, as Jansen suggests, that the doctrine of the *munus triplex* was peripheral to Calvin's theology, though there are reasons to doubt this claim, we can say that early Particular Baptist attempts to reconstitute the Church exploited the theology of Christ's rights as prophet, priest and king in and over his church to the maximum. The triple formula was also central to Baptist understanding of congregational ministry and polity and fully utilized in the organization of both features of church life.

The trajectory of a church formed according to the Christological formula was begun by Henry Jacob, and bequeathed to those congregations which emerged from his ecclesiological innovation. The impact of this ideological commitment was thorough-going in relation to practices of church life such as baptism, membership, discipline, decision-making, and ministry. In particular, the rule of King Jesus carried within an eschatological imperative and, on account of their Christological focus, Baptists were inevitably influence by, and participated in, the growing millennial expectation regarding the advent of Christ's kingdom, commonly held by advanced Puritans. This explains the urgency of Baptist action in forming congregations, and the willingness of many to undertake personal risk to establish a sectarian, congregational, form of *ecclesia*.

Millennial Christology also determined that convictions which inspired believers in the 1630s to renew the Church according to the teaching and purposes of King Jesus inspired the saints in the 1650s to pressurize the political authorities in England to establish a theocracy. Prominent Baptists like Henry Jessey, John Pendarves, Hanserd Knollys, and unknown others, were drawn towards the militant expression of millenarianism of

---

of this attribute to all believers. Collier avoids this dilemma by upholding the wish of Moses, "would God that all the Lord's people were prophets and that the Lord would put His spirit upon them! Num 11.29." See Jansen, *Calvin's Doctrine*, 50–51.

170. "He hath made all the saints prophets, he hath poured down a spirit of prophesie upon them, that now they are enabled by the spirit of prophesie to speak one to another, for edification, exhortation, and consolation." Collier, *Exaltation of Christ*, 201.

the age, politicized by the Fifth Monarchists. By 1660, however, Charles II was restored to the throne of England, not King Jesus, and it was evident that Christ's Kingdom was not of this world, and the rule of the saints did not include the machinery of government. The Baptist perspective on the spiritual nature of Christ's kingly reign, the spiritual dominion in the lives of the saints, was vindicated, as millenarian enthusiasm waned. From the beginning, however, conformity to the mind, will, and purpose of Christ was the measure of a true ecclesiology.

4

"A Holy and Orderly Communion"

Theology and Practice of Discipline among Early Particular Baptists

> There is not a thing in the world of more grave and urgent importance throughout the whole life of man than discipline. The flourishing and decaying of all civil societies, all the turnings and moving of human occasions are moved to and fro upon the axle of discipline. Nor is there any sociable perfection in this life, civil or sacred, that can be above discipline.[1]

Introduction

THE INDEPENDENT, CONGREGATIONAL PATTERN of the church had as its *raison d'etre*, the intention to be holy devoted to Christ in polity, and in the lives of each and all its members. Among the early Calvinistic Baptists, a rightly ordered church is a congregation properly related to Christ, and living under the rule of Christ, it is therefore essential that members of the body of Christ should live a life of "holy and orderly communion."[2] According to the records of the Abingdon Baptist Association meeting in October 1652, the main purpose of "perticular church communion" is "to keepe each other pure and to cleare the prefoession of the Gospell

---

1. John Milton, writing in 1641: Cited in Hill, *Society and Puritanism*, 188.
2. 1644 London Confession, article XLIV. In Lumpkin, *Baptist Confessions*, 168.

from scandale."[3] In this chapter I want to show that in this area of church life, as with others, the controlling theological principle was the kingly rule of Christ over his people, and, since Christ is king of the Church, his subjects must be worthy members of his kingdom and live in submission to his commands.

The first thing to note is that the practice of church discipline among the early Particular Baptists operated within a theological framework provided by the traditional Calvinistic scheme of salvation. The work of God in electing and redeeming fallen humanity provided the ideological narrative for the ecclesiological commitment to a disciplined church. This pattern is clearly evident in the First London Confession, as set out below. Thereafter, Particular Baptist theology and practice of discipline in the *Association Records* will be considered. In addition, attention will be given to the interpretation of key biblical passages, and the theological concept of the "power of the keys."

4.1 The Purity of the Saints in Particular Baptist Confessions

Discipline in early Calvinistic Baptist churches was not a singular matter of establishing a legalistic basis for church fellowship, but grounded in an understanding of God's eternal saving purposes to create a godly people. On this basis it was regarded as an essential feature of the life and practice of a true church.

The biblical foundation for the exercise of church discipline among early Particular Baptists is set out in the First London Confession. Article 1 states:

> there is ... one Rule of holinesse and obedience for all the saints,
> at all times, in all places to be observed.[4]

The texts cited alongside this principle, 1 Tim 6:3, 13, 14; Gal 1:8–9; 2 Tim 3:15, emphasize the importance of a godly life as a necessary accompaniment to correct doctrine. Purity of doctrine and purity of life are of one piece, so that even as the church is one in its confession of the Trinity,[5] the one, true, holy and apostolic church is united in affirming the "holiness" and "obedience" of its members. This article can be read as a positioning state-

---

3. *ARPB*, 126.
4. Lumpkin, *Baptist Confessions*, 156.
5. First London Confession, article II.

ment by the Calvinistic Baptists, affirming that though they demurred from the *corpus permixtum* of the National Church, they stood in continuity with those saints of all times, and in all places, who prized holiness of life and obedience to Christ. In this regard, the Particular Baptists might be viewed as one expression of English Puritanism seeking to complete the reformation of the church after the primitive pattern of scripture.[6]

The continuity of the Particular Baptists with Puritanism can be seen in the indebtedness of their Confession of 1644 to the Puritan manifesto of 1596, *A True Confession*.[7] In regard to the practice of discipline, dependence is evident as Article 1 of *A True Confession* asserts:

> That ther is but one God, one Christ, one Spirit, one Church, one truth, one Faith, one Rule of obedience to all Christians, in all places.[8]

It can be seen that the London Confession has added the word "holiness" to "obedience," creating a hendiadys, demonstrating a deepening commitment to the Puritan ideal of a godly church comprised of disciplined believers.

The theological rationale for a disciplined church emerges from the London Confession not merely by consideration of the articles which speak directly to this subject, but by examination of the doctrinal narrative which underpins the statement of faith relating to creation, Fall, election and salvation. Article IV of the 1644 Confession, asserts that sin was not a constituent element of original human nature and therefore, by implication, is not natural to human destiny:

> In the beginning God made all things very good, created man after his own Image and likenesse, filling him with all the perfection of all naturall excellency and uprightnesse, free from all sinne.[9]

Baptists believed God's original intention for humanity was that they be characterized by the moral perfection that God himself possesses. God's purposes in redemption therefore include forgiveness and the removal of sin in order to restore humanity to the original state.

---

6. See Collinson, *Elizabethan Puritan Movement*, 29–44.

7. This observation appears to have been made first by Whitley, *HBB*, 94. See also, White, *English Baptists of the Seventeenth Century*, 62; Nelson, "Reflecting on Baptist Origins," 33–46.

8. In Lumpkin, *Baptist Confessions*, 82.

9. Ibid., 157.

Continuing with the biblical narrative, the primary obstacle to the moral reformation of human beings is the corruption of human nature:

> all since the Fall are conceived in sinne, and brought forth in iniquity, . . . children of wrath, and servants of sinne, subjects of death, and all other calamities due to sinne in the world.[10]

Particular Baptists took for granted the Augustinian-Calvinist doctrines of original sin and total depravity[11] in their theological scheme, which only served to emphasize the need for a separatist form of church comprised of the saints. This theological commitment leads to the next Article concerning God's redemptive response to the Fall and consequent corruption of humankind. The Confession states that while humans are,

> dead in sinnes and trespasses, and subject to the eternal wrath of the great God . . . yet the elect . . . are redeemed, quickened, and saved.[12]

Out of the *massa damnata* God has determined to rescue some for salvation and to bring them into union with himself through faith. Article XXVIII asserts:

> Those which have union with Christ, are justified from all their sinnes, past, present and to come, by the bloud of Christ; which justification wee conceive to be a gracious and free acquittance of a guiltie, sinfull creature, from all sin by God, through the satisfaction that Christ hath made by his death.[13]

The final step in God's work of redemption concerns the moral transformation of the elect, as the following article asserts:

> All believers are a holy and sanctified people, . . . whereby the believer is in truth and realitie separated, both in soule and

---

10. Article IV. Ibid., 157.

11. Article V. While Calvin agrees with, and affirms, all that Augustine said about original sin, he also has a nuance not found in Augustine. For Calvin, original sin is undoubtedly hereditary, saying, "Original sin, therefore, seems to be a hereditary depravity and corruption of our nature," but is also a consequence of an ordinance of God, a judgment of God passed on all humanity whereby Adam's sin is imputed to all in the same manner that Christ's righteousness is imputed to believers. See Calvin, *Institutes* III.xxiii.3-9 also II.i.8; also Couenhoven, "St. Augustine's Doctrine of Original Sin," 359–96.

12. Lumpkin, *Baptist Confessions*, 158.

13. Ibid., 164. In the *Appendix* to the second edition of the First London, Samuel Cox heightens the predestinarian element in salvation. See articles 4 and 5 in Underhill, *Confessions of Faith*, 52–53.

> body, from all sinne and dead works, through the bloud of the everlasting Covenant, whereby he also presseth after a heavenly and Evangelicall perfection, in obedience to all the Commands, which Christ as head and King in this new Covenant has prescribed to him.[14]

In this statement, the sanctification of the believer is declared to be "in truth and reality," an experiential event, working change in both "soule and body." The godliness of the elect is therefore an observable event, a measureable quality, a reality which can be monitored by those whom God has appointed overseers in the church. Herein lies the basis for a bifurcation between the elect and non-elect, believers and non-believers, between "Church" and "World," and article XXIX reflects the Baptist commitment to a separated, believers' church comprised of the godly, in contrast to a national and inclusive church.

In a gathered, believers' church, how a member continued to wrestle with sin was almost as important as the crisis event of conversion itself. The Christian life was acknowledged to be a continuing spiritual struggle against internal and external forces:

> That all beleevers in the time of this life, are in a continuall warfare, combate, opposition against sinne, selfe, the world, and the Devill, and liable to all manner of afflictions, tribulations, and persecutions, and so shall continue untill Christ comes in his Kingdome.[15]

What enables Saints to overcome these malign powers, however, is the strength of Christ who,

> assistes them in all their afflictions, upholds them under all their temptations and preserves them by his power to his everlasting Kingdome.[16]

In terms which all Calvinists would have accepted, Baptists believed that God, by his grace, was not only responsible for the creation of a godly people, but also for their perseverance in faith. In words consistent with the theology recently codified in the Canons of Dort, article XXIII states:

> Those that have this pretious faith wrought in them by the Spirit, can never finally nor totally fall away; and though many stormes and floods do arise and beat against them, yet they shall never

---

14. Article XXIX. Lumpkin, *Baptist Confessions*, 164.
15. Article XXXI. Ibid., 165.
16. Ibid.

be able to take off that foundation and rock which by faith they are fastened upon.[17]

It follows, unsurprisingly, from this position that the London Confession describes the church as a "spiritual Kingdome" on earth, which Christ "hath purchased and redeemed to himselfe, as a peculiar inheritance."[18] To emphasize further the exclusive character of the church, it goes on to state that the company of visible Saints are,

> called and separated from the world, by the word and Spirit of God, to the visible profession of the faith of the Gospel.[19]

This teaching of observable holiness was characteristic of provincial Calvinistic Baptists also, as evidenced by a tract of West Country messenger Thomas Collier of 1654:

> Now the ends of God are expressed as followeth, That he might redeem to himself a peculiar people zealous of good works, that he might present his church to himself without spot or wrinkle, or any such thing.[20]

This commonly held understanding of the church, as a body whose identity and destiny is defined in terms of purity from sin and obedience to the word of God, reflected a community which cherished its calling to sainthood and protected its reputation by mutual discipline. This feature of Baptist faith arose from, and supports, an ecclesiology in which the church and world are separate and distinct spheres of human existence, being inimical, and in opposition, to one another.

Pertinent to the subject of discipline, a further series of short statements in the London Confession state that believers who join Particular Baptist churches are to live under Christ's "heavenly conduct and government."[21] Consistent with the Independent view of the power of the keys, authority is given to the Church, "to receive in and cast out, by way of Excommunication, any member" who was erring.[22] According to article XLIV, church discipline is a mutual and communal responsibility, stating, "He hath given

---

17. Ibid., 163. Compare, The Canons of the Synod of Dort, Fifth Main Point of Doctrine, *Perseverance of the Saints*, Article 4: "The danger of true believers falling into serious sin," and Article 8: "The certainty of this preservation." In Pelikan and Hotchkiss, *Creeds and Confessions of Faith in the Christian Tradition Volumes* vol. II, 592–93.

18. Article XXXIII, Lumpkin, *Baptist Confessions*, 165.

19. Article XXXIII, Ibid., 165.

20. Collier, *Right Constitution*, 5.

21. Article XXXIV, Lumpkin, *Baptist Confessions*, 166.

22. Article XLII, Ibid., 168. See Paul, *Assembly of the Lord*, 146–50.

authoritie, and laid dutie upon all, to watch over one another."[23] In true congregational fashion, no church member was exempt, or above, the process of discipline as Article XLIII makes clear:

> every particular member of each Church, however excellent, great, or learned soever, ought to be subject to censure and judgement of Christ; . . . .[24]

This egalitarian view of discipline is supported in the Confession by a number of texts, Gal 6:1; 1 Thess 5:11; Jude 20; Heb 12:15, which speak about the commonality of the spiritual life. The Heb 12:15 text also appears in the Somerset Confession,[25] in its instruction about mutual "watch care," which is regarded as a commandment of the Lord: "see to it that no one fails to obtain the grace of God." This same Confession has a series of commandments exhorting the community to Watching, Caring, Exhorting, Discovering (presumably "examining"), Loving, Reproving one another as a means of practicing loving discipline in gathered church.[26]

Evidently, in the formative phase of the emergence of the Particular Baptists church discipline of members was a matter of vital importance, and it is therefore interesting to note how little is said about the idea of a "pure Church," or mutual discipline, at the time of the Second London Confession in 1677, and nothing is said regarding excommunication.[27] This is not to say that the 1677 Confession is entirely silent about the issue of correction and discipline, but by comparison with the earlier document it is muted. A summary of its position is as follows. The saints are still those who have professed "faith and obedience unto God,"[28] but it is conceded that communities are not perfect since they "are subject to mixture and error." In light of this, the Confession affirms the dominical instruction in Matt 18:15–20 that the faithful are to "walk together in particular societies, or Churches, for their mutual edification," which implies the need for mutual correction

---

23. Lumpkin, *Baptist Confessions*, 168.

24. Ibid., 168.

25. This was issued 1656 by the Particular Baptists in the West Country. It was largely written by Thomas Collier with the intention of proving to the London leadership that the churches of Somerset had not relaxed their grip on orthodox Calvinism, in spite of the pressure from the General Baptists.

26. See Commandments 4–9. Lumpkin, *Baptist Confessions*, 210.

27. Another testimony to the practice of discipline in a Particular Baptist church in the late seventeenth century is the Discipline Book of the "Church of Christ assembling in George Yard in Thames Street." This is a record of about twenty cases of discipline kept by the then pastor Robert Steed. Robinson, "Baptist Church Discipline 1689-1699," 112–28, 179–85.

28. Chapter XXVI. Lumpkin, *Baptist Confessions*, 285.

and discipline.[29] Article 7 states explicitly that Christ has given to each particular congregation power to administer "discipline" and, therefore, believers who bind themselves to a particular congregation, and are admitted to the privileges of the church membership, must submit to the censures and government of the church, according to the Rule of Christ.

What this survey of the 1644 Confession has demonstrated is that the *true* Church, as understood and envisioned by the early Baptists, is rooted in the redemptive activity of God, who determined to create a godly people through the saving work of Christ.

4.2 Church Discipline in Hermeneutical Perspective

Among the Calvinistic Baptists, ecclesiastical discipline derived its importance from the belief that discipline was an essential component of the New Testament Church. Committed to the principle of organizing their congregations in conformity to scripture, discipline was likewise considered a vital element in the life of their churches. In this section I will examine the use of key biblical texts in Particular Baptist literature to formulate policies and procedures for the exercise of discipline within their congregations, and highlight ways this contributed to their theology of the church as a "holy and orderly communion."

The *locus classicus* for questions about church discipline in Particular Baptist congregations was Matt 18:15–18.[30] This text was regarded as providing the *modus operandi* Christ prescribed for dealing with sin in the *ecclesia*, and from the rise of English Puritanism separatist churches constructed disciplinary procedures accordingly.[31] There are hermeneutical issues in this text, however, that show the Baptist manner of reading and applying the text was not without prejudice.

---

29. Ibid., 286.

30. See, for example the discussion in the Abingdon Association recorded in *ARPB*, 188. In response to a question, it is stated that brotherly discipline must conform "exactly" to the rule of Christ in Mt 18. Also, White cites an unpublished record from the Leominster Churchbook MS in which the church is advised how to deal with a minister who persists in taking state pay. They were to proceed according to the steps of discipline laid down in Matt 18:15–17. White, "English Particular Baptists," 28.

31. See Collinson, *Elizabethan Puritan Movement*, 346, 350, 353. Collinson recounts the testimony of John Udall before the Star Chamber that, on the basis of Matt 18, he desired a church governed, "as Christ's holy discipline doth require." See Chidley, *The Justification of the Independent Churches*, 9 and 45, who regarded this text as the fundamental rule of Christ, "the King of peace," for the establishment of righteousness in the church.

In the first instance, Matt 18:15 has an important textual variation. The majority of manuscripts, but of lesser importance, read, "If your brother sins *against you* . . ." emphasizing the second person singular pronoun. The alternative reading, found in two of the most important manuscripts, Vaticanus and Sinaiticus, reads more simply, "If your brother sins, go speak to him . . ." Much hangs on this variation, since the reading which specifies sin "against you," personalizes the offence, making the essence of the failure relational. This reading implies what is at stake in the moral failure of a saint is the unity of the church. The alternative reading makes the general moral conduct of another disciple, or church member, a matter of interest to other church members, implying the holiness of the church is the primary concern. Most modern commentators[32] regard the longer text, "sins against you," as original, based on the instruction following, namely, to speak to the offender, brother to brother, "when the two of you are alone," though certainty on this question is impossible.

Another point of uncertainty in the text is the meaning of *harmartēse*, sin. Luz suggests that "sin" in this context is, "an open word"[33] that Matthew does not define with specificity because those who are addressed are expected to take the initiative in determining its occasion. In the light of its generality, it is therefore probably too limiting to restrict the sin to "a personal offence committed against a fellow believer,"[34] and better to think in terms of "grave transgressions against the community."[35]

Another point of controversy in the text centers on interpretation of the word *ecclesia* in v. 17, and what it means to "speak to the church; and if the offender refuses to listen even to the church, ..." Traditional Catholic interpreters, both before and after the Reformation, almost always spoke of *ecclesia* in terms of office holders,[36] and many Reformers took the same line. Calvin argues that when Jesus spoke of the *Church* he was thinking of the Old Testament arrangements and the administration of justice by the Jews, therefore it follows that, "the power of excommunication belonged to the

---

32. For example, Dale and Allison, *International Critical Commentary*, Gundry, *Matthew*, Luz *Matthew 8–20*. France, *Gospel of Matthew*, disagrees regarding the "against you" as a reading back from v. 21.

33. Luz, *Matthew 8–20*, 451.

34. Davies and Allison, *Matthew*, 2:782.

35. Schnackenburg, *Gospel of Matthew*, 176.

36. Luz, *Matthew 8–20*, 456. This is not necessarily true of modern Catholic commentators. For example, McKenzie equates *ecclesia* with "the local church community" in *The Jerome Biblical Commentary*, ed. Brown, *et. al.*, II.95.

elders who held the government of the whole *Church*."[37] Bucer, Bullinger and Beza followed the same line.[38]

Early Baptist interpretation reflected the view of the church found in Elizabethan Puritans like Henry Barrow, who understood "tell it to the church" to mean the whole company of the congregation.[39] Around the turn of the century Henry Jacob took up the argument against the Puritan/Presbyterian view[40] asserting that New Testament references to *ecclesia* in the singular indicated,

> an ordinarie Congregacon; & not any provinciall nor universall Church nor ruling sinod.[41]

Jacob further argued that "all the Greek authors" as well as the New Testament and Christ could be cited in support of the reading that,

> the sense of the word *ecclesia* Mat. 18.17 was of a parish and not of any sinode, senate, or consistory.[42]

Jacob also appealed to the tradition of interpretation in Zwingli and unnamed others, though Tyndale might have been cited, stating:

> But all authors of credit doe give to the word Ecclesia . . . the sense only of one ordinarie Congregacon, they never give it the sense of all, the destinct Congregacon through a nation or province, much les through thee world nor yet doe they ever take it for a sinod; not for a sinnat or consistory nor for any supreame person.[43]

In his work, *An Attestation of Many Learned, Godly, and Famous Divines* Jacob made it clear that he did not deny that synods could make doctrinal judgments and decrees, but discipline belonged to the local church:

---

37. Calvin, *Commentaries* vol.XVI, 356.

38. See Luz, *Matthew 8–20*, 456 n. 65. On Bucer and Bullinger, see Sunshine, "Discipline as the Third Mark," 471, 473.

39. See Collinson, *Elizabethan Puritan Movement*, 350.

40. For example, see John Udall: "Tell the Churche: that is sayeth he, the governors of the Church." In Udall, *A Demonstration of Discipline*, 67. A more extreme view than that of Udall was put forward by Convocation in 1606 with the assertion that Christ, by the words "Tell it to the church" had authorized church courts as were administered by the Church of England, as the last remedy against an erring and unrepentant brother. See Hill, *Society and Puritanism*, 266.

41. Jacob, *Defence of Certain Christians*, cited in Ha, *English Presbyterianism*, 52.

42. Cited in Ha, *English Presbyterianism*, 52.

43. Ibid., 52.

> I grant Synods may discusse and determine of errors, and may pronounce them wicked and accursed errors. But actually excommunicat mens persons, the Apostles never did without the concurrence and consent of that Congregation where they were members.[44]

Jacob's contribution to the emergence of Congregationalism was to propose a model of congregational discipline which could operate within a framework of trans-local church oversight, which Particular Baptist churches would later adopt and utilize in the 1640s and 1650s.

In the London Confession of 1644 the Particular Baptists defined *ecclesia* as "Congregation," thus identifying with the traditional separatist view.[45] Thomas Collier in the West Country likewise defined the Baptist view against alternative positions:

> What is the Discipline and government of the Church of Christ?
>
> *An.*1 Negative. not an Episcopall Government by Lord Bishops, not a Presbyterian Government of many, to rule over one.
>
> But every Assembly of Saints thus gathered, as is before mentioned, are to elect and to Ordaine Officers, and to them Christ hath given full power to performe every duty of a Church, that is, to watch over one another, to admonish one the other, to Censure such as are disorderly, in a word, to receive in such as they conceive the Lord hath added, to cast forth such as walke disorderly.[46]

The reading of *ecclesia*, as a reference to the congregation rather than one man, or a subset of the congregation, was axiomatic for Baptists, the plain reading of the text being normative.

This hermeneutical decision is evident in the policy of congregational discipline as codified in the First London Confession. By means of a series of proof texts they systematize diverse New Testament teaching about the way Christ's church is to kept holy and orderly. In the first article dealing with discipline it was stated:

> Christ has likewise given power to his whole Church to receive in and cast out, by way of Excommunication, any member; and

---

44. Jacob, *An Attestation of Many Learned, Godly, and Famous Divines*, 117.
45. Article XLII. In Lumpkin, *Baptist Confessions*, 168.
46. Collier, *Certain Queries*, 22–23.

> this power is given to every particular Congregation, and not one particular person, either member or Officer, but the whole.[47]

Particular Baptists believed that the power Christ had given to the Church universal was available to each congregation locally. Each local congregation was competent in itself to be a church, since Christ was fully present in each gathered community.[48] The authority of a particular Congregation to act in the name of Christ, by receiving in and casting out,[49] was established by the Apostolic instruction in 1 Cor 5:4, "In the name of the Lord Jesus . . . hand this man over to Satan." Since Paul had written this to the church at large, the Confession emphasized that the power to pass judgment on a sinner was a corporate responsibility, "and not one particular person, either member or Officer."

The next article, XLIII, dealt with the question of who in the church was subject to discipline. It asserted:

> And every particular member of each Church, how excellent, great, or learned soever, ought to be subject to this censure and judgement of Christ.[50]

This egalitarian approach to the church was justified on the basis of Acts 11:2-3 which was cited as evidence against an aristocratic system of discipline, since it shows that even Peter was not immune from defending his actions before the church.[51] In similar vein, 1 Tim 5:19-21 affirmed the right of the church to exercise universal censure and discipline, even over the officers, however, care was to be taken when disciplining an elder, requiring the testimony of two or three witnesses, but, notwithstanding the difficulties, the church dare not shrink from its responsibility.

Article XLIV addressed the issue of who should exercise discipline in the congregation. Having stated in article XLII that excommunication was a congregational responsibility, this article spoke of the particular responsibility of church officers in "keeping the Church in holy and orderly communion." It stated,

---

47. Article XLII. In Lumpkin, *Baptist Confessions*, 168.
48. See Kiffen, *Briefe Remonstrance*, 11.
49. Article XLII. See also Collier, *Certain Queries*, 23 who uses this text to make the same point.
50. In Lumpkin, *Baptist Confessions*, 168.
51. Article XLIII. Ibid., 168.

> And as Christ for the keeping of this Church in holy and orderly Communion, placeth some speciall men over the Church, who by their office are to governe, oversee, visit, watch . . .[52]

Paul's farewell speech to the Ephesian elders in Acts 20:27–28 was the inspiration for this arrangement of ministerial work in the church. There was, however, no question that church officers were above other members of the congregation as the article continued to make clear,

> . . . So likewise for the better keeping thereof in all places, by the members, he hath given authoritie, and laid duty upon all, to watch over one another.

While the officers in the church may be appointed to the function of watch-care, according to Mark 13:34 and 37, this did not absolve the remainder of the membership from a mutual responsibility to watch over each other. Galatians 6:1 was added as biblical authority for this practice, so that if someone was caught in sin, other members should restore him in a spirit of mutual help and gentleness, since every believer is subject to temptation. Likewise, Jude 3, 20 which exhorts the congregation to, "contend for the faith," and "build yourselves up!," suggests that discipline could be not only punitive, but edificatory in purpose, designed to strengthen the church. Finally, a communal exhortation to ensure that no one fails to obtain the grace of God was found in Heb 12:15. This text implies that mutual correction served not only the end of a pure church, but had salvific significance for each individual. For Calvinistic Baptists the importance of maintaining faith was not because salvation in the elect could be lost, but persevering was experiential evidence of that very election.

In summary, in the formulation of their theology and practice of discipline early Particular Baptists followed the traditional separatist reading of Matt 18.17 as an instruction given to the *ecclesia*, understood as the congregation. The work of Henry Jacob was undoubtedly influential in their commitment to this hermeneutical decision, and in the 1640s it was applied systematically to the formulation of an agreed practice of church discipline. Proof texts were used to buttress this egalitarian, congregational policy of mutual watch-care. In such an arrangement every church member had equal opportunity to administer the power and authority of Christ in relation to fellow believers. In this way they believed they were faithfully fulfilling Christ's purposes for the church, and preserving the gathered community as a "holy habitation to the Lord."[53]

---

52. Ibid.
53. Kiffen, *Briefe Remonstrance*, 11.

4.3 Church Discipline in Early Particular Baptist Records

Having considered the biblical and theological foundations of church discipline in Particular Baptist Confessions, the practical application of these principles can be observed through the *Association Records of the Particular Baptists*.[54] The *Association Records* are a material witness to the questions and concerns of Baptist congregations through England Ireland and Wales throughout the 1650s. Discipline is an often discussed theme, and the *Records* make possible an assessment of the degree to which biblical proof texts, and ideological commitments to discipline, translated into experience.

According to the Abingdon Association records, church discipline was to be routinely practiced as an essential element, or *nota*,[55] of church life. The hopeful instruction of associational Messengers was that churches,

> would in like manner consider the dutie of all saints to deale lovingly and faithfully one with another not onely instructing and exhorting but also, as need shall require, admonishing and reproving, considering the word of the Lord in Lev. 19.17, Thou shalt not hate thy brother in thine heart: thou shalt in any wise rebuke thy neighbour and not suffer sin upon him. Also in Prov. 28.23, He that rebuketh a man shall find more favour afterwards than he that flattereth with the tongue. And againe, Prov. 27.5, Open rebuke is better than secret love. Also in Mat. 18.15, If thy brother trespasse against thee, goe and tell him his fault betweene thee and him alone. In Col. 3.16,24, The word of Christ dwell in you richly in all wisdom, teaching and admonishing one another. In 1 Thess. 5.14, Warne them that are unruly, or, disorderly. In Gal 6.1, If a man be overtaken in a fault, ye that are spirituall, restore such a one in the spirit of meeknesse and in Heb 3.13, Exhort one another daily while it is called today lest any of you be hardened through the deceitfullnes of sin. And in Heb. 10.24, Let us consider one another to provoke unto love and good works. And that saints may not be unwilling to receive both wholesome admonition and also seasonable and necessarie reproof, it is desired that the saying of David may be well minded, Let the righteous smite me, it shall be a kindness, and let him reprove me, it shall be an excellent oyle which shall not breake mine head.[56]

---

54. White, *Association Records of the Particular Baptists of England, Wales and Ireland to 1660*, 3 volumes and index. A substantial introduction to the *Association Records* is the review article of Nuttall, "Association Records of the Particular Baptists," 14–25.

55. ARPB, 142.

56. Ibid.

In typical Baptist fashion, discipline was regarded as a thoroughly biblical feature of the church, and a means by which saints might serve one another in love. Discipline was evidence that the word, or rule, of Christ was "dwelling richly" in his people.

In the following sections I will examine the records recounting the occasions of discipline in early Calvinistic churches, and the pastoral procedure followed in the practice of discipline. These accounts will provide the basis for extrapolating the theology of discipline validating its exercise.

4.3.1. Occasions of Discipline in Baptist Records

Cases of discipline among early Calvinistic Baptists encompass a range of issues including moral, social, ecclesiastical, and doctrinal deviance. In the Loughwood Church Books[57] from 1653, one of the earliest first-hand accounts of church discipline is recounted in some detail. The manner of dealing with offenders includes a number of disciplinary themes repeated often throughout the seventeenth century. The entry for 25 April 1654 reads:

> 1. That Bro. Phillipp and Bro. Jno. Demmige having neglected to assemble with the church on the first day and at that tyme meett with those persons who hold the doctrines of freewill, falling from grace and generall redemption; and doe upon examination profess themselves to be of that judgement, and beinge warned to come to the church that soe their scruples touchinge these doctrines might be removed. But doe neglect the same and refuse to heare the church therein. It is ordered that Bro. Jno. Davy and Bro. James Hitt doe sometyme this weeke warne the to doe their duty in cominge to the church the next first day in order to their satisfaction.[58]

The multiple offences referred to in this citation include the common charge of "forsaking the assembling of the saints" according to Heb 10:25.[59] More prominent was evidence of holding General Baptist doctrines of "freewill, falling from grace and general redemption."[60] It is known from the

---

57. Loughwood is located in East Devon, and the Meeting House is now owned by the National Trust.

58. Cited in Whitley, "Church Discipline," 288.

59. This charge appears also in the *Reading Church Book* for 1656, 3.

60. General Baptists were active in Tiverton from at least 1623. See Burrage, *EED* 1, 273. The founding date of a separate congregation is uncertain, but Parish records recount that as early as 1617 some members were absenting themselves from church services, and it appears likely that these were the nucleus of the Anabaptists who are

appearance of the Somerset Confession in 1656 that West Country Baptists were suspected of non-Calvinistic views, and of being out of harmony, doctrinally, with the London Particular churches.[61]

While Thomas Collier was endeavoring to counter Arminian theology on the wider scale, local churches were trying to persuade individual members of their erroneous doctrine and bring them into line with Calvinistic orthodoxy. Richard Copp of Axminster, another member at Loughwood was similarly charged with holding Arminian views.[62] In addition to doctrinal error these brothers were also refusing to "heare the church therein," thus rejecting the authority of the gathered community, showing themselves unwilling to submit to the rule of Christ in the congregation. On three counts, then, these brothers had offended the church and transgressed the law of Christ, and disciplinary proceedings were instigated against them.

Marriage outside the fellowship, and outside the faith was considered a grave sin. Where this arose in a church of the Midland association a woman who had so transgressed was charged with a still greater "evil," which was not heeding to the church when they had endeavored to keep her from making this marriage.[63] In the Hexham church records for November 1658, Thomas Rewcastle was sanctioned, "for marrying with an unbeliever."[64]

Non-participation in the Lord's Supper could also become an occasion for discipline in the case of repeated offence. This was a difficulty faced by the church at Andover, and members were encouraged to ascertain the basis of refusal of the Supper, whether "from prophanenesse, or want of clear light and of satisfaction in his conscience."[65]

A tragic case of attempted suicide in the Bedford church in 1659 was made the subject of disciplinary action by the church. A certain John Taylor had self-administered poison on account of being

> in a distracted condition partly through a melancholike frame and also . . . overcome by earthly mindedness and distrust.[66]

---

identifiable as the Baptist church in Tiverton in correspondence of 1626. See Tucker, "Salisbury and Tiverton about 1630," *TBHS* 3.1, 1–7; Burgess, "James Toppe," 193–211.

61. See Collier's *Epistle Dedicatory* to the Somerset Confession, Underhill, *Confessions of Faith*, 63f.

62. Whitely, "Church Discipline in Loughwood," 290.

63. *ARPB*, 31.

64. Underhill, *Records of the Churches*, 297.

65. *ARPB*, 187.

66. Ibid., 193.

Since the attempt to end his own life had failed the church had seen insufficient "sound Gospell [repentance] in him," which rendered him liable to the sentence of "withdrawing."

A serious sin was believed to have been committed when the principle of separation from an excommunicated person was not observed.[67]

A common offence in a number of records was that of "disorderly walking," more specifically defined as drunkenness. For example, at Loughwood:

> Bro. Gill from the Brethren at Honiton informed the church that Bro. Lamby was drunke in the open streete on Satturday last to the reproach of the gosple.[68]

A more grievous case of disorderly walking was the instance of Edmund Subdean, recorded in the Porton and Broughton Churchbook for 14 May 1672. He was tried by the church:

> for being guilty (as himself confessed) of these actions following: first for endeavouring abusing himselfe with mankind, condemned as sinful by the Lord his servants in Rom 1.31 [sic] 1 Tim 1:9-10.[69]

Charges of homosexuality were rare,[70] but this instance is recorded to illustrate the range of conspicuous issues Baptists were facing in the quest to form a godly people. What was defined as "sin" was anything condemned as unlawful by scripture, or anything commanded as Christian duty, by scripture.

---

67. Ibid., 196.

68. Whitely, "Church Discipline in Loughwood," 290. In The Church Book of Bunyan Meeting, 1650–1821, Harrison observes that drunkenness was the most common failing for which members were punished. The record for 1673 recounts the case of John Rush who was cast out because he was: "above the ordinary rates for drunkerds for he could not be carried home from the Swan to his own house without the help of no less than three persons, who when they had brought him home could not present him as one a live to his familie, he was so dead drunke." See, *A Booke Containing a Record of the Acts of a Congregation of Christ in and About Bedford and a Brief Account of their first GATHERING*, X and f.53.

69. *Porton and Broughton Churchbook*, n.p. The biblical text of Rom 1.31 is almost illegible and the reference is a best guess at what is written.

70. This is only reference to homosexuality in Baptist church books of the period that I am aware of.

4.3.2. Pastoral Procedure in Discipline

According to the Association Records, the refining of procedures of discipline was a major concern to Baptists throughout the 1650s. The congregational nature of churches made possible either laxity in discipline, with the attendant danger of bringing the name "Baptist" into disrepute,[71] or excessive zeal, resulting in judgmental and critical attitudes. Both forms of deviation from the mean are evident in Associational debates about discipline, and required Messengers to construct a moderate policy of pastoral practice to guide churches how to protect their reputation, while promoting a spirit of forbearance among the congregation. In accordance with their ideological commitment to the rule of Christ in the church, the Messengers adopted a method of strict adherence to biblical ordinances about discipline, thus holding in tension the twin objectives of truth and love, according to Eph 4.15. The practical guidelines for correct disciplinary procedure can be identified according to the following pattern, although what is set out here might be described as the ideal scenario.

4.3.2.i. Confronting the offender.

The first step in dealing with believers deemed to have fallen into sin was to show them their sin in the light of scripture, in the hope that confrontation with the Word would turn offenders from their error. In 1658, the Abingdon Association was asked for advice about dealing with a member who refused to take the Lord's Supper, though in all other respects their conduct was orderly. The rule by which the church should proceed was as follows:

> The church, in the first place, ought by scripture light to shew him his sin and then to admonish him to turne from it.[72]

In the case of some church members in the Midlands who advocated taking tythes for preaching the Gospel it is clearly stated that offenders must be made fully aware of their fault and the consequences of persisting therein,

> [they] are to have theyer sinn layd before [them] and to be admonished to repent of the same and to breake it off. And if, being thus seriously dealt with, and this more then once, they still continue in theyer evill, then they are to be withdrawn from.[73]

---

71. See *ARPB*, 132.
72. Ibid., 187.
73. Ibid., 31.

In this instance of perceived misconduct, the authority to confront the miscreant lay with the church according to article XXV.17 of the Somerset Confession: "PUBLICK rebuke to publick offenders."[74] In the case of less public sins the confrontation might be private, as made evident from a question put by the Thistleworth[75] church:

> When a brother knowes another to have sinned or trespassed as that he judgeth himself bound to deale with him according to the rule in Mt. 18.15 etc., whether he may finish that whole dealing in one day, if the church doe that day meet or whether it doe necessarily require some longer space of time?[76]

This question supposes that one brother is in possession of information concerning another, and further knows his responsibility to confront the offender. What is in doubt is how to proceed if his opportunity to deal with the matter is a day when the church will meet and may be required to pass judgment on the offending brother. The Messengers counselled patience, since haste risked losing the brother rather than winning him to repentance.

The importance of strict adherence to scriptural procedure is seen in another statement from the Abingdon Messengers,

> ... If the opportunitie of dealing with the offending brother the first and second time according to the rule, have bene let slip, or such opportunitie cannot be gained and made use of before the time of the next church meeting, whether in this case the brother offended may carrie the matter to the church before he have satisfied the rule in that behalf in Mt. 18? Answer. He may not; but ought exactly to conform to the rule of Christ.[77]

This advice dealt with the possibility that one church member not proceed in the correct manner to deal one to one with someone who has offended, and go directly to the church. This was expressly forbidden, being contrary to the teaching of Christ, even if the process of dealing with an erring member be slowed considerably.

The means by which sins came to light in Baptist churches reflects the small size of their congregations and their close knit fellowship. In contrast to the consistorial method of continental and English reformed churches, which used the visitation and examination of members by elders prior to

---

74. In Lumpkin, *Baptist Confessions*, 210.
75. That is, Isleworth in London. *ARPB*, 214 n. 106.
76. Ibid., 187–88.
77. Ibid., 187 and 188.

"A Holy and Orderly Communion" 115

admission to the Lord's Supper,[78] Baptist congregations maintained a watching brief over the lives of one another.[79] Naturally, suspicion and watching out for instances of sin in the lives of fellow church members might become the preoccupation of some, and on occasions could be maliciously abused. At Loughwood on 28th. 10 mo. 1655 two women came before the church accusing each other of speaking ill of the other:

> Sister Barnes chargeth Sister Burgis with calling of her durty beast, dogged woman; threatening to throw her cup to her head, and at least hinting to one of the world as if she had more than ordinary familiarity with another woman's husband.
>
> Sister Burgis responded by making some lesser charges against sister Barnes, and initially the church was uncertain as to who was in the right. Eventually, after investigation of the complaints, the church pronounced Sister Burgis the guilty party, subsequently leading to her excommunication.[80]

Abuse of disciplinary procedure may be the reason Messengers of the Midlands area instructed churches that the open reproving of a member before the church by a "private brother" not be encouraged, but reserved for elders, and also in exceptional circumstances, a "ministering brother," although this must not be contrary to any judgment of the local elders.[81] Another issue churches wrestled with was whether a testimony against a believer might be received from someone "of the world."[82] When this question arose in the West Country it was decided that the local church should judge for itself whether the testimony be satisfactory.

Christopher Hill, in a sociological analysis of puritan discipline, highlights the enormity of what was taking place at this point in ecclesiastical history, as congregationalism "brought a new kind of layman into the government of the Church."[83] Henry VIII had revised canon law to permit lay practitioners of civil law to exercise ecclesiastical jurisdiction, but the idea that a layman, without specialized legal training, could pass judgment upon a minister, or anybody else in the church, was beyond imagination.[84]

---

78. See Ha, *English Presbyterianism*, 155.
79. Somerset Confession, Article XXV.4. In Lumpkin, *Baptist Confessions*, 210.
80. Whitely, "Church Discipline in Loughwood," 291.
81. *ARPB*, 34.
82. Ibid., 59.
83. Hill, *Society and Puritanism*, 190.
84. Ibid., 190.

In this first phase of discipline, as indeed throughout, churches were advised to proceed "in the tenderness of love,"[85] since the purpose of discipline was the "gaining" of the offender.[86] The importance of a formal mechanism for making an accusation of wrongdoing against a church member, however, was to avoid gossip, and that an offender might know their status in relation to the congregation. In 1657 the Warwick church sought clarification when a member might be said to be "under dealing by a church." The response states that until an accusation with substance, that is, with "good testimony," be laid before the church, "a member cannot be said to bee under dealing by a church."[87]

4.3.2.ii. Punishing the Offender

Churches dealing with transgressing members had a variety of punishments available to them, from verbal rebuke, to exclusion from the Lord's Supper, and the ultimate sanction of excommunication.

An offender, following admonition by the church, might experience the withdrawing of the church, a form of "disfellowshipping" short of excommunication.[88] In the Abingdon Association discussion took place regarding the potential difference between "noting" and "withdrawing from," and whether these constituted a full "cutting off." The question was rationalized into this form:

> whether in case a church member be withdrawn from or noted as one with whom the saints would have no companie, according to 2 Thess. 3.6, [or if a] church have any further worke to doe in cutting [off].[89]

The distinction between the sentences of "withdrawing from" and "cutting off" is explicit in the case of an immoral brother reported by the Stoke and Andover church to the Association meeting in 1659:

> Two brethren are under dealing, of which one, though he be not totally cut off and cast out, yet he is withdrawn from and since

---

85. *ARPB*, 37.
86. Ibid., 187 and 188.
87. Ibid., 32.
88. Ibid., 54.
89. Ibid., 184. Words in square brackets are supplied by the editor due to manuscript damage.

his being withdrawn from, he hath increased his sin by going naked.[90]

The term, "withdrawing from" was often preferred to that of "excommunication" as it emphasized the action of the church in relation to the offender, in contrast to the sentence imposed upon the offender.[91] In the Loughwood Church Books for 29 December 1658, Sister Hossiter of Honiton was sentenced to be withdrawn from as a result of failing to heed several warnings regarding attendance at Quaker meetings.[92] In the same church another brother who had been warned by two elders regarding absence from the assembly, having failed to reform, was asked to "forbear from breaking bread."[93] This was an uncommon form of discipline among Particular Baptists, probably because of the restricted nature of entry to the church, via believer's baptism, and the covenanted gathering of the congregation. Exclusion from the Lord's Supper represented such a serious breach of community that, for anyone so disciplined, it was tantamount to excommunication.[94]

Prior to admonition an offender was not to be rejected, even in cases of gross offence, in the hope that discipline would provoke repentance bringing restoration to the fellowship.[95] Such a well-meaning policy of restoration might, however, also have the undesired effect of relapse leading to repeated episodes of discipline, as was the case in Hexham, according to Church records for 3 April 1653:

> John Huspeth, who before was suspended and again embraced, was now excommunicated.[96]

In June 1655 the Hexham church was in disarray,[97] and a challenge to the authority of pastor, Thomas Tillam, had broken out regarding the

---

90. Ibid., 192. Nakedness may be a reference to contact with radical Quakers. See Carroll, "Early Quakers," 76–83.
91. See for example, ARPB, 187.
92. Whitely, "Church Discipline in Loughwood," 289.
93. Whitely, *From Backwoods to Beacon*, 7.
94. Baptist practice of barring from communion contrasts starkly with that of Presbyterians in the same period, who used suspension of communion as a central plank in their evangelical project to bring reformation and inward conversion to parishioners. See Vernon, "Ministry of the Gospel," in Durston and Maltby, *Religion in Revolutionary England*, 125–30.
95. ARPB, 54.
96. Underhill, *Records of the Churches of Christ*, 291.
97. This internecine warfare was caused not least by the debacle surrounding the imposter and supposed Jew, Joseph ben Israel. See Underhill (ed.), *Records of the*

doctrine of imposition of hands. Mr. Anderson, a church member, openly opposed Tillam on this issue and as a result,

> he was by the elders, with the joint approbation of the church, delivered unto Satan with Thomas Ogle.[98]

On the 4 November, the church also withdrew from John Warde and John Redshaw.

At Loughwood, on 13th. 11 mo. 1656 it was recorded:

> The church thus proceeded to the excommunication of sister Elizabeth Burgis for divers evils which she stood guilty of and for which she brought forth noe satisfactory repentence after longe waiting.[99]

At the twenty-first General Meeting of the Abingdon Association in 1659, the Reading church reported that since the last meeting "one member hath bene cast out."[100] The Hadnam church likewise reported, "one member is under dealing and likely to be cast out."[101] The Watlington church also stated that, "one sister hath bene cast out since the last meeting."[102] The perfunctory manner in which these cases are recounted, and the absence of further detail, implies that excommunication was not an uncommon occurrence.[103] The woman in the Midlands case who had made an "unequal" marriage was liable to be "put away as an impenitent person," unless she "repent unfaignedly."[104]

According to the Midland Association records, excommunication might happen in an open service of pubic worship as a witness to onlookers that the Baptist experiment in separatist ecclesiology was a serious attempt to form a godly people:

> Wee judg allsoe the pronouncing of the sentence of excommunication may be done before the worlde that they may see the church doth not bear with sinne and sinners and that it may minde them of the wofull condition of wicked man and that

---

Churches of Christ, 292. The story is told fully in Bell, *Apocalypse How?*, 238–41,

98. Underhill, *Records of the Churches of Christ*, 295.

99. Whitely, "Church Discipline," 290.

100. *ARPB*, 190.

101. Ibid., 191.

102. Ibid.

103. Other examples could be cited from Kingston, Stoke and Andover, Abingdon and Wantage. See ibid., 199, 203.

104. Ibid., 31.

God will denounce that terrible sentence against them, Goe, ye cursed.[105]

For sentences less than excommunication, the church was to announce admonition in "closed session," out of view of the world, in hope that the offender might be recovered.[106]

The power and effectiveness of excommunication derived, as Christopher Hill notes, from the reality of close community. Hill notes that the story of "the breakdown of excommunication as an effective censure [in the National Church] is the story of the breakdown of the medieval communities."[107] The opposite reality pertained in the churches of the Particular Baptists, where members were covenanted to Christ, and one another through baptism. In such contexts of a "society within society," where congregations functioned as self-regulating communities, where discipline was by the people for the people, or at least with their passive participation,[108] the sentence of excommunication retained considerable emotional and spiritual impact.

4.3.2.iii. Responses of the Offender

It is clear from church records that responses to disciplinary procedures by offenders could be varied, ranging from contrition and repentance to indifference, and insincere repentance. In the West Country, in October 1655, a church was wrestling with the question how to deal with a believer who had sinned greatly, been reproved and admonished openly by the church, but had responded in silence and displayed no clear signs of repentance. Should the church "appoint him a day when to tender his repentance to the church," or "whether the church is to leave him in respect of time to his own liberty and to God's work upon his heart?" The Messengers replied that the church,

> may appoint him a day wherein to come before them in order to their satisfaction, either to acquit him of his fault on satisfactory repentance or else to reject him.[109]

---

105. Ibid., 27.
106. Ibid.
107. Hill, *Society and Puritanism*, 305. See also Hill, "Theory and Practice," 1–11.
108. See Hill, *Society and Puritanism*, 325.
109. *ARPB*, 61.

In this scenario, the church becomes a court in which the congregation function as judge and jury, and members are subject to the ruling of their peers. At Loughwood on 14th. 12 mo. 1655:

> Sister Sprague, having offered satisfaction by repentence before the church is received into full communion againe.[110]

A similar circumstance is recorded in the Longworth church in 1659, according to the Records of the Abingdon Association:

> Five members have bene added viz., four [have been] baptized and one that had formerly strayed now [showing re]pentance againe received.[111]

At Loughwood, however, Sister Hossiter again appeared before the church on 29th. 10 mo. 1658 when she was admonished, but subsequently told on 16th. 12 mo. 1658 that her repentance was to be further inquired into. When it was discovered two months later that she was continuing to disobey the church by meeting with the Quakers, she was excommunicated.[112] In the Hexham church on 26 December 1658 John Johnson and John Orde were received back into the church after a period of discipline for drunkenness.[113]

Discipline in a Baptist congregation could be an untidy process, resulting in a mixture of reform and rebellion among transgressors. This suggests that members held a range of estimations of the authority possessed by the local church, exercised in the name of Christ.

4.3.2.iv. Shunning the Impenitent

The disposition adopted by churches towards impenitent offenders, excommunicated from the congregation, was hard but not entirely lacking mercy. The instructions of the Midland messengers to their churches in 1656 was,

> our carriage to a person cast out of the church ought to be as towards a heathen or a publican, Mt. 18.17. If wee find him hardened and persisting in sinne then to leave him and take no more notice of him that of another wicked person. But if wee find him

---

110. Whitely, "Church Discipline in Loughwood," 290.

111. *ARPB*, 191. Square brackets indicates words are supplied by the editor (B. R. White) of the manuscript.

112. Whitely, "Church Discipline in Loughwood," 289.

113. Underhill, *Records of the Churches of Christ*, 297.

willing to heare us and soe likely to be gained then to use such meanes as the Scriptures affordeth for the regaineing of him.[114]

This procedure was almost identical to that operating in the Western Association where, when the occasion demanded, churches could pronounce severe sanctions couched in scriptural terms, as in the case of Richard Copp of Axminster:

> . . . but he still stiffly persisting therein and indeavouring to cause divisions in the church and to draw away others after him, was by the church in the name of Christ – delivered up to Satan, and was judged fit to be no further communicated with than a heathen or publican. And that upon these scriptures (viz) 1 Tim. 6:3,5 verses, Romans 16:17, Titus 3:10.[115]

In this instance the terms of excommunication, namely "shunning," were every bit as uncompromising as that associated with the ban used by continental Anabaptists.[116] Procedures of this type had also been available to the ecclesiastical courts prior to their emasculation in 1641, when the sentence of "greater excommunication" could be passed on a sinner, depriving them of ordinary social support and common benefits, though this was not commonly employed.[117] When this judgment was given, however, the excommunicated suffered social and economic ostracism, being unable to buy or sell, not to be employed, unable to sue or give evidence in court, thereby depriving them the opportunity to recover debts. Neither could they give bail, make a will, or receive a legacy. Such "discipline by the purse,"[118] which effectively cut a person off from common civil rights, compares harshly with the spiritual penalties applied in Baptist congregations.

Following excommunication, churches in the Abingdon Association agreed to notify neighboring churches of their decision to prevent an

---

114. *ARPB*, 26–27.

115. Whitely, "Church Discipline in Loughwood," 290.

116. See Williams, *Radical Reformation*, 485–99.

117. One example from the early seventeenth century is noted by Marchant who cites the appeal of a parish priest to the archdeacon's register in Nottingham on behalf of Mary Bell a pregnant parishioner on the brink of giving birth:
"I have received a writ of Excommunication against Marie Bell (my parishioner) and I dare not stay it without warrantie from your Court. Will you be pleased to be certified, that she waites her every houre, and not able to travaile halfe a mile out of the towne. Let mee entreat so much favour of you (if it may bee) as to reverse that which is done, or els to absolve her againe, that she be not deprived of womens helpe, which now shee is like to stand in need of. I hope you will pittie a woman in her case." Cited in Outhwaite, *Rise and Fall*, 12.

118. So called by Bishop Hacket. See Hill, *Society and Puritanism*, 307.

offender joining an adjacent congregation. However, if the offender subsequently showed satisfactory repentance, the neighboring churches would likewise be informed of this change of status.[119]

It was acknowledged that restoration had been the intention of excommunication in its Christian origins, a means of warning rather than mere punishment. Excommunicated persons were not supposed to be cast out of the church permanently, but until such time they repented.[120] If repentance was not forthcoming then shunning was to be fully implemented. In Oxford, the church resolved that,

> a person lawfully cast out be looked upon as one whom the saintes doe and must put away from among themselves, and whom they doe and must turne away from, and whom they doe and must avoid and reject.[121]

The imperative in this resolution reflected the fear of spiritual contamination by contact with an excommunicant, and those who failed to observe the rule of shunning were also in danger of being cast out. What about the situation, asked the Midland and Abingdon Associations, of listening to the preaching and praying of an excommunicant? This question presupposed someone being cast out for a difference of theological conviction, regarded by some as anathema, and by others as a brother. In response the Messengers asserted,

> it is not lawful at any time to heare an excommunicated person preach unless some necessity shall be found to require some able brethren to heare in order to a present discovery and refutation of his errors.[122]

One circumstance which gave rise to a dilemma such as this was the question of laying on of hands as an ordinance of Christ.[123] Those who insisted on making laying on hands a divisive and schismatic issue were to be put out of the church. But what then of those who disagreed with the grounds of excommunication and being sympathetic to this theology sought them out to receive the laying on of hands? This was the response:

---

119. *ARPB*, 130.

120. See Hill, "Theory and Practice," 1-2. In this article Hill also draws attention to the pre-Christian origins of excommunication among the Druids.

121. *ARPB*, 196.

122. Ibid., 38.

123. See the Midland Records for October 1658, ibid., 39.

wee judg it his greater evill under a twofold consideration. First, not seeking reconciliation to the offended brethren Mt. 5. 23f., and, next, in that hee goeth after an excommunicated person for to have hands layd upon him who should have bine to him as an heathen or a publican for which evill the church is to deale with [him] as a great offender.[124]

By hearing an excommunicated preacher the decision of the church, from which he was excommunicated, was rendered null and void, and the authority of the church compromised. The Abingdon messengers warned the churches that such behavior

> doth utterly make voyd the authoritye given of Christ to the churches to excommunicate such members as Gospell rule requires to be layd by and so doth open a wide dore to confusion and licentiousness.[125]

This was a plea for congregational unity when discipline was imposed, and personal dissent, leading to a breach of the ban, compromised the authority of Christ in his church risking spiritual and moral anarchy.

This discussion of the practice of discipline among the Particular Baptists has shown that observance of scriptural principles in their congregations was a conviction of first importance, and those who defied the authority of the local church were dealt with with a degree of severity. The agreed policy of church leaders was that those who had been admonished and excommunicated should be regarded no longer as a brother or sister. Their judgments, however, were not always supported by rank and file members of the church, who clearly understood the implications of democratic church government.

4.4. Theology of Discipline among Particular Baptist

Arising from the practice of discipline among early Particular Baptists a number of theological commitments, which legitimized the application of corrective procedures to members, may be identified.

4.4.1. *The Authority of the Church*

In the 1644 London Confession, Baptists stated that,

---

124. Ibid., 39.
125. Ibid., 205.

> Christ has given power to his Church to receive in and cast out, by way of Excommunication, any member; and this power is given to every particular Congregation.[126]

This statement shows that Baptists assumed the authority and competence of the universal church was fully realized in the local congregation. Any judgment passed by a particular congregation represented the judgment of the church universal and was universally applicable. A person excommunicated from the local church was *de jure* excommunicated from the universal church, even if *de facto* they might appear a week later as a preacher in another congregation.[127] As the Messengers in the Abingdon Association recognized, however, such reprehensible behavior was "to make voyd the authoritye given of Christ to the churches."[128]

Terry Dowley has argued that among Baptists the "refusal to hear the Church," by offenders, was the greater part of any sin committed by a church member. He contends that the failure to take seriously the rebuke of the church constituted a slight to the authority of the body of Christ, and was, "theoretically at the base of all their [Baptist] disciplinary activity."[129] This observation highlights the importance of ecclesiology, which cannot be divorced from Christology, and the perceived significance of the local church, in Baptist practice of discipline. In the Baptist form of congregationalism, a failure to submit to the church amounted to a failure to submit to Christ.[130]

The difficulty faced by churches in the Midlands was that of individuals defying the authority of the local church by pursuing their own interpretation of scripture.[131] Those who regarded the laying on of hands as an ordinance of Christ refused to be bound by the church meeting that decreed it not to be so, and had suffered excommunication for being schismatic about the issue. However, a separatist church, which had been formed on the basis of liberty of conscience in the interpretation of scripture, could not hold back those who challenged their officers in matters of Christian practice which to them were issues of conscience. Baptists had denounced the hierarchical structure of episcopal authority in the Church of England, and seen little attraction in the trans-local, synodal approach to authority in the Presbyterian system. Now they were faced with members who rejected the

---

126. First London Confession article XLII. Lumpkin, *Baptist Confessions*, 168.

127. As in the Abingdon case mentioned above. *ARPB*, 205.

128. Ibid., 205.

129. Dowley, "Baptists and Discipline in the Seventeenth Century," 163.

130. This was a view shared with Independents like Katherine Chidley, as in *The Justification of the Independent Churches*, 18.

131. See *ARPB*, 38–39.

authority of the congregation in preference to individual conscience before scripture. The seeds of fissiparity latent in the Reformation principle of *sola scriptura* were bearing their inevitable fruit.[132]

4.4.2. The Glory of Christ

Secondly, discipline among early Baptists was inspired by the quest for a church living under the rule of Christ, existing to give glory and honour to God alone. In the West Country, Thomas Collier described praying for "strength and light to purge out every persistent impenitent sinner." His zeal for bringing the ungodly to discipline was fuelled by the belief that evil doers in the church were "enemies and traytors to the crown and dignity of our Lord Jesus." Believers continuing in sinful ways were "living short of a true sight and sense of God's majesty in his churches and among his saints." In Old Testament prophetic style, he warned the cold-hearted and impenitent sinners,

> You have but, as it were, played with God. You have not trembled in his presence. You have been wanton before him, having been without the terrour of his majesty . . .[133]

Benjamin Cox, in similar terms to Collier, asserted that though the elect can have no sin imputed to them, yet believers in Christ must guard against the practice of sin, because "it tends to the provoking and dishonouring of God."[134] Sin in the life of a Christian is a thing which "the most holy God declares himself to loathe and abhor."[135] Thus while unbelievers may resent and resist the imposition of discipline by the church seeking to instil piety into society, the godly will welcome discipline because they experience the grief of sinning "against their holy and glorious God, and merciful and loving Father."[136]

4.4.3. Purity of the Body of Christ

Thirdly, church discipline can be understood as a concern to establish a pure church, which validated Baptist claims to be a true church. A pure church

---

132. See Collinson, "Sects and the Evolution of Puritanism," 129–44.

133. All citations from *ARPB*, 93–94.

134. Cox, *An Appendix to a Confession of Faith*, article XII. In Underhill, *Confessions of Faith*, 56,

135. Ibid.

136. Ibid.

and a true church were not necessarily synonymous, since a true church also required preaching of the true Gospel and correct administration of the sacraments. Purity, however, was an essential component in the Baptist ecclesiastical project since the *ecclesia* was to be the pure and spotless bride of Christ.

The Baptist commitment to a pure church might be contrasted to the Presbyterian program in the same period. The Presbyterian ambition of a national church, based on a parish system, was intended to impose Christian discipline on the whole of society through the work of the ministry. In particular, Presbyterians were anxious to make preaching the keynote of parochial reformation, and evidence shows that in both London and Lancashire, where the Presbyterian classis system was most fully implemented, Provincial Assemblies focused on the competence of hopeful incumbents as preacher when making ministerial appointments.[137] Unsurprisingly, given that preaching was intended to play such an important role in the eradication of sin from society, proper observance the Sabbath became a major concern for Presbyterians. To this end, they were able to make use of the parliamentary ordinance of April 1644, "for the better observation of the Lord's Day," which required everyone including wandering beggars and vagabonds to attend church, hence to be under the Word of God.[138] This gave rise to the "ministry" of Sunday tavern raiding by Presbyterian elders intent on catching transgressors of the law.[139] These measures, which appeared intrusive and overbearing to many people, were intended to Christianize society, and Presbyterians hoped that the strict observance of religious duties would lead to the inward conversion of sinners.

From the sectarian perspective of Particular Baptists, Presbyterian disciplinary policy practice enacted the "salt of the earth" model of missionary endeavor, which blurred the distinction between church and the world.[140] This resulted in popular resentment of ecclesiastical authority and achieved little in terms of social reform. Increased numbers in churches represented nothing more than formalism and hypocrisy, resulting in *corpus permixtum*.[141] In order to address this situation, which was felt most acutely at

---

137. Vernon, "Presbyterians during the English Revolution," 120. See also, Collinson, "Shepherds, Sheepdogs and Hirelings," in *From Cranmer to Sancroft*, 46–47.

138. See Durston, "Preaching and Sitting Still," in Durston and Maltby, *Religion in Revolutionary England*, 213.

139. Evidence of such work is confirmed in the minute book of the Fourth Classis in London for December 1646. See Vernon, "Presbyterians during the English Revolution," 120.

140. Kiffen, *Briefe Remonstrance*, 5.

141. See Luomanen, "Corpus Mixtum," 469–80.

times of communion, the London Provincial Assembly in 1655 published its *Exhortation to Catechizing*, which is, apparently, not to be "viewed as a last ditch effort to reform ignorant parishioners."[142] Presbyterians had similar ambitions to the sectarian Baptists to organize a "pure church," but the Presbyterian task was more difficult because they were seeking the internal reformation of the lives of the unconverted as well as the converted members of the parish. In addition to the application religious laws, the aim of catechizing was:

> to advance, the glory of God's *grace*, to staine the pride of mans nature; to make the Saints walke much more the *comfortably* . . . [and] to damme up that cursed fountaine of *self conceit*, whence daily issue so many impure streames.[143]

In contrast to Presbyterian policy of using biblical law as a means to inward conversion, Baptist ecclesiology proceeded on the basis that inward conversion was the necessary presupposition of obedience to God's law. The gathered church, in Baptist perspective, was Christ's spiritual kingdom where Christ exercises his power to the purification, preservation and ultimately, the salvation of the elect. To the elect Christ applies the benefits of his priesthood:

> namely, to the subduing and taking away of their sinnes, . . . regeneration, sanctification, preservation and strengthening in all their conflicts against Satan, the World, the Flesh, and the temptations of them.[144]

In Baptist theology, the purity of the church could only be spoken of as a reality, but must be spoken of as a reality and not merely an aspiration, because Christ had committed himself to the sanctification of the saints by his priestly sacrifice for sins and kingly power over his people. The purity of the church was not a condition that a gathered community could achieve by external submission to canon law, parliamentary ordinance, or church rules. A "godly people" was that which God brings into being by the effectual work of the Gospel in the hearts of the elect.

Church discipline served this end, not directly, but indirectly, because external behavior, or misbehavior, may more or less approximate to the true state of heart of any believer. Discipline was necessary in the church, however, as God's appointed means of goading believers, and, when necessary,

---

142. Vernon, "Presbyterians during the English Revolution," 123.

143. [The Provincial Assembly at London] *An Exhortation to Catechizing*, 15. Italics as per original. Cited in Vernon, "Presbyterians during the English Revolution," 123.

144. 1644 London Confession, Article XIX. Lumpkin, *Baptist Confessions*, 161–62.

their rebuking one another. Discipline was the exercise of mutual watch-care, as believers walked together in covenant community. William Kiffen asserted,

> wee conceive our selves bound to watch over one another, and in case of sinne, to deale faithfully one with another, according to these Scriptures.[145]

Far from abandoning the world outside the church, the primary commitment to the purity of the Church meant Baptists contributed to social reform taking place in English society in the mid seventeenth century, albeit on their own terms. Among Baptists there was no dissent from the shared conviction that the task of the church was to promote the Christianizing of society, though disagreement did exist regarding the means by which it should be achieved. According to Baptist theology, the first step was to have its own house in order, and its own family under discipline, since the church was the kingdom of Christ and his kingly rule demanded obedience and submission. This, in turn, would constitute a rebuke to sinful society. A disciplined, gathered church, in Baptist thought, was a "light set on a hill."

Summary

This chapter has examined the logic of ecclesiastical discipline in Particular Baptist church perspective and has shown that Baptist ecclesiastical discipline was one instance of the concern for Church discipline recognizable in English Puritan and Separatist tradition. In turn, the Puritan and Separatist application of discipline grew out of the Reformation program to define, and create, a true church modelled on the pattern of the New Testament *ecclesia*. Throughout the 1640s and 1650s, congregational discipline among Particular Baptists was regarded as an essential mark of true church, necessary for maintaining a believer's church, a godly fellowship, a communion of saints. Discipline was the means by which the church preserved its identity as the church of King Jesus, in contradistinction to the world. The controlling sociological concept in the exercise of discipline was that of the "sect," but the decisive religious concept was that of a community living under the Rule of Christ. Discipline, however, was not simply concerned with creating a rules-based church, a legalistic form of religion. Discipline was regarded as a necessary means to the end of creating a godly people, free from sin, according to God's original intention in creation, the fulfilment of God's redemptive purposes in Christ.[146]

145. Kiffen, *Briefe Remonstrance*, 13.
146. See 1644 London Confession, article XXIX.

5

"An Intolerable Usurpation"[1]

Theology and Practice of Ministry among Early Particular Baptists

5.1. The Choosing of "Meet Persons": Baptist Lay Ministry

ONE OF THE MORE radical developments achieved by early Calvinistic Baptists, a direct result of utilizing the rule of Christ as the controlling precept of church life, occurred in the area of ministry within their congregations. Although Henry Jacob intended that the church he gathered in 1616 should have a professional ministry,[2] his ecclesiology made possible a contrary development that came to flower in the late 1630s.[3] Jacob had permitted lay members of the church to "exercise" before the congregation, and when separatist churches began to proliferate after 1638, it was not considered extraordinary within the constituency that the majority of leaders were tradesmen, not dependent on the congregation for their living.[4] In the words of Murray Tolmie,

---

1. Ricraft, *Looking Glasse*, 11.

2. Jacob, *Confession and Protestation*, B9, B4, C7. The first three ministers of this congregation, Jacob, Lathorp and Jessey were university educated and ordained clergymen.

3. The political background, including the collapse of episcopal administration in December 1640 is discussed in chapter 2.

4. One prominent example would be William Kiffin. See Orme, *Remarkable Passages in the Life of William Kiffin*, 22–23. Hanserd Knollys supported himself as a

The custom of lay preaching, incipient in the 1616 congregation, had flowered into a fully elaborated lay pastorate by the beginning of the revolution.[5]

Since most Baptist congregations in the early 1640s were small in number, and resources meagre, provision for a professional ministry was in most instances impractical. The social standing of ministers in Baptist churches was not lost on their accusers and opponents who at first ridiculed them[6] and later petitioned Parliament to silence them.[7] One of their most outspoken enemies, Daniel Featley, regarded it as a manifestation of anarchy among the Baptists that the most unsuitable persons imaginable ministered among them:

> [In their meetings] a brewers Clerk exerciseth, A Taylor expoundeth, A Waterman Teacheth – the lowest of the people.[8]

Josiah Ricraft, wrote to William Kiffin to warn him,

> That you are so far from having any warrant to be a Minister of any such congregation, as that you have not the least warrant to be a Minister of any at all. But your taking upon you to bee a Minister to dispense the Word and Sacraments, is a greater sinne and disorder than ever any was in the constitution of the Church of England since Reformation. And for ignorant illiterate men, the lowest of the people such as yourself, to take upon

---

schoolmaster which pastoring a Baptist church in London.

5. See Tolmie, *Saints*, 42. The growth of the "lay tradition" in Puritanism is discussed at some length in Cross, *Church and People*, especially chapter 9. Also, MacLear, "Making of the Lay Tradition," 113–36.

6. The satirical poet John Taylor compared to rise of sectarian ministry to a plague of insects:
These kind of Vermin swarm like Caterpillars
And hold Conventicles in Barnes and Sellars
Some preach (or prate) in Woods, in fields, in stables,
In hollow trees, in tubs, on top of tables.
Taylor, *A Swarme of Sectaries, and Schismatiques*, 7.

7. A legal prohibition on lay preaching was issued by Parliament on 26 April 1645: "An Ordinance for none to preach but ordained Ministers, except alowed by both Houses of Parliament." *Acts and Ordinances of the Interregnum, 1642–1660* (1911), 677. A petition was submitted to Parliament against lay preachers by the Lord Mayor and Common Council of London 19 December 1646 asking of Parliament: "give authority to suppresse all such from publike Preaching, as have not duely been Ordained, whereby their gifts for the Ministry, and their soundnesse in the Faith might be evinced." Responses from the separatists included John Saltmarsh, *Sparkles of Glory* and Edmund Chillenden, *Preaching Without Ordination*. See Greaves, "Ordination Controversy," 226.

8. Featley, *Dippers Dipt.*, B4 Preface. See also *The Clergyes Bill of Complaint*, 5.

> you to be a Minister of God, a guide of soules, is such an intolerable usurpation & profanation of God's name, that without great repentance you will find one day to your cost that fulfilled of the Saviour, The blinde lead the blinde, and both fall into the ditch.⁹

Thomas Edwards, another prominent critic of Baptists in the mid-1640s, tried to arouse the fear and loathing of the nation towards Baptists by writing:

> Is it fitting that well meaning Christians should be suffered to goe and make Churches, and then proceed to chuse whom they will for Ministers, as some Taylor, Feltmaker, Button-maker, men ignorant, and low in parts, by whom they shall be led into sinne and errors, and to forsake the publicke assemblies [?]¹⁰

Edwards feared the slow progress of the Westminster Assembly in organizing a new national church settlement was allowing sectaries to grow in strength and gain credibility for their egalitarian ecclesiology, and urged Parliament to act. Baptists, however, were undeterred by Parliament's ordinances and their critic's comments and continued to refine their theology and practice of calling forth those they deemed suitable to officiate in the offices of Christ.

Attitudes of the period, to lay ministers, from wider afield are reflected in Cromwell's response to the governor of Edinburgh on 12 December 1650 concerning the claims of Scots ministers:

> You say, You have just cause to regret that men of Civil employments should usurp the calling and employment of the Ministry; to the scandal of the Reformed Kirks. Are you troubled that Christ is preached? Is preaching so exclusively your function? . . . We have not so learned Christ. We look at ministers as helpers of, not lords over, the faith of God's people.¹¹

But the exigencies of social class was not the only cause of Baptists elevating lay ministry in their churches, their practice was also theologically motivated. The first attempt to explain their theology and practice of ministry was in the London Confession of 1644, and here they asserted that in their gathered churches,

---

9. Ricraft, *A Looking Glasse for the Anabaptists*, 11.
10. Edwards, *Reasons Against the Independent Government*, 23.
11. Cited in MacLear, "Making of the Lay Tradition," 135 n. 39.

> ought all men to come . . . to be enrolled amongst [Christ's] household servants . . . to present their bodies and soules, and to bring their gifts God hath given them.[12]

This was re-emphasized in article XLV which stated:

> That also such to whom God hath given gifts, being tried in the Church, may and ought by the appointment of the Congregation, to prophesie, according to the proportion of faith, and so teach publickly the Word of God, for the edification, exhortation, and comfort of the Church.[13]

Every baptized believer joining a Baptist congregation was under an obligation to employ their spiritual gifts and graces for the edification of the body. Ministry was not the preserve of university educated and state-validated men, but the responsibility of all the saints, a view which led some critics to accuse Baptists of desiring the abolition of universities.[14] The General Baptist Edmund Chillenden, had a "doctrine of obligation" which required believers who were spiritually gifted, so to minister: "God requires it of them and they may not neglect it," he wrote.[15]

The Baptist theology of ministry was further elaborated in the 1644 Confession, article XXXVI:

> every Church has power given them from Christ for their better well-being, to choose to themselves meet persons into the office of Pastors, Teachers, Elders, Deacons, being qualified according to the Word, as those which Christ has appointed in his Testament, for the feeding, governing, serving, and building up of his Church, and that none other have power to impose them, either these or any other.[16]

In this statement it is evident that Baptist theology and practice of ministry was ordered with reference to Christ. As was observed in relation to church discipline, they believed they had authority from Christ to order their own affairs which included the right "to choose meet people for offices of ministry." It was expected that Christ would exercise his kingly authority over his kingdom, the church, and call servants according to his own will,

---

12. *First London Confession* articles XXXIV and XXXV, in Lumpkin, *Baptist Confessions*, 166.

13. Ibid., 168.

14. See Brown, *Political Activities*, 36.

15. Chillenden, *Preaching without Ordination*, 24.

16. Lumpkin, *Baptist Confessions*, 166. In the second, and subsequent, editions, "Pastors, Teachers," are omitted in favor of the two fold offices.

to undertake the work of ministry. The spiritual calling of ministers was not thought to be in tension with the statement, "appointment of the congregation," since they understood Christ to mediate his authority through the gathered congregation of believers. The authority of Christ, and the decisions of the church, were regarded, theologically, as coincidental.

The Episcopalian Daniel Featley made known his confusion and frustration with such arrangements:

> If all be Pastours, where are their Flocks? if all be Teachers, where are their Scholars?
>
> ... It is true, we grant that all who have received gifts from God, ought to make use of them for the benefit of others; and if any abound in knowledge, he ought to communicate to them that lack, and freely give *lumen de lumine* ... Notwithstanding, this necessary duty of imploying our talent, whatever it may be, to our Masters best advantage, none may take upon him the cure of soules without commission; nor divide the word and dispense the Sacraments, without ordination, and imposition of hands: ... none may open and shut the Kingdome of Heaven, except they have received the *Keyes* from *Christ*; neither a calling without gifts, nor gifts without a calling, make a *man of God*. ... But this is the error of the Anabaptists, whereby they overthrow al order in the Church and confound Shepherds and Flocks, Masters and Scholars, Clergy and Laity.[17]

The Puritan tendency toward the subordination of the ministry to the congregation[18] was now, among Baptists, accelerated to a more radical dismantling of the "professional barrier which even in Congregationalism had stood between clergy and lay."[19] It was not the case that the Baptists confused, or denied, the distinctions between clergy and laity, they simply did not believe these categories were from Christ, and hence had no validity in a rightly constituted church. Every baptized believer was a minister, in Baptist theology, though some ministries, on account of the authority invested therein, might require extraordinary validation.

This highlights the distinctive nature of Baptist ministry, since in the gathered churches of the Independents, Thomas Goodwin, for example, set out the scriptural arguments for the professional pastoral office as instituted

---

17. Featley, *Dippers Dipt*, 183–84.

18. Evident, for example, in the first General Baptist minister John Smyth. See Whitley, *Works of John Smyth*, ii.393. For analysis of Smyth's view see David Hall who judges that among the separatists it was Smyth who "most radically subordinated the office of the ministry to the gathered church." Hall, *Faithful Shepherd*, 38.

19. Maclear, "Making of the Lay Tradition," 125.

by Christ, though the occupant be chosen by the congregation. He argued that the institution of ministry be of God, "yet the designment, who should be a minister, is immediately by men."[20] The practical significance of this ideology was Goodwin's insistence that a scholarly pastor should be financially supported in a manner "suited to the dignity and labour of his place and calling."[21]

Did this policy mean that Particular Baptists were anti-clerical in their understanding of ministry?[22] B. R. White has argued this was the case, stating that, "in the thought of the men who framed the 1644 *Confession*, the ministry was more firmly subordinated to the immediate authority of the covenanted community." And again he states, "Baptists laid less stress [than Separatists generally] upon the distinctive functions of the ministry considered apart from the congregation."[23] White's argument can be supported on the basis that Baptist church officers were often chosen from among the congregation, appointed by congregational election, and sustained financially by the gifts of the congregation.[24] These factors would suggest absolute anti-clericalism. On the other hand, if early Baptist ministry is considered from the perspective of the service performed, rather than in terms of status, there is evidence of great appreciation of ministers, and a longing in many churches to have a separated ministry. In the church at Kilmington, for example, the congregation was served in its early years by approved elders who exercised their teaching gifts, and no evidence exists, nor even the suggestion, that the church was not well served by these men, and yet the first recorded decision by the church, dated 14th of the 12mo. 1653 states:

---

20. See Goodwin, *Works* XI, 294 and especially 352; also Chidley, *Justification of the Independent Churches*, 4–8.

21. Goodwin, *Works* XI, 380.

22. Popular views about the clergy among Independents can be gauged by a comment by Cromwell in respect of the Irish Church. He said "So Antichristian and dividing a term as clergy and laity were unknown in the primitive church. It was your pride that begat this expression, and it is for filthy lucre's sake that you keep it up, that by making the people believe they are not so holy as yourselves, they might for their penny purchase some sanctity from you; and that you might bridle, saddle and ride them at your pleasure." Cited in Hill, *God's Englishman: Oliver Cromwell and the English Revolution*, 122. See also MacLear, "Popular Anticlericalism," 443–70.

23. White, "Doctrine of the Church," 581. "More firmly" suggests a comparative judgment, and Baptists were generally more anti-clerical than the Independents for example.

24. The numbers of fully qualified clergymen amongst the ranks of the Particular Baptists were few. Hanserd Knollys, Benjamin Cox, Henry Jessey and John Tombs were prominent ex-clergymen.

> It lyinge as a grievance uppon the spiritts of many of the members that there is not a pastor amongst us. It is agreed uppon that Bro: Hitt draw upp an epistle to Bro: Pendarves to desire him (if he be not otherwise ingaged) to be the man.[25]

John Pendarves was minister at Abingdon at the time and declined the invitation to move to Kilmington, and three years later was dead, however, the Kilmington record demonstrates the yearning to supplement the gifts of its elders with those of a recognized pastor.[26] This suggests that Baptist attitudes towards ministers was more nuanced than the language of anti-clericalism suggests, and while professional ministers might be regarded as unnecessary, or even undesirable, by many congregations, a separated ministry was by no means rejected. In his study of the progress of lay ministry during the Civil War era, James MacLear makes the point that, "both Luther and Calvin taught the priesthood of believers, though they also stressed the retention of a distinct ministerial order in the midst of that priesthood."[27] This neatly captures the theology and practice of ministry which developed among Particular Baptists, namely, a recognized ministry of pastoral oversight exercised by one called and appointed to this office, operating within a context of congregational ministries performed by church members.

The emerging theology and practice of lay ministry in Particular Baptist congregations came to be tested in relation to the question, who amongst them was permitted to dispense the sacrament of baptism.[28] The 1644 London Confession stated in article XLI:

> The persons designed by Christ, to dispense this Ordinance [baptism], the Scriptures hold forth to be a preaching Disciple.[29]

This assertion in relation to baptism looked to some observers of Baptist practice like a covert form of clericalism, tying administration of the ordinance to a particular office, that of "preaching disciple." Daniel Featley, for example, ridiculed this categorization of ministry, suggesting that a

---

25. Whitely, *From Backwoods to Beacon*, 11.

26. George Allome was elected the first pastor of the church on 10 May 1669. Whitely, *From Backwoods to Beacon*, 11.

27. Maclear, "Making of the Lay Tradition," 114.

28. Baptists were silent about officiating at the Lord's Supper, but where the 1644 London Confession follows the True Confession we maybe find some help in this regard. When describing the authority of officers in the church, the True Confession forbids the administration of the sacraments until a Pastor or Teacher be ordained in the church. The London Confession prescribed no such ban, thus suggesting that any church member, or "disciple" might preside at the Lord's Supper or perform baptism.

29. Lumpkin, *Baptist Confessions*, 167.

"preaching Disciple" sounded as strange as a "Scholar Master," or a "Lecturing Hearer."[30] The Baptists replied, in defense and clarification of their position, that this rule was based on a literal observation of Christ's command in Matthew 28.19 which unites the work of "preaching and baptising" in one person.[31] However, Baptist leaders were sufficiently troubled by Featley's remarks to change the wording of the article in the second, and subsequent, edition(s) of the Confession, published in 1646. Article XLI was rewritten:

> the person designed by Christ to dispense baptism, the scripture holds forth to be a disciple.

The word "preaching" having been removed, for further clarification they added,

> it being nowhere tied to a particular church officer, or person extraordinarily sent, the commission enjoining the administration, being given to them as considered disciples, being men able to preach the gospel.[32]

That the question about who was qualified to administer baptism remained a live and contested issue for Baptists is evident from the Abingdon Association records of 1656, which show that the Messengers discussed the possibility of allowing a brother to administer baptism who was not gifted to preach the Gospel, a church having a preaching brother who was unable to baptize. This was judged unwarrantable, and the church was instructed to call upon a neighboring church for help.[33] This judgment reveals something of the literalist mind-set with which Baptists read the Bible.

In their controversy with Daniel Featley the Baptists were defended by Hanserd Knollys who explained that in appointing a minister in the church

---

30. ARPB, 158, For the London Confession see Lumpkin, *Baptist Confessions*, 158. Also, Featley, *Dippers Dipt*, 183.

31. The phrase "preaching disciple" occurs in the work of Thomas Killcop, *Unlimitted Authority*. This demonstrates the popular usage of this title among Particular Baptists.

32. London Confession, 2nd ed. In Underhill, *Confessions of Faith*, 42. W. J. McGlothlin was correct when he judged that removing the term "preaching" from this article the Baptists conceded nothing substantial to Featley, they only removed an "unhappy phrase. McGlothlin, "Dr. Daniel Featley and the First Calvinistic Baptist Confession," 588. Hanserd Knollys had his own convictions about this change and commented, "We do not affirm, that every common Disciple may Baptize, there was some mistake in laying down our Opinion, . . . Where it is conceived, that we hold, Whatsoever disciple can teach the Word, or make out Christ may Baptize, and administer other Ordinances. We do not so." Knollys, *Shining of a Flaming-fire in Zion*, 9.

33. ARPB, 158.

the call and gifting of the Spirit was primary, though the congregation had a vital role in testing and affirming the charisms of a candidate:

> Nor do we judge it meet, for any Brother to baptize, or to administer other Ordinances; unless he have received such gifts of the Spirit, as fitteth, or inableth him to preach the Gospel. And those guifts being first tried by, and known to the Church, such a brother is chosen, and appointed thereunto by the Suffrage of the Church.[34]

If we ask about the theological foundation for lay ministry as practiced among the Particular Baptists, four factors can be identified as important. First, it is suggested an open, intelligible, perspicuous Bible was an essential prerequisite for the rise of lay ministry. In his study of the lay tradition in revolutionary England, James MacLear speaks of the importance, for understanding the strength of the lay spirit, of "Puritan scripturism," which had, "stimulat[ed] a self-reliant religiousness."[35] Puritan scripturism, he argues, accounts in part for lay preaching based on the conviction that with the Bible in hand, each believer had access to the final authority on all matters of faith and life. "Here [in scripture] the divine will was revealed to the simplest believer in independence of all priestly or churchly mediation." Any saint, possessed of the Spirit, and possessing a Bible, might bring a message from God to the congregation. In article XLV of the 1644 Confession, we see the outworking of this principle:

> To whom God hath given gifts, being tried in the Church, may and ought by the appointment of the Congregation . . . [to] teach publickly the Word of God, for the edification, exhortation, and comfort of the Church.[36]

As Samuel How had argued, it was no longer necessary to study theology, learn languages, understand the rudiments of hermeneutics in order to minister the Word of God to the people. The "gift" of reading, explaining and applying the scriptures, recognized and approved by the congregation was sufficient.[37] The one safeguard against ministry anarchy in Baptist

34. Knollys, *Shining of a Flaming-fire in Zion*, 9.
35. Maclear, "Making of the Lay Tradition," 115.
36. In Lumpkin, *Baptist Confessions*, 168.
37. The tendency of the age to private interpretation of scripture is reflected in the account of Colonel John Hutchinson coming to anti-pedobaptist views. According to his wife's memoire, "he himself became as unsatisfied, or rather satisfied against it [i.e. infant baptism]. First, therefore, he diligently searched the Scriptures alone, and could find in them no ground at all for that practice." Thereafter he consulted all the treatises he could find on both sides, and subsequently invited to dinner "all the ministers" to

churches, it can be observed in article XLV, was that prophecy and preaching were subject to the testing and approval of the congregation, the arbiters of all ministry in the church, lay and ordained.

Second, the immediacy of the Holy Spirit to each believer fully and completely meant that any member of the congregation could be the means of spiritual encounter between God and his people. In his stout defense of lay preaching and prophesying, Samuel How spoke for many separatists, including Baptists, when he prioritized the enabling of the Spirit:

> *The Spirit searches the deep things of God*, and *the spirituall man discernes all things*; if then the Spirit searcheth the deep things of God, and that discernes all things, what need we more: and with this agrees the Apostle *John*, saying, *And ye need not that any man teach you, save as the Anoynting teacheth you*. Then I conclude, *That we need not that any man teach us, not the Master, nor any of his followers, for the Disciples of* Jesus Christ *doe learne (as the truth is) in him, and of him, and they have received the Spirit of* God, that they might know the things of God; therefore we may well be without any mans *learning*, and have no need of it; and so the point is cleare and plain, *That such as are taught by Gods Spirit without that Learning, do truly understand the Word*.[38]

Ministry which relied on worldly education is here set in opposition to ministry reliant on the Spirit.[39] While this was something of an ideological statement, "the uneducated man's and woman's way of rejecting the hegemony of the learned élite,"[40] How's argument was also the justification of the necessary, since amongst Baptists a preaching ministry that depended more upon the zeal and fervor of the preacher, than erudition and scholarship,

---

propound his doubts to them. Since none of them could defend their practice satisfactorily, his new born baby was not baptized. Hutchinson, *Memoirs of the Life of Colonel Hutchinson*, 289f.

38. How, *Sufficiency of the Spirits Teaching*, C1. Italics as original.

39. Oliver Cromwell reflected the attitude of many sectaries when he said, in 1657, "what pitiful certificates served to make a man a Minister! If any man could understand Latin and Greek, he was sure to be admitted." Abbot, *Writings and Speeches of Oliver Cromwell*, vol. 4, 495–96; c.f. also, 272. This is one cause of Richard Baxter's antipathy towards sectaries. "Education," he wrote, "is God's ordinary way for the Conveyance of his Grace, and ought no more to be set in opposition to the Spirit, than the preaching of the Word." Cited in Nuttall, *Holy Spirit in Puritan Faith and Experience*, 84. Thomas Goodwin also took the contrary view to that of How: "There is a generation of men that are against acquired knowledge, or that which is sought out by study, or received from others, and would have all infused." Goodwin, *Works* XI, 377.

40. Reay, "Quakerism and Society," in McGregor and Reay, *Radical Religion*, 146.

was indeed what most had to offer.⁴¹ This was not lost on opponents such as Robert Baillie, who pointed out to Parliament,

> In their Pastors they required no secular learning, yea to them all secular learning was abominable, they did burn all books but the Bible as impediments and hurtful instruments to the Ministery of the Gospel. They required their illiterate Pastors to work with their own hands for their livings.⁴²

This accusation was no embarrassment to Baptist preachers, who believed that even as God worked secretly in the soul of sinners to effect in them salvation by unmediated grace, so he might reveal his thoughts to those who waited upon him, again by his grace. William Kiffin testified to this type of experience in his own life. Having found faith and soul-rest in Christ through the preaching of John Goodwin, he began to meet with other young men to, "read some portion of Scripture, and [speak] from it what it pleased God to enable us."⁴³ This has been characterized by James Maclear as a "spirit of religious self-reliance."⁴⁴ Prophets, so moved by the Holy Spirit in the heart, following the preaching of the word, were prompted to offer a mixture of biblical exegesis, personal testimony and exhortation for the benefit of the gathered company.⁴⁵

A third explanation for the rise of lay ministry was the erosion of the culture of deference which coincided with the Civil War.⁴⁶ For the generation of Englishmen willing to cut off the head of the reigning monarch, it was a smaller step to denigrate the ministry of clergymen. Samuel How identified the significance of the changes of the times, writing in 1639 about the rising tide of lay preaching:

> It may teach all men to cease pinning of their Faith upon the Sleeves of Learned Men, for there is no good cause why we should so doe; but to see with our own eyes, seeing that the just is to live by his own Faith, and to believe what the Lord hath said, which is, that he hath hid those things, that is, the mysteries of the Gospel . . . from the wise and learned.⁴⁷

41. This is not to say that most ministers did not work hard to improve their knowledge. William Kiffin describes his labors in self-study of the Bible. Orme, *Remarkable Passages*, 22.
42. Baillie, *Anabaptism the True Fountaine*, 31.
43. See Orme, *Remarkable Passages*, 7–12.
44. Maclear, "Making of the Lay Tradition," 116.
45. Nuttall, *Holy Spirit in Puritan Faith and Experience*, 75.
46. This is highlighted by Brailsford, *Levellers and the English Revolution*, 34.
47. How, *Sufficiencie of the Spirits Teaching*, 21.

Baptist theology of ministry both participated in, and contributed to, the Puritan movement towards democracy, and a levelling of the social classes.[48] As was shown in the previous chapter, in the Baptist Confession of 1644 it was stated that, "every particular member of each Church, how excellent, great, or learned so ever," was subject to censure, judgment, even excommunication. Within this society of gathered believers there was equality before the law of Christ. In terms of social egalitarianism Baptists did not go nearly so far as Quakers who refused to show deference to anyone,[49] but a believer, called by Christ, and empowered by the Spirit, though lowly in world status, might be prominent in the ministry of Christ's kingdom on earth.

A fourth factor contributing to the rise of lay ministry was the Reformed doctrine of the universal priesthood of believers.[50] The 1644 London Confession, article XVII, stated that Christ in his Priesthood "makes his people a holy Priesthood," proof texted with 1 Pet 2.5.[51] The emergence of this doctrine in the Reformation goes back to Luther, who first, in a letter to Spalatin in 1519, argues against a distinction between clergy and laity.[52] In *An Open Letter to the Christian Nobility* (1520) Luther developed this theme arguing there is only one Christian estate, "*des christlichen Standes*," which encompassed all believers, both "clergy" and "laity."[53] He wrote,

> All Christians are truly of the spiritual estate and there is no difference among them except that of office . . . because we all have one baptism, one gospel, one faith, and are all Christians alike; for baptism, gospel, and faith alone make us spiritual and

---

48. See Luther's strong statements about equality of all citizens under the Gospel: "It is, indeed, past bearing that the spiritual law should esteem so highly the liberty, life, and property of the clergy, as if laymen were not as good spiritual Christians, or not equally members of the Church. Why should your body, life, goods, and honor be free, and not mine, seeing that we are equal as Christians, and have received alike baptism, faith, spirit, and all things? If a priest is killed, the country is laid under an interdict: why not also if a peasant is killed? Whence comes this great difference among equal Christians? Simply from human laws and inventions." Luther, *Address to the Christian Nobility*, in *Luther's Works* 44, 132.

49. Reay, "Quakerism and Society," 162.

50. Here I trace the Lutheran, rather than Calvin's interpretation of this doctrine. See Avis, *Church in the Theology*, 95–96.

51. Lumpkin, *Baptist Confessions*, 161.

52. Luther did not use the term "Priesthood of All Believers," but rather the concept of *allgemeine Priestertum*, literally "universal or common priesthood." See Wengert, "Priesthood of All Believers." Also, Norman Nagel, "Luther and the Priesthood of All Believers," 277–98.

53. Luther, *Open Letter to the Christian Nobility*, in *Works* 44, 127.

a Christian people . . . we are all consecrated priests through baptism, as St Peter says in 1 Peter 2, "You are a royal priesthood and a priestly realm," and The Apocalypse says, "Thou hast made us to be priests and kings by thy blood."[54]

Luther's proposal eliminated the category of "laity" as a separate type of Christian existence and stated that we are all priests because "priest" means "a Christian or spiritual human being."[55]

In contrast to later developments of the doctrine typical of Pietism,[56] Luther's doctrine is derived from his Christology, not his doctrine of the church. In speaking about priesthood, Luther asserts that in the New Testament *sacerdos* only applies to Christ, or by extension to all believers in Christ communally.[57] The same approach is evident among Particular Baptists, who state in the First London Confession,

To be Prophet, Priest, and King of the Church of God, is so proper to Christ, as neither in the whole, nor in any part thereof, it can be transferred from him to any other.[58]

According to Norman Nagel, Luther was not addressing an ecclesiological problem, the concentration of ministry in a select order to the exclusion of others, but a Christological aberration, since Christ was displaced from his rightful place in the Church.[59] Having established that the essence and origin of priesthood is in Christ, Luther expounds the nature of secondary priesthood from 1 Peter 2. In the *Babylonian Captivity* he writes,

we are all equally priests, as many of us as are baptized, and by this way we truly are; . . . we are all priests, as many of us as are Christians.[60]

Wengert argues that Luther's interpretation of this text was in terms not of a "priesthood of all believers" but a common priesthood given "to all

---

54. Ibid. See also, *Babylonian Captivity of the Church*, in *Works* 36, 112–13.
55. *Works* 44, 127, 129. See also *Works* 36, 140.
56. The first major discussion of the category is that of Philipp Jakob Spener in 1675. In fact Spener does not talk of *allgemeines Priestertum*, but of *geistliches Priestertum*, a *Spiritual Priesthood* which is available only to those who are anointed with the Holy Spirit. See Wengert, "Priesthood of All Believers," 2; Nagel, "Luther and the Priesthood All Believers," 295.
57. *Works* 36, 138–39.
58. Article XIII. In Lumpkin, *Baptist Confessions*, 159.
59. Nagel, "Luther and the Priesthood All Believers," 281.
60. *Works* 36, 112–13.

Christians communally."⁶¹ In other words, the functions of ministry do not belong to the individual who performs them, they are the common property of all Christians.⁶² Luther's own thoughts on this matter come in a response to his opponent Jerome Emser who disputed his exposition of 1 Peter. Luther says,

> But all of these things we have said concerning the common authority [*ius*] of Christians. For, because all of these things are the common property of all Christians, as we have demonstrated, no one is allowed to proceed into the midst [of Christians] by his [or her] own authority and seize for himself [or herself] what belongs to all.⁶³

In Luther, the Priesthood of All Believers does not focus on the individual, the privilege and responsibility of each church member. The "royal priesthood," the "holy priesthood," is a communal gift with a strong congregational emphasis.⁶⁴

Luther did not suggest that there should be no ministers, or that *anyone* in the church had the right to preach, baptize, and administer the sacraments. In the *Babylonian Captivity* he argued that although we are all priests by virtue of our baptism, some are authorized to exercise the pastoral office.⁶⁵ That authorization, however, comes via the community's permission and entrustment. In his *Letter to the German Nobility*, Luther imagines a scenario where there is no bishop, no ordained minister, and ministry must of necessity be instituted by the congregation, which it has every right to do by virtue of its possession of the Gospel and its spiritual priesthood:

> if a little company of pious Christian laymen were taken prisoners and carried away to a desert, and had not among them a priest consecrated by a bishop, and were there to agree to elect one of them, born in wedlock or not, and were to order him to baptize, to celebrate the mass, to absolve, and to preach, this man would as truly be a priest, as if all the bishops and all the Popes had consecrated him.⁶⁶

Thus to be a minister is to "hold" an office, to be *trusted* with an office according to a necessary human arrangement. A minister is only a

---

61. Wengert, "Priesthood of All Believers," 25.
62. *Works* 36, 141.
63. Ibid., 151; *Works* 39, 237.
64. Ibid., 312–13.
65. *Works* 36, 112.
66. *Works* 44, 128; cf. *Works* 39, 310.

functionary, and if he should be deprived of his office he would return to be a citizen, like everybody else.[67] This is not to say that any believer can be a minister, or everybody is a Pastor. The shoemaker does not belong in the pulpit any more than the pastor should operate a lathe.[68] They have different tasks which belong to their God-given office, and there is no question that the office of ministry is superior to any other.[69] This was precisely the point Knollys was making about the Baptist understanding of ministry in response to Daniel Featley, the Spirit's distribution of gifts for ministry is to be entirely respected.

Many parallel lines of theology and practice can be traced between Luther and Particular Baptists. Christology was the first principle in thinking about ministry in both. Church, and congregational ministry, is rooted in the ministry of Christ, and since every baptized believer is in Christ, ministry is universal. Ministry is not concerned with the status and office of the individual minister, but a practical necessity of the church which requires to be met. The text, 1 Peter 2 was important to both, since ministry was regarded as the sovereign gift of Christ to his people, each believer having the calling and privilege of service, since by baptism each one is a priest.[70] The one caveat to this, however, concerned the ministry of women.[71] The ministry of women was not regarded in priestly terms, and their role in the congregation was limited to assisting deacons.[72] From a modern perspective this policy appears inconsistent at best, a capricious outworking of the doctrine of the universal priesthood.

In the Association Records of the Particular Baptists we gain an insight into the progress of Baptist lay ministry in the 1650s, its failures and successes. In a letter from the Irish Baptists to their London counterparts in June 1653 we read of the intention to set aside one day every month to pray with fasting and mourning for the following deficiency:

> Our litle sincere love to the Lord and his people and our litle knowledge of the office and proper place of each member as God hath sett him in the body of Christ, to the end that every

---

67. *Works* 36, 117; *Works* 44, 129.
68. Ibid., 130.
69. Ibid., 129.
70. *Works* 39, 233.
71. According to Luther, "As preaching is a public matter, some people—women, children and other "unqualified persons" (*untüchtige Leute*)—are excluded straight away as unfit to hold any public office." See Avis, *The Church in the Theology of the Reformers*, 106.
72. *ARPB*, 11.

particular member might be now effectually improved for the mutuall edification of the whole.[73]

This quaint statement appears in the context of the Irish churches seeking greater efficacy in the work of the Lord and believing this could be achieved by the mobilization of the saints into the work of Christ. Further details about the Baptist causes in Ireland follow, and indicate that in Limerick the church was "in a decaying condition for want of able brethren to strengthen them." From Galloway it was reported that the church likewise, "have few able amongst them to edifie the body." Similar conditions existed in Wexford and Carrick Fergus.[74] The numerically small size, and ministerially weak condition, of some of the Irish churches gave impetus to the desire to see their theology of lay ministry become reality.

In 1659 in the West Country there was likewise acknowledged a scarcity of ministers, which was the more serious on account of the vulnerability of the churches to Quaker missions in the region. Quaker activities were described in terms of, "the enemyiyes endeavours to cast fire in the sanctuary," though "the Lord hath preserved the churches in a good measure in peace and unity."[75]

More positively, we read in the record of the Abingdon Association meeting at Tetsworth in 1659 that in a number of churches God was stirring up gifts of ministry among the congregation. The report stated:

> One church (margin: viz., Stukeligh) declared that God hath drawne forth some gifts among them which formerly lay hid. And another (margin: viz., Watford) that some members were hopefully coming on to the carying on of the worke of the Lord. A third (margin: viz., Kensworth) also signified that some hopefull branches doe appear among them very comfortably growing up as to the worke of the Lord for whom they desire the prayers of the saints.[76]

In one region of the country, at least, the practice ministry in Baptist churches approximated to the theology of "universal priesthood." Among emerging Particular Baptists ministry was no longer the preserve of a special class, there was no more a division between clergy and laity, only a division of function. This brings us to a consideration of the discrete roles of ministry among the Baptists.

---

73. Ibid., 118–19.
74. Details of all three churches are found in Ibid., 120.
75. Ibid., 99.
76. Ibid., 194.

5.2 Offices of Ministry in Particular Baptist Churches

In spite of the openness of early Particular Baptists to lay ministry there is ample evidence in the Association Records of the 1650s that Baptists, unlike Quakers,[77] believed in the God-given gift of separated ministry in their churches. In the Abingdon Association General Meeting of 1654 the messengers issued a statement to be affirmed by the churches:

> That the offi[ces of E]lders and deacons are ordained of the Lord for the [good] of his church and, therefore, it is the duty of everie church verie diligently to endeavour, and very earnestly to seeke unto the Lord, that they might enjoy the benefit of these his gracious appointments, remembering God's promise to give his people pastors according to his owne heart, Jer 3.15.[78]

The pattern of ministry among churches was remarkably consistent, though the multitude of names given to their officers suggests greater variety. The usual arrangement was that of elder and deacon, as the Abingdon Association affirm in a letter to the London church of Pettie France in 1656:

> we understand, to our great comfort and rejoicing, that you have long had upon your hearts the will and counsaile of the Lord touching church officers, viz., touching elders and deacons.[79]

The twofold pattern was also affirmed in the second edition of the London Confession (1646), and in subsequent editions.[80] Evidently, however, the usual practice had not yet become established because the Abingdon messengers requested of the Pettie France church in London a letter outlining their pattern of ministry, with accompanying scriptural proofs, that they might disseminate the same model to the churches throughout their association:

> We humbly desire you thus to communicate your light in a letter to the church at Abingdon and another (if it shall not seeme too burdensome unto you) to the church of Kensworth who will communicate the same to the rest of the churches and in the same to hold forth fully the scripture directions and grounds which the Lord hath given you to see touching the election and

---

77. On the rejection of a separated ministry in Quakerism see Nuttall, *Holy Spirit in Puritan Faith*, 87.
78. *ARPB*, 134.
79. Ibid., 168.
80. Underhill, *Confessions of Faith and Other Public Documents*, 41.

> tryall and ordination of these officers, in what manner and by whom they ought to be chosen, tryed and ordained.[81]

This indicates that by 1656 there was a desire to establish a common pattern of ministry in the regions along the lines of the London churches thus strengthening the sense of denominational unity.

In the West Country there was a degree of regional variation of church officers. Thomas Collier followed the older structure consisting of Pastor-Teacher, to feed the flock, Ruling Elders to govern the church, and Deacons to care for the poor.[82] In Wales, a similar situation prevailed from 1651, when the church at Llanharan rectified the "unsettledness" afflicting the congregation on account of having no officers. After a day of prayer and fasting they,

> found the Lord soe ordering all things among us that with one consent brother John Myles was chosen and declared to bee pastour of this church, brother Morgan Jones was chosen and ordained elder and assistant to our sayd brother Myles in the government thereof, and brother Leison Davies was chosen and ordained deacon.[83]

By 1654, the structure of three was still in operation, but the titles were changed and comprised of: "1. Pastors. 2. Teachers. 3. Helps, or those who rule."[84] It is then added that, "These three are called Elders, Bishops, Watchmen," suggesting that titles were interchangeable, depending on whether they were considered from the perspective of office or function.

The lack of uniformity may in fact have derived from London, since although they appear to have usually had a two-fold pattern of elders and deacons, a variety of names were available for the twin offices, as was seen in Article XXXVI of the 1644 Confession, cited above. That the list of offices given in article 36, "Pastors, Teachers, Elders and Deacons,"[85] did not refer to four distinct people, but to the four-fold responsibility of ministers, is made clear by Thomas Collier who wrote:

---

81. *ARPB*, 168.

82. Collier, *Certain Queries*, 23; *Right Constitution*, 19f.

83. Owens, *Ilston Book*, 20. For comment see White, "John Miles," 45.

84. *ARPB*, 11. The influence of the 1596 *True Confession* may account for this unusual grouping of ministry gifts including Helps. Article 19 speaks of, "this publick ordinarie Ministrie of Pastors, Teachers, Elders, Deacons, Helpers to the instruction, government, and service of his Church." In Lumpkin, *Baptist Confessions*, 88.

85. This list may have been taken from the Separatist *True Confession* of 1596, article 19, but if so the ministry of "Helpers" was dropped. In Lumpkin, *Baptist Confessions*, 88. For comment see White, "London Calvinistic Leadership," 34.

Ministry have several titles given to it, not to distinguish (as some think) the Ministery into so many offices, but rather to discover the fullness of the work.[86]

The fullness of pastoral ministry is evident from the Welsh Association Records, which lists the corporate responsibilities to be undertaken by Elders, Bishops and Watchmen:

1. To take care of the church.

2. To consult on controversies.

3. To order things in the church.

4. To advise in matters of doubt.

5. To govern.

6. To visit the sick, if sent for.

7. To care for the distribution of collections.[87]

These were the generic duties of "all the elders," but scripture permitted the work of ministry to be divided and apportioned to specific offices. Among the offices in the church, however, that of pastor was primary,[88]

First, the pastor's office is to do all that tends to the feeding of the flock, Jer 3.15; Matt 24.45 as to

1. Exhort.

2. Reprove with authority.

3. Cast out.

4. Lead the sheep, he is to be the mouth of the whole.

5. Watch.

6. Administer all the ordinances in the church.

7. Give himself wholly to the word and doctrine.

8. Rule well, which consists (1) in the right ordering of questions and disorderly speaking. (2) in preserving purity of doctrine and discipline, Rev. 2 and 3. The angels are charged with it.

---

86. Collier, *Right Constitution*, 20.

87. ARPB, 11.

88. This was based on the address of the letters in Revelation to "the angle of the church." Ibid., 11; Thomas, *History of the Baptist Association*, 11–12.

This was a role of congregational oversight that would have given the pastor an exalted status in the church on account of the executive responsibility inherent in the office. In Thomas Collier's tract on ministry, preaching and teaching has primary place among the manifold responsibilities of the pastoral office. By means of doctrinal preaching the Pastor protects the flock from enemies.[89]

Next, the duties of the Teacher were specified:

> Secondly, the teacher's particular office is, to wait on teaching, to expound scriptures, and confute errors. And this is no less the pastor's office.[90]

It is not entirely clear whether the later Baptist pattern of Pastor-Teacher is implied here, maintaining a twofold ministry, or whether separate persons are imagined. The latter arrangement seems most likely, so that teaching and scripture exposition were the responsibility of the pastor also. Then,

> Thirdly, the ruling elder's, or helping office is, to oversee the lives and manners of men: to whom also double honour is due. He must also take care of God's house.
>
> Fourthly, the next officer is a deacon, who is to serve tables, that is, the Lord's Table, and the tables of all others in the church, that shall want his service. He also is to be dedicated to the church's service, as the word deacon imports, Acts 6.1 etc.[91]

Here we note that deacons were to officiate at communion, which suggests a hierarchy of sorts did function *de facto* in Baptists churches even if it was commonly believed any disciple might dispense the sacrament of baptism.[92]

A fifth office, established for the assistance of deacons was that of "widows," appointed to help the church, "most probably in looking to the poor and sick."[93] This was deemed an appropriate ministry for women to undertake, since it was named in scripture, practical in nature, and involved no public speaking.

---

89. Collier, *Right Constitution*, 22. See also, Laurence, "Priesthood of She-Believers," 358–59.

90. *ARPB*, 11.

91. Ibid.

92. See *First London Confession*, second edition Article XLI, in Underhill, *Confessions of Faith*, 42. In the Evangelical tradition Luther allowed that women might baptize, though they could not preach. Luther, *Works* 40, 23, 25. Calvin took the contrary view, absolutely forbidding women to baptize. Calvin, *Institutes* 4.15.20–22.

93. *ARPB*, 11.

In addition,

> Sixthly, there are, for the further edifying of the church, ordinary prophets, who, though they be not such as wait on the ministry, or are wholly given up to it as yet, are such as being gifted, may speak, as they be permitted, or desired, to edification, exhortation, and comfort.[94]

This record is the most comprehensive and detailed description of the range of ministry offices in any of the early Baptists records. It shows that the nomenclature of officers was not tightly defined, but the functions and responsibilities of the church's ministry were comprehensively understood and responsibility for their performance allocated.

An additional point of interest in the Welsh record is that in juxtaposition to the duties and responsibilities of church officers are also set out those of church members. Congregational obligations were:

> In relation to their elders, they are to honour them. Submit to and obey them. To provide for them, especially such as labour in the word and doctrine, having dedicated themselves thereto. To pray for them. Not to grieve them. Nor to speak roughly to them. Nor hastily to receive an accusation against them.[95]

These instructions suggest that the entire church, active and non-active members alike, had a share in the health of the ministry operating in and among the church and its congregation. These guidelines about ministry devised at Llantrisant in August 1654 were sent to every church in the Welsh Association, signifying a desire to create a common pattern of ministry among constituent congregations.

Regarding the maintenance of the ministry, which is listed among the congregational cares in the Welsh statement above, it was expected the local church would provide a minister's allowance:

> The true ministers of Jesus Christ are to be supported, as touching their outward subsistence, not by tithes, nor by any inforced maintenance but, as they shall be found worthy and as it shall be found [nee]dfull and convenient and the saints shall be enabled

---

94. Ibid., 12. The role of prophets was also discussed among the Midland churches and their ministry defined according to 1 Cor 14.3 as "edification and exhortation and comforte." See ibid., 28.

95. Ibid., 12. The copious biblical text references validating each instruction have been omitted.

thereunto, [by] the voluntarie contribution of those that are instructed by them.[96]

In the event of a church having insufficient funds, they might be aided by a neighboring church.[97] The details of minister's pay are set out in the records of the General Meeting in Wales for July 1653. William Thomas, who was minister at Carmarthen, and overseer of several small churches around the town, was to be paid £10 for six months of ministry. It was agreed that £2.10 be provided by the church at Llantrisant, the same from Carmarthen, and £5 from the church at Ilston.[98] It was also decided that the church at Hay would assist in the financial provision for William Richard soon to be the minister at Abergavenny.[99]

Throughout the Civil War period the question of payment of ministers in Baptist churches was a subject of debate, and despite the strong views of some ministers, uniformity of practice did not emerge. The London leaders stated in the 1644 Confession:

> That the due maintenance of the Officers aforesaid, should be the free and voluntary communication of the Church, that according to Christs Ordinance, they that preach the Gospel, should live on the Gospel and not by constraint to be compelled from the people by a forced Law.[100]

Despite this statement, the London churches did accept government money for ministry in individual cases, such as that of John Miles and Thomas Proud.[101] These two men were sent out by the Glaziers Hall congregation in 1649 as evangelists and church planters under the government sponsored, "Act for the better propagation and preaching of the Gospel in Wales."[102] In 1658, the policy of taking state money for ministry was decisively rejected in a letter penned by Benjamin Cox to Richard Harrison. Cox denounced government maintenance as "unlawful," and "shameful," be-

---

96. Ibid., 151. Also Thomas, *History*, 6.

97. See 6.2 in the following chapter.

98. *ARPB*, 7.

99. Ibid. At a subsequent meeting in August 1654, the Llantrisant church was asked to help the Abergavenny church with a £5 gift towards their minister. See ibid., 10; Thomas, *History*, 11. Given that this was half the six month salary the church at Abergavenny must have been especially poor.

100. Article XXXVIII, in Lumpkin, *Baptist Confessions*, 166–67.

101. See White, "Organisation of the Particular Baptists," 211.

102. "*February 1650: An Act for the better Propagation and Preaching of the Gospel in Wales, and redress of some Grievances*." Acts and Ordinances of the Interregnum, 1642–1660 (1911) 342–48.

cause it perpetuated the system of tithes that was hated by commoners and sectarians alike.[103] Cox further argued that the maintenance of the Gospel ought to be provided by the church, and this was allowed for in scripture.[104]

In the 1646 revision of the London Confession, Pastors, Teachers, Elders and Deacons were reduced to two offices, that of Elders and Deacons.[105] The twofold ministry thus became the settled pattern of pastoral offices in Calvinistic Baptist churches.[106]

5.3 The Calling of Ministers in Early Baptist Congregations

As already observed, article XXXVI of the 1644 London Confession confirmed that each congregation had from Christ the privilege and duty of calling its own ministers,

> every Church has power given them from Christ for their better well-being, to choose to themselves meet persons into the office of Pastors, Teachers, Elders, Deacons, being qualified according to the Word.[107]

To defend the practice of appointing ministers from within the congregation, Baptists appealed, not to the power of the keys as did other Independent groups,[108] but to biblical precept and Apostolic practice. The Confession cited two texts alongside article XXXVI, Acts 1:2 which speaks of Christ "giving instruction through the Holy Spirit to the Apostles," and Acts 6:3 which describes the Apostles commanding each congregation in Jerusalem to "select from among yourselves seven men of good standing, full of the Spirit and of wisdom, whom we may appoint to this task." Since Christ, during his earthly ministry, instructed the Apostles "through the Holy Spirit," there was no reason the ascended Christ, who had promised to

---

103. *ARPB*, 44.

104. See also the Somerset Confession (1656): "a ministry labouring in the word and doctrine, have a power to receive a livelihood of their brethren, whose duty it is to provide a comfortable subsistence for them, if they be able." In Lumpkin, *Baptist Confessions*, 212.

105. Article XXXVI, in Underhill, *Confessions of Faith*, 40.

106. See the confirmation of this pattern in the Second London Confession (1677 & 1688), article 8. In Lumpkin, *Baptist Confessions*, 287.

107. Ibid., 166. This was a core conviction of Congregationalism as seen in Cotton, *Keys of the Kingdom of Heaven*, 12.

108. Appeal to the power of the keys was fundamental in the theology of John Cotton, John Owen, and Thomas Goodwin. See Beeke and Jones, *Puritan Theology*, 628–39.

be in the midst of the gathered congregation, could not continue to direct his people in its choice of officers, by the Holy Spirit.[109]

When Featley challenged the Baptists to justify the calling of uneducated,[110] lay members to prophesy and expound scripture in the church, they responded with the inclusion of article XLV in the 1644 Confession:

> That also such to whom God hath given gifts, being tryed in the Church, may and ought by the appointment of the Congregation, to prophesie, according to the proportion of faith, and so teach publickly the Word of God, for the edification, exhortation, and comfort of the Church.[111]

Among Particular Baptists, a calling to ministry was a spiritual event[112] to be assessed by those spiritually competent to judge the gifts of the candidate. This was a Gospel church gathered in the name of Christ, as Thomas Collier argued,

> For a Church of Christ to whom Election belongs, are a company of Believers, Saints gathered out of the world, by the power of the Lord, in the ministry of the Gospel.[113]

This policy was directly challenged by Presbyterians, who stated that a gifted brother not lawfully ordained may not preach, and acted contrary to faith.[114] Baptists, however, viewed the gathered church as the primary testing and proving place for ministry,[115] since the church possessed the power

---

109. It was this principle that led modern Baptist historian Ernest Payne to write, "the very notion of episcopacy implies an impoverished doctrine of the work of the Holy Spirit." Payne, *Free Churches*, 10.

110. Not all Baptist ministers were uneducated. Jessey and Knollys, Benjamin Cox and Christopher Blackwood, Paul Hobson and John Pendarves were university educated, as was John Myles, though this in itself seems to have carried little weight among Baptists. In the Broadmead records for 1657 Terrill recounts the ridicule Presbyterians heaped upon Baptists because of their lack of university education. Underhill, *Records of a Church of Christ*, 57.

111. Lumpkin, *Baptist Confessions*, 168.

112. See Collier, *The Pulpit-Guard Routed*, 3. The messengers in the West Country discussed the possibility: "whether some brethren have not, without any clear call from God, taken up a trade of preaching to get into a trade of maintenance." The possibility that men were tempted to practice preaching for the money highlights the extremity of the economic conditions of the time. *ARPB*, 143.

113. Collier, *Pulpit-Guard Routed*, 20.

114. See [Provincial Assembly of London], *Jus Divinum Ministerii Evangelici*, 91.

115. There are numerous references to congregational testing of preaching gifts in Wales in Owens, *Ilston Book*, 12, 13, 19, 36.

to appoint to office.[116] This explains the introduction of a procedure in the Midlands Association in 1656, that a gospel minister could not be chosen as an officer of the church, "unless he be orderly a member of the same."[117] The validity of ministry to a congregation was guaranteed by the involvement of the congregation in the appointment of its officers, according to 1 Thess 5:21, which teaches the people to test or "prove all things." In the case of a preaching gift, this would be examined by church members only, with unbelievers excluded from the testing.[118] Presbyterians suspected this gave too much power to the congregation, leaving their officers vulnerable to popular opinion.[119]

In 1656, the Abingdon Association asked the London church at Petty France[120] for their "judgements from scripture touching the tryall, election and ordination of elders and deacons."[121] In the reply we have one of the fullest descriptions of "rules and grounds" of early Baptist practice of appointing officers:

> upon the tryall and examination of the person's giftes and graces and endowments by scripture qualifications (after solemne seeking God for direction and assistance therein) she doe solemnely signify by distinct acts upon each qualification, her approbation of the person or persons as being in some good measure fitted by the Lord and the most fit amongst them to serve the Lord and his people in the respective offices to which they are to be appointed. And then that she doe by one single act of lifting up the hand, choose or elect the person or persons to the offices accordingly.[122]

In an accompanying letter, the London church outlined the process by which they had come to this procedure. The first principle was the biblical question, "unto whom Christ Jesus had given such gifts as the fruit of his ascension for the gathering and edifying of his church." According to Eph 4.8–14, "the church." This, they conceded could mean the universal church,

---

116. *ARPB*, 143.

117. Ibid., 26.

118. Ibid., 27, Owen, *Ilston Book*, 12.

119. See Beeke and Jones, *Puritan Theology*, 624.

120. The history of this church is told in, Dowley, "London Congregation," 232–39. The correspondence is briefly discussed in White, "London Calvinistic Baptist Leadership," 34–45.

121. *ARPB*, 170.

122. Ibid., 171.

but since Paul was writing to a particular congregation, they took it in this way.

The second principle was: "by whose authoritie these gifts are orderly to be called forth unto their actuall services and administration." According to Acts 1.13–end; Acts 6.2–5, 14.23, they concluded the Apostles had sought the advice of ordinary disciples about the "tryall, election and ordination" of those suitable to succeed to office and therefore the congregation should conduct the trying, electing and ordaining of ministers.

The third principle dealt with the question, whose authority is operative in the appointment of officers in the church. They stated:

> Acts 14, Luke informs us that elders were ordained in everie church by lifting up of the hand, so, in the originall, by election, so it is in the old translation which we must imply the action of the church. Wherein we doe agree with the *Paraphrase* of Beza, and others, upon the place, which is in these words: <u>The apostles did not thrust the elders upon the churches through briberie or lordly superioritie, but chose and placed them by the voice of the congregation.</u>[123]

It appeared obvious to early Particular Baptists that spiritual ministers could not be imposed upon churches from above, by bishops, or presbyteries, or committees of "Triers"[124] since, "Christ hath placed the authoritie of tryall and electing, viz., in his church." Although, Presbyterians like Thomas Edwards regarded the election of officers by the raising of hands among church members as extraordinary,[125] and the Presbyterian defense *Jus Divinum* argued that only Paul and Barnabas were involved in Acts 14,[126] among Separatists and Baptists it appeared obvious, and Apostolic.[127] To proceed to the appointment of officers by means other that this was to usurp the authority of King Jesus.

Early Baptist ecclesiology stressed the competence of the local gathered congregation to identify and appoint its own officers according to the ordinance of Christ, and the apostolic pattern. Yet, although churches might

---

123. Ibid., 171. The words underlined were cited verbatim from the marginal notes in Beza's translation of the Bible, Acts 14.23 n. 9. The marginal notes in the Geneva Bible were regarded with almost the same respect as Scripture. See Hill, *Society and Puritanism*, 18.

124. On the role of the Triers see Collins, "Church Settlement," 18–40.

125. Edwards, *Reasons Against the Independent Government*, 1–29.

126. [Provincial Assembly], *Jus Divinum*, 129–31.

127. See the defense of this practice in the separatist circle of Catherine Chidley in *Justification of the Independent Churches of Christ*, 4.

act congregationally to appoint officers, they may not act with such independence to do anything against the common good. No church, therefore, ought to choose an officer whom other churches could not approve.

5.4 Ordination among Early Calvinistic Baptists[128]

When the Westminster Assembly gathered in 1643, the question of ordination was high on the agenda, and twelve propositions setting out the doctrinal basis for ordination were prepared for Parliament on 3 April 1644.[129] In the Presbyterian settlement it was laid down that classical presbyteries, comprised of at least seven parishes, would supervise the ordaining and settling of minsters. Ordinands would present their degrees and references to the classis, and satisfy the ruling elders and ministers of their godliness and preaching ability through disputation. Thereafter, a successful candidate would be appointed to a parish, and subject to continuing supervision by the classis.[130] Against the background of a national theological debate about ordination, and the organizing of an English Presbyterian system, sects like Particular Baptists were formulating their own distinctive theology and practice.

Particular Baptist ordination may be explored by the example of Thomas Collier who was appointed to the office of West Country messenger of in 1654. The record of his ordination is brief but illuminating in a number of details.[131] Firstly, Collier had for some time been performing the work for which he was to be ordained, namely evangelism and church gathering, and was now to undergo, "a further and more orderly ordaining and appoyntinge . . . to the worke of ministery to the worlde and in the churches."[132] For a number of years Collier had ministered without ordination, a practice not regarded as an impediment to the proper exercise of his ministry. This suggests that the churches in the West Country regarded the importance of ordination as only relative, not essential. From another

---

128. By ordination is meant the formal setting aside of called and chosen persons to a church office. See Renihan, *Edification and Beauty*, 102–3.

129. See Shaw, *A History of the Church During the Civil Wars* vol.1, 323; Paul, *The Assembly of the Lord*, 328–29, especially n. 88. Also Greaves, "Ordination Controversy," 225–41.

130. Vernon, "Ministry of the Gospel," in Durston and Maltby, *Religion in Revolutionary England*, 117.

131. The record is based on a letter that was sent from the Western Association in May 1654 to the newly founded Lyme church, and transcribed by Ivimey, *HEB* IV, 292f, collated with the Lyme Churchbook. The composite text is found in *ARPB*, 103.

132. *ARPB*, 103.

perspective, which was also key to Baptist theology of ordination, Collier had proven his gifts and calling, ordination serving as a recognition and validation of the ministry he had from God.[133]

Secondly, ordination was an action of the congregation, not requiring any person to administer apostolic succession. This principle had been established by Henry Jacob, an implacable opponent of successionism, who stated,

> Wee believe that the essence of Ministers calling under the Gospell, is the Congregations consent.... Therefore the Congregations consent is essentiall ever, and every where in the making of a minister.
>
> [W]e believe that to think we doe, or can receive a Ministery essentially from a former Minister or Prelate (in these dayes) is an errour, and the thing received is a nullitie in that respect.[134]

Jacob's separatist ideology was rooted in the theology of the Reformers,[135] and was restated in the work of William Ames, who had a strong influence upon the Particular Baptists.[136] Ames argued that, "no external means properly have the power to communicate grace to us in any real sense." This meant that true spiritual ministry could not be received by succession from a Bishop or priest, for "the Spirit bestows Christ and all his benefits on us."[137]

The principle of congregational ordination was affirmed as normal Baptist practice by the West Country messengers at the General Meeting on 18–20 September 1654, in the dealing with a question from the churches:

> Query 1. Whether the seting apart of any to administer officially in the church of Christ is not to be done by that church of which the person set apart is a member?
>
> Answer: 1. That it is in the power of the church to ordain and send forth a minister to the world, Acts 13.2f. Secondly, that this person sent forth to the world and gathering churches, he ought

---

133. See the comment of Cromwell to Sir Walter Dundas, "Approbation [i.e., ordination] is an act of conveniency in respect of order; not of necessity, to give faculty to preach the Gospel." Cited in Greaves, "Ordination Controversy," 228.

134. Jacob, *Confession and Protestation*, B4 and B7.

135. It is evident, for example, in Luther, *Works* 44,128; 36, 116; 41, 154. For comment see Hendel, "Doctrine of the Ministry," 27.

136. Their use of his *Marrow* in the 1644 Confession was discussed in chapter 2.

137. See Ames, *Marrow of Theology*, 182.

with them and they with him to ordain fit persons to officiate among them, Acts 14.23, Tit 1.5.[138]

Thirdly, it was widely recognized that ordination was an ordinance of Christ still in force, and hence to be practiced still, though no biblical reference was offered.[139] Fourthly, the manner of ordination was a matter of dispute, in particular whether it was necessary to employ laying on hands.[140] Initially, the messengers who had gathered to ordain Collier could not agree on this point, and those who scrupled the practice included John Pendarves from Abingdon.[141] After debate they agreed not to oppose those who were in favor, though they did not give their assent either. The act of ordination was performed by two men from Luppit in Devon who had been "formerly ordained and now called thereunto." This instance of laying on hands in ordination, officiated by two ex-clergymen, savored of apostolic succession, and may explain why Pendarves, and others, refused to participate. For them, the issue was not only what was done, but by whom.

Although we are grateful for this brief account of Collier's ordination, and the insights into early Calvinistic Baptist practice, much remains opaque about this event. For example, why was Collier ordained at this time when he had been gathering and confirming churches for maybe ten years?[142] Furthermore, to what office precisely was Collier ordained? In his *History of the English Baptists*, Ivimey understood the Association record in these terms,

> The office to which Mr. Thomas Collier . . . had been ordained, was that of a messenger of the churches, exercising a kind of general superintendency over all the associated churches.[143]

Ivimey's statement that Collier was appointed to "a kind of general superintendency" became, in subsequent histories of the Baptists, the assured conviction that he was appointed to be, "General Superintendent and

---

138. ARPB, 56.

139. In the Directory for Ordination produced by the Westminster Divines, it was also stated that "Ordination is always to be continued in the church, Tit. V. 1 Tim. V.21, 22." See Paul, *Assembly of the Lord*, 329 n. 88.

140. Point 4, in the Presbyterian Directory, stated, "Every minister of the Word is to be ordained by the imposition of hands, and prayer, with fasting." Ibid., 329 n. 88.

141. See Land, "Doctrinal Controversies," 246–48.

142. This based on the supposition that Benjamin Cox was describing the work of Collier in his *Appendix* to the second edition of the first *London Confession* in 1646. See Underhill, *Confessions of Faith*, 58, article XIX.

143. Ivimey, *History of the English Baptists* IV, 292.

Messenger to all the Associated Churches of Wessex."[144] B.R. White reconstructs Collier's ordination differently. He states that Collier may have been engaged in his missionary work already for a decade, without ever being formally set apart for the work, before the brothers at Bridgewater sought to correct this anomaly with "a further and more orderly ordaining."[145] This would appear to make best sense of the information about Collier's ordination on this occasion.

Interestingly, in addition to the above historical information about Collier's ordination, we have his own theological reflection on what this ritual meant. In *The Right Constitution and True Subjects of the Visible Church of Christ* he asks, "How and by whom should [the] Ministry be ordained in the church?"[146] He answers, ordination is to be performed, "by fasting and prayer with the Laying on of hands." Given the controversy over the laying on of hands at Collier's own ordination, this makes evident where his sympathies lay. In this act he understood two things to happen. First, it represented a formal recognition of the minister "by the authority and in the presence of the Church." Second, Laying on hands, linked to prayer and fasting, was "the exercise of faith in the expectation of an increase of the gifts of the Spirit, and fitness to the work of ministry."[147] This suggests a "sacramental" element in Collier's thinking, in so far as the preacher expected "an increase of the gifts of the Spirit," for the work of ministry.

One of the clearest statements about early Baptist ordination occurs in the letter from the Petty France church to the Abingdon Association in 1656, after the latter had sought advice about the appointment of ministers for their churches. In an account which shows remarkable consistency with that set out by Collier, the London congregation explained their practice:

> we shall briefely lay downe the rules by which we were guided in the matter of ordination. By ordination first, we meane, a separation or setting apart publikely and solemnely of the person (chosen as aforesaid by the power and authoritie of Christ in his church) by fasting and prayers, together with the laying on of hands by an orderly evangelist or eldership, where such as [sic] to be had or, in case of that defect, by such gifted brethren of the same congregation as may be called prophets and teachers, as those were, Acts 13.1. By all which you may perceive our judgement is, and accordingly was our practice, that the sole

---

144. Whitley, *HBB*, 72. He was possibly following Fuller, *Brief History*, 9. See *ARPB*, 109 n. 51.

145. Ibid..

146. Collier, *Right Constitution*, 31–34.

147. Ibid., 33.

authoritie, as in trying, electing and ordering, so in ordaining, resides in the church (specially since the apostolicall power is ceased) the reason being the same.[148]

That fasting and prayer was to accompany ordination was a sign of its "weightienesse," as well as conforming to scripture (Acts 13.3 and 14.23). Laying on of hands was understood in practical, and non-sacramental terms:

> That the laying on of hands is to be added appeares, not onely because some publike ceremonie is needful to signifye a person set apart but mostly because the Lord hath of old made choise and use of this rather then any other.[149]

The use of evangelists or elders to administer ordination also warranted further defense from London. First, they noted this was the Apostolic custom according to the example of Timothy and Titus,[150] who were especially appointed to this office, amongst others. Second, they argue that, "the reason of the thing seems to evince it, not onely to maintain an orderly succession," by which is meant, ideally, ordination from a baptized minister, or failing this, "the persons laying on their hands, be persons of aproved wisedome, experience, gravitie and fidelitie," but principally so the church and officers might understand fully their duties and authority.[151] In order to secure an orderly ordination at Petty France under the latter circumstances, they sought assistance from "orderly elders from other congregations and others beside us have since done the like."[152] Baptist sensitivities about this matter were no doubt due in part to how their ordination was perceived by outsiders. In a recent article, Curtis Freeman makes the point that in the eyes of the Church of England and Parliament all Baptist ministers were regarded as lay preachers, because they were ordained by neither bishops nor presbytery, and hence their public ministry was warrantless.[153]

The instructions of the Petty France church to the Abingdon Association, it is to be noted, were offered as advice not a rule. They were commended, but not commanded, as a blessing and guidance of the Lord. Their importance, however, is that it was the model of ordination that other

---

148. *ARPB*, 171.

149. Ibid.

150. Collier also referred to the practice of Timothy and Titus (*Right Constitution*, 34).

151. *ARPB*, 172.

152. Ibid.

153. Freeman, "Visionary Women," 265–66.

Baptist churches were adopting as the pattern for their own practice. This is evident from the letter the Abingdon messengers subsequently sent to the member churches of the Association, commending the Petty France guidelines as the basis for "a regular practice in this matter."[154]

Summary

In this chapter we have traced the theology and practice of ministry in early and emerging Baptist congregations and a number of points may be noted as significant. In respect to their practice Baptists found theological justification for their ministry in the primitive pattern of the New Testament church, as well as the Reformed tradition emerging from Luther. The majority of ministry was conducted by lay men, without university education, and not ordained by other clergy. The order of lay ministry created the need for a system of election, approbation and ordination of those members of the church who could serve the needs of the congregation for hearing the Word of God, and receiving the sacraments. Such a system developed and was formalized in the pronouncements issued by the Association Messengers to the churches under their oversight. Baptists were aided in the development of their theology and practice by the favorable political conditions of the period, and the personal sympathies of Cromwell.

Baptist theology and practice of ministry was consistent with congregational church government, in which Christ was the true minister. This ecclesiology regarded all members as equal in status, and equal receptors of the gifts bestowed by the ascended Lord through the Spirit. There was also a place for ordination, as the honoring of those especially called and gifted for public ministry, recognition by the congregation of the first among equals. Though Baptist ministry was regarded by their enemies as "an intolerable usurpation," they believed it to be an attempt to reconstitute the primitive church in which the sovereign calling and gifting of the Spirit was given priority.

---

154. *ARPB*, 173.

6

"The Counsel and Help of One Another"

Independency and Interdependency: Particular Baptist Churches in Association[1]

6.1 The Origins of Particular Baptist Associations to 1660.

THROUGHOUT THE PERIOD 1640–1660, it is possible to trace the intentional organization of a network of churches by which Particular Baptists related to one another, and their reasons for so doing.[2] In this final chapter I propose to examine the impact of Christology on the Calvinistic Baptist doctrine of the church in relation to the organization of their congregations in Associations. I want to suggest that from the early 1640s Baptist ecclesiology, although determined by separatist and congregational principles, did not regard independence of the local gathered congregation as the ideal ecclesiological stance. In the words of W. T. Whitley, Baptists, "sought to maintain sisterly intercourse between local churches,"[3] a posture that was theologically motivated by the image of the church locally, and translocally as the "body of Christ."

Early attempts to explain the origins of Particular Baptist associationalism generated two historical theories. The first was that of Whitley in his

---

1. The substance of this chapter was published as the winning essay in the Payne Memorial Competition. Birch, "Counsel and Help of One Another."
2. See, for example, White, "Organisation of the Particular Baptists"; Nuttall, "Association Records," 14–25.
3. Whitley, *HBB*, 86.

History of the English Baptists, 1923, followed later by R. G. Torbet in 1950, though he added little of substance to the main argument. The Whitley/Torbet theory[4] states that the organization of Particular Baptist congregations in associations was patterned after the formation of the county militia by Cromwell in the First Civil War. In a series of articles, B. R. White subjected the Whitley/Torbet theory to historical scrutiny and found it unsatisfactory in a number of details.[5] Subsequently, in an article of 1974 White proposed a more organic, evolutionary process in which Particular Baptist associationalism was foreshadowed in the theology of church relations proposed by Henry Jacob.[6] In 1988, White's suggestion, for it was little more than this in the original paper, was developed into a full theory by Sladen Yarbrough. In his paper, "The Origin of Baptist Associations," Yarbrough stated that he would, "present and defend the position that the theory of voluntary associational cooperation came to the Particular Baptists through the teachings of Henry Jacob."[7] He proposed that the Dutch English classis,[8] which flourished between 1621–1633, modelled Jacobean associational theory thereby providing the London Particular Baptists with a historical example of inter-church cooperation when they compiled the London Confession in 1644.[9] Some consideration of the thinking of Henry Jacob will enable us to see the importance of his pioneering thought for later Baptist developments.

In *A Confession and Protestation of the Faith of Certaine Christians*, Jacob propounded a theology of the church congregational and associational, holding the twin poles of local and universal church together. In the section headed, *of Christes true visible politicall Church in more speciall manner*,

---

4. Ibid., 86–91. This theory is also advanced in Whitley's biographical essay on Edward Harrison, in "Edward Harrison of Petty France," 216. And, Torbet, *History of the Baptists*3, 43–45.

5. See White, "Organisation of the Particular Baptists," 209–26; White, *English Baptists of the Seventeenth Century*, 67–70; White, "Doctrine of the Church," 585–89.

6. Ibid., 582, 588–89; White, "English Particular Baptists," 22. White also proposes that a debt to John Cotton's influential work, *The Keys of the Kingdom of Heaven*, may also be evidenced in early Baptist writing about inter-congregational cooperation.

7. Yarbrough, "Origin of Baptist Associations," 14–24, esp.15.

8. In the reformed tradition, a classis is a group of churches within a geographical area which has authority to deal with matters concerning its churches in common and its decisions are binding on the churches in its region. On the Dutch English classis see Burrage, *EED* 1, 296; Sprunger, "Archbishop Laud's Campaign," 310; Sprunger, *Dutch Puritanism: A History of English and Scottish Churches of the Netherlands in the Sixteenth and Seventeenth Centuries*, 373; Stearns, "New England Way in Holland," 755; Ha, *English Presbyterianism*, 128–29. See also Jewson, "St Mary's Norwich," 108–17.

9. Yarbrough, "Origin of Baptist Associations," 18. Yarbrough writes in detail about Jacob's theological and personal relationship to the Church of England in "Ecclesiastical Development," 183–97.

Jacob first defined the independence and competence of the local congregational church,

> A true visible politicall Church under the Gospell is but one ordinary Congregation. . . . That by Gods ordinance, this one ordinary congregation of Christians is a spirituall bodie politike; and so it is a free congregation independent. That is, It hath from God the right and power of spirituall Administration, and Government in it selfe, and over it selfe by the common and free consent of the people independently, and immediately under Christ, always in the best order they can.[10]

In a subsequent section entitled, *Of synods and councells*, he speaks, in terms which reflect a Puritan background, of the complementary pole of the church universal,

> Howbeit we acknowledge with all, that there may be, and that on occasion there ought to be on earth a consociation of Congregations or Churches, namely by way of Synods: but not a subordination, or surely not a subjection of the congregations under any higher spirituall authoritie absolute, save only Christs, and the holy Scriptures. They who deny this, mainteyning a Diocesan and Provinciall (and neither wee nor they themselves know what universall) visible politicall Church both proper and representative, doe herein vary farr from the rule of the Gospell.[11]

Jacob's commitment to independent congregationalism clearly did not rule out a role for voluntary associations of churches, or translocal synods, though he was careful to circumscribe their authority over the local church. He allowed that synods could make doctrinal judgments and decrees, and were beneficial for advice and counsel. Synods could contribute to the unity of churches, and churches might benefit in government from the resources of the synod, however, the local church could never be subordinated to the synod, especially in matters of discipline.[12] No external authority could be exercised over an independent congregation, since their only authority was Christ and the scriptures.[13]

---

10. *A Confession and Protestation of the Faith of Certaine Christians*, no page number.

11. Ibid., B2.

12. See Jacob, *Reasons Taken out of God's Word*, 31–33. See also Yarbrough, "Origin of Baptist Associations," 18. Ha, *English Presbyterians*, 54 and 222 n. 40 has further bibliographic information for Jacob on this point.

13. See Yarbrough, "Origin of Baptist Associations," 18.

This was a carefully thought through theology of the church upholding its independent congregational basis, while resisting any drift towards congregational isolationism. While it is difficult to trace with absolute certainty the pedigree of an ideology, and no Baptist writings of the 1640s and 1650s make reference to Jacob's *Confession*, White and Yarbrough have rightly shown that the idea of inter-congregational cooperation was known in the Jacob-Lathrop-Jessey congregations prior to the London initiative of 1644.

6.1.1 The Origins of Associations in the Association Records of the English Particular Baptists

The attempt to explain the origins and nature of Particular Baptist Associations was given significant momentum in 1960 with the discovery by Geoffrey F. Nuttall of the records of the Baptist Western Association 1653–58, in the Library of the Society of Friends in London, and the library of Bristol Baptist College.[14] Subsequently, Ernest Payne located the records of the Berkshire churches 1652–60, of Wales, the English Midlands and Ireland.[15]

The first group of churches to be formed into a mutually supportive network was in South Wales. The South Wales churches owed their beginning to John Myles and his associates, who founded their first church in Ilston, near Swansea, on 1 October 1649.[16] By August 1652 five congregations had been formed on the basis of "closed communion," that is, membership of these churches was restricted to those who underwent believer's baptism.

The first joint meeting of South Wales churches took place on 6–7 November 1650 at Ilston comprising the three congregations, Hay, Llanharan, and Ilston.[17] The second gathering, on 19 March 1651, incorporated the host church Carmarthen, expanding the association to four.[18] The third meeting took place during the summer of 1651, the fourth on 14–15 July 1653, when the churches from Llantrisant and Abergavenny were represented for the first time,[19] and the fifth on 1–2 March 1654. The last recorded meeting was on 30–31 August 1654, at which it was agreed to hold a general meeting every six months thereafter.[20]

14. See Nuttall, "Baptist Western Association," 213–18.
15. White, "Organisation of the Particular Baptists," 209–26.
16. Thomas, *A History of the Baptist Association in Wales*, 5.
17. *ARPB*, 3; Thomas, *History*, 6.
18. *ARPB*, 4; Thomas, *History*, 7, who uses the Welsh spelling "Caermarthen."
19. *ARPB*, 6.
20. Ibid., 9.

At the first meeting, to facilitate the cultivation of "one minde and one heart," it was agreed that a "declaration" from the Hay church would be considered by each congregation successively and questions arising would be discussed at a subsequent meeting convened for the purpose. No extant record of this "declaration" remains, nor of any discussions that followed;[21] however, the detail does indicate that the churches in fellowship sought a measure of unity and uniformity between them in doctrine and practice.[22]

At subsequent meetings discussions took place regarding the supply and remuneration of ministry to the various churches.[23] Other matters of common interest were the manner of singing Psalms, "whether laying on of hands be an ordinance of Christ; and if it be so, then upon whom?"[24]

At the fifth meeting on 1–2 March 1654, the question of Psalm singing was raised again, and the record provides an insight into the strength of relationships between the united churches. The congregation at Abergavenny was rebuked for failing to "forbear to sing Psalms," and it was desired that "satisfaction be made for the offence given the churches, in not asking their advice and counsel therein."[25] No explanation is given as to what "satisfaction" might consist of, but presumably an apology was intended, and evidently one church was willing to submit to the collective discipline of the association.

During the sixth General meeting, 30–31 August 1654, a question about the continuance of fast days, an initiative promoted by the Irish correspondence of 1653,[26] reveals the extent of the Particular Baptist network developing throughout the three kingdoms, by means of correspondence. The relevant answer was,

> It is judged, that the appointed fast days should be continued; for that is the agreement of the churches in England, Ireland, and Wales, and our promise to God and them to observe it.[27]

The desire for uniformity on this matter across national boundaries indicates a growing sense of common identity and desire for interdependency among kindred churches.[28]

---

21. Ibid., 14 n. 13.
22. See ibid., 4.
23. Ibid., 4–5.
24. Ibid., 16 n. 47; Thomas, *History*, 7.
25. ARPB, 8.
26. See ibid., 114 and 118.
27. Ibid., 9.
28. I am not suggesting that early Baptists were self-consciously setting up a rival to the National Church, but these gathered congregations accepted the status of sectaries

The Association Records of the Calvinistic Baptist churches in the Abingdon region recount their meetings from 8 October 1652. Three churches from Abingdon, Reading and Henley first joined together in Wormsley to discuss matters of inter-congregational concern.[29] At the next meeting, on 3 November, representatives from Kensworth in Hertfordshire and Eversholt in Bedfordshire attended. In March 1653, the church representatives, now called "messengers" met at Tetsworth in Oxfordshire to sign "The Agreement of certain Churches,"[30] setting out the basis for fellowship and co-operation in missionary activity:

> true churches of Christ ought to acknowledge one another to be such and to hold a firme communion each with other in point of advice in things remaining doubtfull to any particular church or churches as also in giving and receiving in case of want and povertie of any particular church or churches and in consulting and consenting (as need shall require and as shall be most for the glory of God) to the joint carrying on of the worke of the Lord that is common to the churches.[31]

The messengers also agreed to hold in common principles and constitutions, and each committed himself to walk in these ways. They agreed to continue meeting together, and between meetings to correspond by letter, "as need shall require."[32] Hence, by means of messengers' meetings and letters, a relationship of mutual interest and joint activity was established and consolidated.

One other decision from this meeting in March 1653 is significant, namely the intention to refer matters agreed among the messengers back to the churches, "for their approbation therein."[33] This protocol determined at the outset that while gatherings of church representatives might

> discerne [whatsoever else] the word of God require[s] true churches to hold communion in, [their deliberations and decisions] held no coercive power over individual congregations.[34]

---

and were organizing themselves in a manner necessary for their continuance. See Hill, "History and denominational History," 65–71, esp. 68.

29. For the Reading church see White, "Baptists of Reading," 256–63.
30. *ARPB*, 129.
31. Ibid.
32. Ibid.
33. Ibid., 130.
34. Ibid., 129.

At the following meeting, on 10 June 1653, the messengers drafted a letter to fellow Baptists in London conveying news about the formation of an association[35] of congregations in and around Abingdon. The letter set out the basis of their communion and the intent and purpose for the churches so joined. The address of the letter is noteworthy, as a further indication of the sense of "denominational" unity growing among Calvinistic, closed-communion Baptist churches:

> To the church of Christ of which our brethren John Spilsbury and William Kiffin are members and to the rest of the churches in and neere London, agreeing with the said church in principles and constitutions and accordingly holding communion with the same, the churches of Abingdon, Reading, Henlie, Kensworth, and Eversholt send greeting.[36]

From this address it may be discerned that in and around London there was a "communion" of churches holding an agreement of "principles and constitutions," though there are no extant records of meetings held between London Baptist churches for the period currently being considered.[37] It would also appear that the church of Spilsbury and Kiffin had status above that of the other churches. The address also provides clear evidence that strong links existed between the London churches and those in the provinces.

At the tenth General Meeting of the Abingdon Association held on 26 December 1654, a letter was drawn up in response to a request from the church at Warwick seeking advice how to form a new association of churches, "neere unto them."[38] The response of the messengers at Tetsworth was threefold. First, they encouraged the Warwick church, and others, to bring to fruition their desires to enter into a solemn association with other churches that are "rightly constituted and principled." Second, they promised to send out papers setting out, "on what grounds and after what manner we ourselves did enter into our association." Third, they agreed to send representatives from the Abingdon Association churches to a meeting of the Warwick churches to advise and assist them in any way that might be ben-

---

35. This letter contains what is thought to be the earliest use of the term "association" to describe a group of Calvinistic Baptist churches. Ibid., 131.

36. Ibid. White first noticed the dual reference to Spilsbury and Kiffin identified with just one church. In the London Confessions of 1644 and 1646 they signed as leaders of different congregations, and how they came to be united as one is unknown. See White, "The Organisation of the Particular Baptists," 217 n. 3.

37. See White, "Organisation of the Particular Baptists," 209.

38. *ARPB*, 136.

eficial in forming an association. In particular, Abingdon proposed to have John Pendarves, of the Abingdon church, and Benjamin Cox of Dunstable, attend the meeting, and requested Warwick to convene the meeting away from Easter or Whitsuntide.[39]

At the eleventh General Meeting, 19–20 June 1655, the Association welcomed four further churches into membership. These were Wantage, Watlington, Kingston and Hadnam, an indication that the Baptist cause was continuing to expand.[40] On 17 October of that year, Pirton was received into association[41] and at the meeting of 11 March 1656, the churches of Oxford[42] and Hempsteed[43] were added.[44]

A significant moment in the life of the Association occurred on 16 October 1657. The churches at Kensworth, Eversholt, Pirton and Hempsteed requested permission to meet as a district association on account of their distance from Tetsworth. They further submitted that there were several other local congregations which might join a new association who were yet unwilling to join the existing association. This request was unanimously approved by the messengers.[45] At the following meeting on 30 March 1658, being the start of the new year,

> the said messengers of the churches of Abingdon, Reading etc., did solemnly commit and commend the said churches of Kensworth, Eversholt etc. to be henceforth a distinct association.[46]

The amicable nature of the partition between the groups of churches is confirmed by an agreement to maintain a relationship through

---

39. Ibid., 135–36. In 1932, Whitley commented that while churches enjoyed "fraternal intercourse" within associations, there was none between associations as such. This is now known to be incorrect. Whitley, *HBB*, 92. See additional comment on this inaccuracy in White, "The Organisation of the Particular Baptists," 218 n. 1.

40. *ARPB*, 139.

41. Ibid., 140.

42. In his article, "Baptist Churches till 1660," 251, Whitley stated that the Oxford church joined the Berkshire Association in 1653. This was based on the Longworth Church book and transcribed in The Gould Manuscript. This has now been proved to be incorrect and the date of 1656 firmly established. See Kreitzer, "1653 or 1656: When did Oxford Baptists Join the Abingdon Association," in Thompson and Cross, *Researching the Past or History?*, 207–19.

43. That is, Hemel Hempstead.

44. *ARPB*, 145.

45. Ibid., 180.

46. Ibid., 181.

correspondence, and continuing to send two messengers to the Abingdon Association meetings.[47]

At the meeting beginning 14 September 1658 representatives of four additional congregations were present, Longworth, Andover, Newberrie and Thistleworth.[48] The meeting of 7 April 1659 affords a glimpse of developments in the sister association which met at Dunstable on 3 and 4 March. The original four churches had now become nine by the addition of Luton, Stukeligh, Watford, Newport Pagnell and Bedford. The meeting also considered an application from a recently formed congregation at Woolaston in Northamptonshire. It was agreed to receive the church into membership; however, Woolaston first desired to consider the sixteen articles of faith and order, together with the twelve conclusions, by which the association was constituted.[49]

The final meeting of the period on 20 June 1660, only three weeks after the Restoration of the monarchy, records encouragement to the several churches to seek the Lord by prayer and fasting, "that they may be kept stedfast in the day of tryall."[50] From each church only one representative was in attendance,[51] which was almost certainly due to the anxiety generated by political developments at large. B. R. White speculates that already a number of Baptist leaders were in jail.[52]

In Ireland, the Baptist cause had been established as a result of the English military campaign from 1649.[53] The significant numbers of Baptists in the New Model Army resulted in Irish garrisons forming their own Baptist congregations.[54] In the correspondence between the Irish churches and London in June 1653 a letter, with two accompanying documents, indicates the existence of ten Calvinistic congregations together with names of their leaders.[55] These were in Dublin, Waterford, Clommell [sic], Killkenny, Corke, Lymrick, Galloway, Wexford, Kerry and Carrick Fergus.

According to document (i), "The agreement concerning matters requiring prayer by the churches," it is evident that the Irish congregations

---

47. Ibid., 182.
48. Ibid., 193.
49. Ibid.
50. Ibid., 206.
51. Ibid., 193.
52. See White, "Organisation of the Particular Baptists," 220.
53. See White, *Baptists of the Seventeenth Century*, 80.
54. See Whitley, "Association Life," 19.
55. *ARPB*, 115, 119–20.

had already met on at least one occasion, since they describe their commitment to meet regularly for spiritual exercises:

> [we] doe agree together, through the Lord's assistance, to sett apart one day in every month, solemnly to seeke the face of our God and, by prayer and fasting, humbly to mourne before him for the things following which is alsoe recommended to our deere frinds the churches of Christ in England and scattered brethren in severall places, who have obtained like pretiouse faith with us.[56]

The first Irish letter to London gives further evidence of growing links between the Particular Baptist congregations, and associations across the four kingdoms. The Irish speak first of the mutual benefit derived from correspondence between them:

> The Lord haveing put it into the hearts of all his congregations in this Iland to keepe a more revived correspondency with each other by letters and loving epistles . . . in the practice thereof [we] have found great advantage not only weakning Satan's suggestions and jealousyes but it hath begot a closer union and knitting upp of heart.[57]

Having profited so greatly from this union by letter, they ask the same of churches elsewhere:

> Wee heerby earnestly request and begg the same brotherly correspondence with you and from you desireing the same things by your meanes with all the rest of the churches in England, Scotland and Wales whom we trust you will provoke to the same feelings and which wee hope, once in 3 months, may be mutually obtained.[58]

The Irish churches also sought from the London leaders a list of congregations with whom they were in contact. They further desired the London churches to send out two or more competent leaders to the churches known to them throughout England, Scotland and Wales to, "visit, comfort and confirme all the flock of our Lord Jesus."[59] There is no extant evidence that this visitation took place. It signifies, however, the prominence of the

---

56. Ibid., 118. As noted above, this suggestion was taken up by the Welsh churches, though its continuance was later questioned. See ibid., 9.

57. Ibid., 114.

58. Ibid., 115.

59. Ibid.

London churches among British Particular Baptists, and the growing sense of union between such churches.

On 24 July 1653, the Glasshouse church wrote a covering letter to accompany the Irish correspondence sent out to the congregations throughout the three kingdoms. In addition to the requests made by the Irish Baptists, the London leaders asked of the churches,

> your care and paines in visiting the severall weake and scattered brethren in your parts, that from a thorough knowledg of, and acquaintance with, theire present standing, wee may receive information from you and our brethren in Ireland, according to their desires, from us.[60]

The pastoral concern of the authors is to the fore, born of a sense of inter-relatedness among Baptists.

The records of the associational gatherings of Particular Baptists in the "county of Somerset and the counties near adjacent" were kept and published, probably in 1658, by Thomas Collier.[61] They show that churches from Gloucestershire to Cornwall were linked together under the general oversight of Thomas Collier.[62] The first meeting took place on 8–9 November 1653 at Wells to discuss the practice of laying hands on all baptized believers, and whether this was an ordinance of Christ. It was decided that it was not. In the communication of this decision, however, greater attention was given to the matter of dissention within churches and the growing incidence of separation between churches over the practice, which was considered most undesirable.[63] The third part of the response warned churches that did not practice imposition of hands that they ought not to allow to preach in their pulpit a member from a church that did so practice, if they scrupled about this matter as a basis for fellowship. It is thus implied that the messengers regarded imposition of hands as an *adiaphora*, or non-essential issue, and that union among the church should not be jeopardized on account of the practice, or non-practice, of this custom.[64]

"Association"[65] amongst the Western churches was achieved as a result of the efforts of Thomas Collier, who in 1651 put out, "A Second General

---

60. Ibid., 111. The inclusion of this request in a longer letter to the Welsh General Meeting can be found in Owens, *Ilston Book*, 63.

61. *ARPB*, 53. These are the records discovered by Nuttall described above.

62. See White, "The English Particular Baptists and the Great Rebellion," 21.

63. See *ARPB*, 54.

64. See ibid.

65. Collier did not use the term "association" but spoke of "general meetings of Messengers." See White, "Organisation of the Particular Baptists," 221 n. 4.

Epistle to all the Saints,"[66] to generate a sense of kinship among them.[67] Meetings began in 1653, and thereafter Messengers usually gathered twice a year, in autumn and spring. For the wider relations of the Western churches with the national Baptist constituency, a number of links are evident. First, through Thomas Collier's contact with the London churches, London leaders, and London theology.[68] Second, John Pendarves of Abingdon is known to have had contact with the Western churches, and was present at the Chard meeting in September 1655,[69] and the Wells gathering in April 1656.[70] Third, in 1656 the congregation at Tiverton invited the counsel and advice of other churches and leaders following the mental breakdown of their pastor William Facey.[71]

In addition to correspondence with other Baptists that was positive in nature, and designed to encourage, the letter of the Western Baptists to the Irish churches, dated 18 April 1655, demonstrates a willingness to chide. News had reached them of "things amiss" in the Irish churches which they felt duty bound to address.[72] These included "pride in apparel," "dependency of the ministry on the maintenance of the magistrate," both of which were deemed contrary to the Gospel constitution in 1 Cor 9.14, "they that preach the Gospel should live of the Gospel."[73]

The relationality underpinning this rebuke of the Irish churches by the Western Association was that of "faithful friends."[74] The messengers claimed:

> we have not written these things to shame you, but to warn you not as having dominion over your faith but as helpers of your joy.[75]

The significance of this statement is that it evidences a pattern of inter-church relationship of the Henry Jacob type, that was non-hierarchical, and

---

66. See Lumpkin, *Baptist Confessions*, 200 n. 37.

67. See Whitley, "Association Life," 20.

68. The Somerset Confession of 1656, principally the work of Thomas Collier, was designed less to state the doctrinal position of the Western churches and more to shew their theological consensus with London. See Lumpkin, *Baptist Confessions*, 200–1.

69. ARPB, 78.

70. Ibid., 80.

71. The account is detailed in, Ballamie, *Leper Clensed, or the Reduction of an erring Christian*.

72. ARPB, 73.

73. Ibid., 74.

74. See ibid., 75.

75. Ibid.

quite different from the synodal approach of Presbyterianism. One Association, in Baptist ecclesiology, had no "dominion" over other associations, or individual churches within them.[76]

In the period up to 1660, the fifth Association to form was the Midland, holding its inaugural meeting 2 May 1655 in Warwick.[77] Although there were fourteen Particular Baptist churches in the eight counties, only seven were willing to associate in the first instance.[78] These were, Warwick, Morton, Bourton-on-the-Water, Alchester,[79] Teuxbury, Hook Norton and Derby, and they agreed to associate on the basis of a Confession of Faith comprised of sixteen articles.[80] The Midland Confession is marked by a number of features, namely, its brevity, its orthodox Calvinism with a strong emphasis on the doctrine of election, and its teaching that baptism be delayed until profession of faith in Christ be evidenced by fruits. At the second meeting on 26 June 1655, an Agreement among the churches was formulated and subscribed to. The doctrinal statement stressed a voluntarist ecclesiology, asserting that those who are baptized by immersion as believers ought to "walke together by free consent as God shall give opportunitie in distinct churches or assemblyes."[81] Such language, concise and yet precise in its definition of the church, emits a growing confidence among Baptists to affirm their convictions about the nature of the *ecclesia* formed after the pattern of Acts 2.42, 46.[82]

The churches of the Midland Association owed their existence to the evangelistic endeavors of Daniel King.[83] The evidence of his connections to four prominent London leaders, Thomas Patient, John Spilsbery, William Kiffin and John Pearson in his tract of 1650, *A Way to Sion*,[84] suggests that

---

76. Polly Ha notes that congregational polity did not only develop in response to episcopacy but also in reaction to Presbyterianism. However, she also cautions that neither system was rigidly fixed, and there was ecclesiological ambiguity throughout this period. See Ha, *English Presbyterianism*, 49.

77. *ARPB*, 20.

78. General Baptists were much stronger in the Midland region, by comparison with the Particulars. In 1651 the General Baptist Confession was signed by thirty congregations. See Lumpkin, *Baptist Confessions*, 195.

79. In some places spelt Alcester.

80. *ARPB*, 19–20. For a complete version of the Confession see Lumpkin, *Baptist Confessions*, 198–200.

81. *ARPB*, 20. Also, "Midland Association Confession," 15th Article. Lumpkin, *Baptist Confessions*, 199.

82. See *ARPB*, 20.

83. See White, "Organisation of the Particular Baptists," 223; Lumpkin, *Baptist Confessions*, 196.

84. See the epistle dedicatory of, King, *Way to Sion Sought Out*, n.p.

King had been commissioned by them to form churches and build up associations in the Midland region.[85]

One factor prompting the organization of an Association in the Midlands was the evangelistic activity of Quakers in the region. Throughout 1654 and 1655, George Fox engaged Baptists in disputations at Biddesley, Warwickshire and at Sileby, Leicestershire[86] which undoubtedly created a sense of urgency among messengers to protect the Baptist flock.[87]

At the second meeting of the Association in June 1655, the messengers agreed a statement of mutual recognition and a basis for cooperation,

> [we] doe mutually acknowledg each other to be true churches and that it is their duty to hold a class communion each with other according to the rule of his worde and soe be helpefull each to other as God shall give opportunitie and abillitie . . . and are faithfully to holde such communion each with other and to endever to be helpfull each to other.[88]

The ways in which churches in association might be helpful to each other was set out in five articles of action.[89] First, giving advice in matters of controversy which one particular church could not settle alone, according to the pattern of Acts 15.[90] Second, alleviating the poverty of any church suffering financial want, according to the example of Rom 15.26.[91] Third,

---

85. It is no surprise that a mission sponsored by the London Baptist churches should be anxious about the formation of associations, since they had enshrined this ecclesiology in the First London Confession, article XLVII.

86. See Langley, "Seventeenth Century Baptist Disputations," 113–14.

87. The threat posed by the Quakers to the churches in the Western Association is reflected in the minutes of the meeting at Bridgewater 5–6 November 1656 where churches are exhorted: "that saints be very wary and weighty in their spirits how they receive any apprehensions that seem to lead us besides plain and positive scripture grounds of practice." *ARPB*, 65. Likewise, in the Epistle Dedicatory to the Somerset Confession of 1656, a warning is given against those, "who lay aside Christ, scripture, and obedience all at once, subjecting themselves to a suggestion or voice within them, more than to the mind of God, written in the holy scriptures." In Underhill, *Confessions of Faith*, 65.

88. *ARPB*, 20–21.

89. Ibid., 21. The citation of biblical texts at every point was a deliberate attempt to prove that association was required according to the rule of scripture.

90. In the Abingdon records, the Abingdon church applied this principle of wider consultation to the question regarding the trial, election and ordination of elders and deacons. See ibid., 172.

91. The issue of financial assistance for poorer churches was taken up in the Abingdon Association in response to a letter from the London leaders about the poverty of churches in the Western Association. News from Abraham Chayer (or Cheare) to the London leaders had resulted in a proposal to establish a central fund "towards the maintenance of a Gospell ministrie abroad in the countreys." The Abingdon Association

the Midland churches agreed to send gifted persons to provide ministry in churches which lacked able leaders. This was deemed biblical on account of the example of Barnabas in Acts 11.22. Fourth, where, "any worke of the Lord that is common to the churches" might be undertaken jointly, as was taught in 2 Cor 8.19. Fifth, there was agreement to watch over each other, in order to maintain "puritie of doctrine, exercise of love and good conversation," since the churches are all members of the one body of Christ, according to 1 Cor 12.12, 29.[92] The ecclesiology of "the body" metaphor set Baptists apart from other forms of ecclesial relationships, especially the emerging Presbyterian hegemony, since relationships between Baptist churches were based on a covenantal commitment to mutual fellowship.

This description of the formation of associational relationships formed between groups of Calvinistic Baptist churches has made clear the organic, instinctive impulse towards networking that is characteristic of trans-local Baptist ecclesiology. This provides a platform for considering the theological commitments which underpinned this significant and, for its time, unique development.[93]

6.2 Theology of Particular Baptist Associations

The rationale for the formation of Baptist church groupings was the need for small congregations, lacking professional clergy, to help and advise one another in regulating their affairs, as true churches of King Jesus. The 1644 *London Confession* makes this clear:

> And although the particular Congregations be distinct and severall Bodies, every one a compact and knit Citie in it self; yet they are all to walk by one and the same Rule, and by all meanes convenient to have counsel and help one of another in all needful affaires, as members of one body in the common faith under Christ their onely head.[94]

From a simple and practical necessity of mutual assistance developed a theology of association among early Particular Baptists.[95]

In chronological order, the first system of associationalism occurred among the Welsh churches. The business of the first General Meetings in

---

was asked to commend the relief fund scheme to their churches. See ibid., 174–75.

92. Ibid., 21.
93. See Wamble, "Beginning of Associationalism," 544.
94. Article XLVII. In Lumpkin, *Baptist Confessions*, 168–69.
95. See further, Randall, "Counsel and Help," 26.

1650 and 1651, was to discuss the scarcity and remuneration of ministers in South Wales' churches.[96] The General Meeting in 1654 affirmed the "common design [of Association] was the mutual edification and comfort of the churches,"[97] which was regarded as consequent upon the provision of ministry to each congregation. There is scarcely any theological reflection regarding the basis and nature of the relationship between the churches, but a sense of obligation to assist one another is strong. It might be supposed that the extremity of the circumstances faced by pioneering Welsh churches allowed little time for theological consideration. A "Declaration"[98] was circulated around the churches, however, to foster unity of doctrine and practice among them, showing that their mutual commitment was not lacking in conviction.

The records of the Abingdon Association contain the most mature thinking, among early Particular Baptists, on the nature, purpose and authority of trans-local communion of congregations. In contrast to the Welsh records, the Abingdon churches had considerable interest in the theological rationale, as well as practical purposes, of links between the churches, and the messengers formulated three points in support of translocal relationship.

First, communion and help between the churches was grounded on biblical precedent. It is stated:

> That perticular churches of Christ ought to hold a firme communion each with other in point of advice in doubtfull matters and controversies, Acts 15.1f., 6, 24, 28; 16.4f. Which scriptures, compared together, shew that the church at Jerusalem held communion with the church of Antioch affording help to them as they could.[99]

According to the biblical pattern of the Council of Jerusalem, independent churches may consult together on questions of mutual concern, without threat to the competence and liberty of each.

The second point agreed upon at Wormsley concerned the giving and receiving of financial assistance to churches in cases of poverty, according to the scripture, 1 Cor 16.3.[100]

The third point lays out the most extended reasoning about the basis of association in any of the records. Here it is stated that,

---

96. *ARPB*, 3–4. Owens, *Ilston Book*, 12–13, 16–20.

97. *ARPB*, 8.

98. The contents of the "Declaration" are currently unknown.

99. *ARPB*, 126.

100. Ibid.

> perticular members of one and the same perticular church stand bound to hold communion each with other . . . because there is the same relation betwixt the perticular churches each towards other as there is betwixt perticular members of one church. For the churches of Christ doe all make up one body or church in generall under Christ their head as Eph. 1.22f.; Col. 1.24; Eph. 5.23ff.; 2 Cor. 12.13f. As perticular members make up one perticular church under the same head, Christ, and all the perticular assemblys are but one Mount Syon, Is 4.5; Song 6.9. Christ his undefiled is but one and in his body ther is to be no schism which is then found in the body when all the members have not the same care one over another. Wherefore we conclude that every church ought to manifest its care over the other churches as fellow members of the same body of Christ in generall do rejoice and mourne with them, according to the law of theire nere relation in Christ.[101]

Here it is asserted that a parallel exists between a local church and an association of churches, since in both cases individual members together comprise the body of Christ, whether local or translocal. The assertion is clear enough; but is the parallel use of the body of Christ metaphor a valid juxtaposition of local church and association?

The question can be answered in the affirmative in regard to the five stated intentions for associational communion defined by the messengers. First, by means of relating one to another they believed churches might,

> keepe each other pure and to cleare the profession of the Gospell from scandal, which cannot be done (1 Cor. 5.5) unless orderly walking churches be owned orderly and disorderly churches be orderly disowned, even as disorderly walking members of a perticular church.[102]

Second,

> For the proofe of their love to all the saints, perticular church communion being never appointed as a restraint of our love which should be manifest its selfe to all the churches.[103]

Third,

---

101. Ibid. The sentence underlined was revised at the third meeting making the original intention clearer. It read: "And in his bodie there is to be no schism which is then found in the bodye when all the members have not the same care one over another." Ibid., 128.

102. Ibid., 126.

103. Ibid.

> The worke of God, wherein all the churches are concerned together, may be the more easily and prosperously carried on by a combination of prayers and endeavours.[104]

Fourth,

> From need they have or may have one of another to quicken them when lukewarm, to helpe when in want, assist in counsell in doubtfull matters and prevent prejudices in each against other.[105]

Fifth,

> To convince the world, for by this shall all men know by one marke that we are the true churches of Christ.[106]

As noted above, the West Country churches began to meet in association a year after Abingdon, and drew on the statements of the Berkshire brethren to establish their united gatherings on the same theological principle of the body of Christ.[107] When the messengers were asked to consider whether larger churches should send out preachers to assist congregations without officers, their agreement was based on the principle that,

> in all the churches all make up but one body though many, [and] as members of that body they should assist one another, Acts 8.14, 11.22, 15.22 with 1 Cor 12.25f.[108]
>
> Mutual assistance in ministry was the outworking of "that common interest that all the churches have in the gifts of God given forth in the church it being but one in the Head."[109]

This dealt with a problem inherent in the separatist, congregational, form of church, namely that while churches regarded themselves as competent to be churches, yet some lacked members willing and capable of functioning as officers. Such churches lacked the means of hearing the word and receiving the sacrament from one of their own number, and were required to seek help from elsewhere. Clearly, the theological metaphor of the "body of Christ" permitted Baptists to juxtapose theology and pragmatism to cover

---

104. Ibid.

105. Ibid., 127.

106. Ibid. The underlined "all" is added from the later restatement of the principles at the third General Meeting, and emphasizes the biblical thinking behind the formulation, showing it is dependent on John 13:35, the "marke" in question being "love."

107. Ibid., 60.

108. Ibid.

109. Ibid.

the embarrassment of "a compact and knit citie" which could not provide for its own spiritual needs. In this scenario, the body of Christ metaphor is not merely *descriptive* of the relationship between the singular and plural expressions of church, but also *prescriptive*, impelling churches to assist one another in the ministry and mission of Christ. The messengers rationalized the issue in this manner,

> so if God give plentifully in one, and but sparingly in others it may be for the tryal of the liberality of the one in the right use of it, and for the trial of the patience of the other, citing Eph 4.11f., 6.10.[110]

This principle did not only apply to the want and supply of ministry among churches but also to financial aid, according to 2 Cor 8.1–4, 14.[111]

It is evident that Particular Baptist ecclesiology functioned at two levels, the local and the universal. The body of Christ could equally be the local congregation, and the trans-local communion of churches. What is affirmed in this statement is that while the local congregation is not deficient in anything that is required for it to be a local manifestation of Christ's body, yet the single congregation cannot function in isolation from other believers in the universal body of Christ, to which it is essentially joined.

This doctrinal commitment to the universal church did not always extend to fellowship with the National Church, on account of, "their pretended ministry being Babilonish, Rev. 18.4."[112] Christian friendship with other Calvinistic Puritans might also be problematic since this required joining with unbaptized believers, and in this respect "disorderly" believers.[113] The line could be drawn in such a way as to exclude the possibility of fellowship even with General Baptists on account of their doctrine of Free Will.[114] The universal church to which the Particular Baptists of the Midlands felt essentially joined were those who shared a commitment to live under the rule of God's word and consented to the truths contained in their sixteen articles of faith.[115] Their form of associational theology was unusually dogmatic and confessional.

---

110. Ibid. The various spellings of "tryal" and "trial" are original.
111. Ibid., 62.
112. Ibid., 25.
113. Ibid.
114. See Howard, *Looking-Glass for Baptists*, 5–6.
115. *ARPB*, 20. The "Sixteen Articles of Faith and Order Unanimously Assented to by the Messengers Met at Warwick," are to be found, with introduction, in Lumpkin, *Baptist Confessions*, 198–200.

What makes sense of this dual reality of the visible church existing in local and universal expressions is the Christological *a priori* that over each manifestation of the body is Christ, the head of the church. This was affirmed in the third basis of association, as stated above. Christ, the cosmic Lord, unifies all things in himself, giving primacy to the universal reality of the body of Christ, from which particular manifestations of the body derive. This is affirmed in the reference to Eph 1:22–23 in the first basis of association, which states:

> and [the God of our Lord Jesus Christ] has put all things under his feet and has made him the head over all things for the church, which is his body, the fullness of him who fills all in all.

The messengers also placed alongside this the reference to Col 1:24 which likewise describes the church as the body of Christ in universal terms. Thus, it seems that in the thinking of the early Baptists, the universal church, as the body of Christ, was not comprised of the aggregate of local congregations here and there, but rather the local congregation is a manifestation of the one universal church of Christ on earth and in heaven. In the words of Paul Fiddes,

> the small bodies exist as an "outcropping" of the whole of the whole body.[116]

The image of the Particular Baptist association as the translocal body of Christ also gives significance to words included in a letter to the London churches informing them of what had transpired in Abingdon. The messengers used the language of covenant in the report,

> we solemnly entered into such an association each with other as this enclosed copie of our Agreement doth manifest.[117]

This statement evidences the strength of bond between individual congregations in communion with one another, the associational arrangement being a gospel imperative, not merely a voluntary arrangement of convenience. It was the covenantal dimension of the relationship between the churches, suggested by the word "solemnly," that enabled them to function in the manner of a single church following the five principles above. At translocal level they worked out in the following way:

---

116. Fiddes, *Tracks and Traces*, 198. Fiddes acknowledges that the image of "outcropping" derives from P. T. Forsyth. Payne earlier cited Forsyth in his description of Baptist Associations in *The Fellowship of Believers: Baptist Thought and Practice Yesterday and Today*, enlarged edition, 29 n. 6. Cf. Forsyth, *Church and the Sacraments*, 66.

117. ARPB, 131.

First, the General Meeting might function like a local church in regard to discipline. In South Wales, the General meeting held on 15 July 1651 was summoned to deal with Thomas Proud, minister of Cheriton in the Gower peninsula.[118] Proud was under discipline for preaching "mixed communion," a form of open membership not requiring believer's baptism of all welcomed to the Lord's Supper. He had rejected the rebuke of his own church in relation to this issue, and was called to account for his conduct at a general meeting of the churches at Llanharan. When Proud did not attend the gathering he was excommunicated by his church, though he may already have departed from them.[119]

As was noted previously, in 1655 the West Country association collectively rebuked the Irish churches for their ostentatious dress, and "taking the king's shilling."[120] To the zealous English Baptists, these were not trivial matters but, "iniquity," "sin," a "device of the devil," an "offence" to other believers. They longed for the Irish to repent and change their ways. They pleaded, "Dear brethren, we desire the Lord to teach you to deny yourselves in this case."[121] The influence of John Pendarves of Abingdon may be recognizable here, for this subject was addressed in his *Arrowes Against Babylon*, in the second section, "Endeavours for reformation in apparel." Pendarves argued that those who claimed to have risen to new life in Christ should abandon the flamboyance of their former life, on grounds of the poverty and suffering of others:

> From the present apparent wants and straights of divers poor precious saints that lack to be supplied with things necessary who, by reason of sickness, weakness or want of stock to manage their honest trades are unable to provide for themselves and their so that they may attend on God without distraction.[122]

The response of the Irish was recorded by the English in a post-script to the letter of 18 April 1655:

> Our brethren in Ireland did never to this epistle return to us any answer which was our trouble.[123]

---

118. See ibid., 14 n. 16.
119. *ARPB*, 5–6. Owens, *Ilston Book*, 19–20.
120. *ARPB*, 73–74.
121. Ibid., 74.
122. Pendarves, *Arrowes against Babylon*, 21.
123. *ARPB*, 76.

It is probably a sign of graciousness on the part of the Irish Baptists that they did not tell their English counterparts to "mind their own business." Clearly, associational authority to administer discipline had its limits.

Second, churches should gather together to manifest love for one another in the translocal body of Christ. It is the *agapeistic* imperative that explains the word "ought" in the third major theological basis for association which states, "every church ought to manifest its care over other churches . . . according to the law of theire nere relation in Christ." This emphasizes the mutual obligation felt among Baptist congregations to be in communion with one another. It was inconceivable that churches would not want to be in fellowship since this was a *sine qua non* of their membership of the body of Christ, given with their "relation in Christ."[124]

The notion of "relation in Christ" appears in the Irish correspondence, evidencing a theology of associationalism based on the image of family. The Irish appeal for closer links between the churches of the four nations is addressed to, "scattered brethren in several places." The purpose of their writing is, "to encourage mutual prayer in order that wee keepe the comfortable fruits of neere relations."[125] This familial language locates the Irish theology of inter-church communion in the same sphere as the *agapeistic* principle in the Abingdon records.

Third, a frequent occurrence in the Association Records is the report of messengers spending time in prayer and fasting for the prosperity of the work of God. A primary purpose of prayer was the felt need among these pioneering, fledgling groups of separatist believers to enquire of God how to form a true church. In the West Country records of 28 September 1655, the Messengers' letter states that the purpose of their meeting is "to enquire of the Lord and one another concerning the laws of his house."[126] In a letter to the churches of 18 April 1657 Thomas Collier writes,

> our Prophet hath taken away the vail from off his people's faces in giving the knowledge of his will in the practical part of the Gospel, in his ordinances and matters of worship.[127]

The determination to be scrupulous in conforming the church to the primitive pattern of the first disciples required a discerning people able to

---

124. This contrasts favorably with the recent document of the Baptist Union of Great Britain which states, "churches *might* and should freely choose to join a communion of churches," which makes the enterprise of trans-local communion appear optional. See *Relating and Resourcing*, 2:5, 4. Cited in Fiddes, *Tracks and Traces*, 200.

125. ARPB, 117–18.

126. Ibid., 76.

127. Ibid., 89.

apprehend Christ's will for his kingdom. Much time was therefore spent in spiritual exercises, as recorded for the Irish Churches:

> The churches of Christ in Ireland, walking in the faith and order of the Gospell, doe agree together, through the Lord's assistance, to sett apart one day every month, solemnly to seeke the face of our God, by prayer and fasting.[128]

In the Midlands, the messengers wrote to the churches to explain their purpose for communal gatherings:

> Deare brethren, we have beene by the precious hande of God our Father brought together from severall partes according to our appointment to seeke the face of our God together by fasting and prayers.[129]

In the West Country, at the fifth General Meeting in 1655, out of four days available for discussion, two were spent in fasting and prayer.[130]

In General Meetings the work of discernment was a twin-track process enquiring both of the Lord, and "one another," what Christ legislated for his house. The practice of double listening, to God and one another, was characteristic of early Baptist spirituality. Hence, it is recorded that at the fourth General Meeting of the Midland messengers on 7–8 April 1656,

> they had joyned together in prayer to seeke the Lord for theyer direction in answer to these quiries following.[131]

In addition to discernment of Christ's will, prayer was also considered essential for church congregations and true Gospel ministry to flourish. The three messengers of the West Country state in a circular letter of April 1656,

> Our heart's desire and prayers to God for you is that you may grow in grace, and that you may flourish in the Lord's house as plants of his own right hand's planting and that you may bring forth much fruit, and that your fruit may remain.[132]

---

128. Ibid., 118.
129. Ibid., 35.
130. Ibid., 60; See also ibid., 87.
131. Ibid., 24. The meeting proceeded to discuss a number of issues raised by the church for which they sought the advice and direction of the messengers.
132. Ibid., 78.

No doubt, the precarious condition of a number of churches in the West Country,[133] lacking both congregational numbers and finance, meant that these sentiments were prayed with sincerity and urgency.

Fourth, associational meetings were contexts where the mind of Christ was sought on all aspects of church practice. Questions included whether it was permissible for sub groups of a larger church to gather for "breaking bread together?"[134] Whether Christ had ordained New Testament churches to sing psalms and in what manner?[135] Whether is a duty of an elder to anoint the sick with oil?[136] "Whether astrology in matters of physick be lawfull?"[137] Whether "it bee lawfull for a church of Christ to hold communion with soldiers?"[138] Also discussed at association level was the division of the church at Kensworth on account of it having grown large, the congregation being unable to settle the matter alone.[139] In response to these questions, the messengers gave their advice taken from the example of New Testament practice or principle. It was not uncommon, however, for the Messengers to supplement their reply with such words as:

> we cannot at present determine this question but desire to waite on the Lord for further light in it.[140]

The General Meeting, in the same manner as the local church, believed that Christ, the head of the Body, would make known to his people his mind and will for his people. The wider, translocal, communion of churches, like the single local church could then live experientially under the rule of Christ.[141]

Fifth, associationalism bore witness to those outside that independent separatist congregations were "true churches of Christ."[142] From the perspective of the National Church, separatists were often viewed as sectarian, schismatic and fissiparous. Baptists, additionally, were accused of Anabaptism

---

133. In 1657 the London churches established a fund to support "Gospell ministrie abroad in the countreys," after learning of the dire state of a number of churches and poverty of their ministers in the West Country. Ibid., 174.

134. Ibid., 58.

135. Ibid.

136. Ibid., 59.

137. Ibid., 65. The popularity of astrology in the seventeenth century was based on its use in millenarian calculations. The saints were divided about its value, and legitimacy. See Capp, *Fifth Monarchy Men*, 17, 187–88; Hill, *English Bible*, 23–26.

138. *ARPB*, 102.

139. Ibid., 146.

140. Ibid., 65. See also ibid., 58–59.

141. See Fiddes, *Tracks and Traces*, 200.

142. *ARPB*, 127.

in its revolutionary, anarchistic manifestation. Isolated congregationalism was, of course, an option for Baptists, however, there was recognition of safety and strength in communion. By joining together under the banner of theological orthodoxy, represented by their Confessions, the early Baptists intended to show they stood in the stream of historic, orthodox Christianity as true churches of Christ.

Although early Baptists, and notably the Messengers, did not speak of associational gatherings, nor associationalism, as "church," they did regard the nature and purpose of their joint meetings in the same terms as the local church.[143] While on the one hand the Messengers assiduously avoided any suggestion that General Meetings were a layer of ecclesiastical polity above, or higher, than the local congregation, they also affirmed that the local church was not the fullness of the visible church. Even as the individual believer requires the gathered fellowship of believers in order to be in Christ, so the local congregation needs to be in relation with other churches to be in the body of Christ.

6.3 Associational Authority and Local Ecclesiology

While the importance of Particular Baptist churches maintaining their independence is frequently affirmed by the common use of the adjective "distinct,"[144] it has been shown above that Calvinistic Baptist churches rejected congregational isolationism. This pattern of ecclesiology, holding in tension the first principles of Congregationalism, together with a doctrine of the translocal communion of churches, required General Meetings to consider the question of authority between the two. The consistent and emphatic response of the messengers affirmed that the Association had no authority over the local church. This conviction had characterized the ecclesiology of Henry Jacob and was a theological commitment the Particular Baptists were never likely to compromise. Jacob asserted,

> that euery perticular congregation and parish church should bee so absolute for the spirituall government of it sel[f] as it should not bee subordinate, nor subject to any ecclesiasticall assemb[ly] to giue an account to them for anything they doe,

---

143. In this regard, Baptists were in harmony with the congregational ecclesiology of Henry Jacob, who introduced the word "synecdoche" to indicate that the people of a particular congregation are called the church. Meanwhile, Presbyterians from the time of Walter Travers applied synecdoche to a plurality of congregations. See Ha, *English Presbyterianism*, 48, 57–58.

144. For example *ARPB*, 20, 77; First London Confession article XLVII.

or receive any ordinances from them, as hauing authoritie ouer them.[145]

According to Jacob, this was the situation in the primitive church in the New Testament:

> under the Gospell Christ never instituted, nor had any one Universall visible church (that is Politicall) either proper, or representative; which ordinarily was to exercise spirituall outward government, over all persons through the world professing Christianity.[146]

Evidence of this Jacobite principle in the records of the Particular Baptists is found in a number of sources. In the letter of the Somerset churches to those in Ireland in 1655 it is stated:

> But, dear brethren we have not written these things to shame you, but to warn you not as having dominion over your faith but as helpers of your joy.[147]

Similarly, the letter of Thomas Collier, General Superintendent of the Western Churches from 1655, issued in the name of the "general assembly" in Chard, to the churches in 1657, asserted,

> I have written these things unto you, not as one that hath dominion over your faith but as a poor helper of your joy.[148]

The locus of authority was not with the General Meeting and its messengers, but in the local congregation. This is clear in the letter from the Pettie France church in London to the Abingdon association who were seeking advice about the appointment of officers in their churches:

> The apostles did not thrust the elders upon the churches through briberie or lordly superioritie, but chose and placed them by the voice of the congregation.[149]

In discussing the means by which elders and deacons should be appointed in a local congregation it is stated,

---

145. Granted that this statement is derived from Jacob's Presbyterian examiners, including Walter Travis, on the occasion of his submission of his plans to found and Independent church to them in 1616, but there is no reason to doubt it was an accurate portrayal of his views. Cited in Ha, *English Presbyterianism*, 51.

146. Jacob, *Confession and Protestation*, B2.6.

147. *ARPB*, 75.

148. Ibid., 92.

149. Ibid., 171.

> By all which it appeares where Christ hath placed the authoritie of tryall and electing, viz., in his church.[150]

And it is affirmed that this principle was also their practice:

> By all which you may perceive our judgement is, and accordingly was our practice, that the sole authoritie, as in trying, electing and ordering, so in ordaining, resides in the church (specially since the apostolicall power is ceased).[151]

That this position on authority was the settled conviction of the Particular Baptists, even at this earliest phase of associational development, is demonstrated by its consolidation in the Second London Confession of 1677 which states:

> In cases of difficulties or differences, either in point of Doctrine, or Administration; wherein either the Churches in general are concerned, or any one Church in their peace, union, and edification; or any member, or members, of any Church are injured, in or by any proceedings in censures not agreeable to truth, and order: it is according to the mind of Christ, that many Churches holding communion together, do by their messengers meet to consider, and give their advice in, or about that matter in difference, to be reported to all the Churches concerned; howbeit these messengers assembled, are not entrusted with any Church-power properly so called; or with any jurisdiction over the Churches themselves, to exercise any censures over any Churches, or Persons: or to impose their determination on the Churches, or Officers.[152]

This principle was re-affirmed when the General Assembly of Particular Baptists met in London in September, 1689, where the first question to be discussed concerned associational authority. The resolution stated,

> we disclaim all manner of *superiority* and *superintendency* over the churches, and that we have no authority or power to prescribe or impose any thing upon the faith or practice of any of the churches of Christ. Our whole intendment is to be helpers together of one another, by way of counsel and advice.[153]

---

150. Ibid.

151. Ibid.

152. Second London Confession, Chapter XXVI.15. Lumpkin, *Baptist Confessions*, 289.

153. Rippon's *Baptist Annual Register*, IV (1801–02), supplement, 48. See also Wamble, "Beginning of Associationalism," 556–57.

The later affirmation of Congregational authority is important in the light of the contrasting tendency among the General Baptists who, towards the close of the seventeenth century, issued a strikingly bold confession elevating the association above local churches. This is worth citing to illustrate the diametrically opposite position adopted by the General Baptists to the Particular:

> General councils, or assemblies, consisting of Bishops, Elders, and Brethren, of the several churches of Christ, and being legally convened, and met together out of all the churches, and the churches appearing there by their representatives, make but one church,[154] and have lawful right, and suffrage in this general meeting, or assembly, to act in the name of Christ; it being of divine authority, and is the best means under heaven to preserve unity, to prevent heresy, and superintendency among, or in any congregation whatsoever within its own limits, or jurisdiction. And to such a meeting, or assembly, appeals ought to be made, in case any injustice be done, or heresy, and schism countenanced, in any particular congregation of Christ, and the decisive voice in such general assemblies is the major part, and such general assemblies have lawful power to hear, and determine, as also to excommunicate.[155]

The Particular Baptist concept of associationalism was a bold attempt to reproduce the dynamic ecclesiology observed in the New Testament, especially at the Council of Jerusalem in Acts 15, which was regarded as a model for local and universal church working in symbiosis.

Although there was no formal authority in the relationship between association and local church, as in the manner of the Presbyterian synod, this did not mean that associations had no influence vis-à-vis the churches. The Association Records, particularly in the West Country and Midlands, contain an extended series of questions posed by the churches, together with messengers' responses.[156] The result is a body of decisions on various issues, without authoritative status, for the guidance of congregations and

---

154. That the General Baptist churches in London in the seventeenth century were so closely linked together that they described themselves as the different parts of one congregation is seen in the Minute Book of the Glasshouse Yard Church, 1682–1740. See Payne, "Glass Yard Minute Book," 321–24.

155. "Orthodox Creed" (1678), Article XXXIX. Lumpkin, *Baptist Confessions*, 327. This position was not universally accepted and in the same year Thomas Grantham published *Christianismus Primitivus* in order to show that according to the pattern of Acts 15 the superiority of Churches one above another is contrary to Scripture.

156. The questions discussed in the Western Association are categorized by Nuttall, "Baptist Western Association," 216–17.

individuals. Queries sent in from several congregations in the West Country concerned such matters as ecclesiastical practice,[157] personal conduct,[158] and social responsibility.[159] Questions about doctrine were rare, but two examples are evident:

> Whether Christ Jesus our Lord dyed for all and every man or for the elect only, and if for all, then how far?[160]

This doctrinal commitment to particular redemption raised the pastoral question:

> Whether a member varying from the faith which at his admission he profest, as in respect of free will, general redemption, and falling from grace, the church may proceed to reject him without some other occasion?[161]

These, and many other, questions were answered on the basis of biblical teaching and Apostolic practice. In some cases the messengers had no clear answer, except that a church should do what they judged best for themselves.[162] This is a clue to the sense of authority and legislative force

---

157. For example, "Whether it be an ordinance of Christ for disciples to wash one another's feet, according to John 13.14?" The answer was that disciples should serve each other humbly, and wash feet only as required. *ARPB*, 60. Or, "Whether a woman may speak in the church at all, and if at all, in what cases?" In the West Country the answer was unequivocally negative, however in the Midlands the response was more nuanced, "women in some cases may speake in the churches." Ibid., 55. See also ibid., 28.

158. For example, "Whether it be lawfull for a believer in the order of the Gospel to marry one that is not in the same order?" Ibid., 55. See also ibid., 21 and 30–31. A remarkable story is recorded of a Baptist church member from the Southwark church, marrying a "Friend" in 1667, and immediately after changing his mind and seeking the marriage annulled on the basis that, "he was a believer, and she an unbeliever." The church agreed to the dissolution of the marriage and the man subsequently married a Baptist. See Payne, "The Glass Yard Minute Book," 324. On another occasion it was asked, "Whether a man in any case in ruling over his wife may lawfully strike her?" The reply instructs men to rule over their wives without striking since domestic violence has no biblical warrant. *ARPB*, 69. Puritans generally protested against wife beating. See Thomas, "Women and the Civil War Sects," in Aston, *Crisis in Europe*, 318.

159. For example, "What is the saints' duty towards the magistrate at this day in this nation?" *ARPB*, 66. See also ibid., 30.

160. Ibid., 61. It is affirmed that "our Lord Christ dyed for all and every man. . . . Yet he died not intentionally alike for all."

161. Ibid., 57. The answer is that such a person should be rejected. This is not surprising given that in the West Country there were tendencies to compromise the Calvinism of the Particular Baptist Churches, and move that was resisted by the issuing of the Somerset Confession in 1656.

162. See ibid., 32 and 68–69.

that the pastoral responses of the messengers were considered to have in the churches.

In the letter sent by the messengers of the West Country Association following the meeting of 26–27 March 1654, the status of the answers to the churches' questions, and the implied authority of the General Meeting is made explicit. Thomas Collier states,

> our answers . . . we commend unto your serious consideration desiring that it may be usefull unto you for the well ordering of the Lord's house.[163]

There is no suggestion that the answers should be taken as rules, or that the General Meeting possessed authority over its constituent congregations, except in cases of serious error. The only force the General Meeting sought to employ was that of moral appeal, trusting that the saints be a "willing people in every good work," and that "love and duty may engage your hearts to a holy, humble and obedient walking with God."[164]

In contrast to Congregationalism which held strongly to independency, to the neglect of the wider body, and Presbyterianism which subordinated the local congregation to the collective synod, the Particular Baptists "could not surrender either doctrine without rejecting biblical evidence on the one hand or violating their own Christian experience on the other."[165]

Summary

This chapter has demonstrated that while early Baptist ecclesiology was sectarian and separatist relative to National Church structures, in relation to one another Baptist churches were closely interconnected in translocal relationships.

Barry White was correct to argue that associationalism developed organically among Baptist churches. The idea that association was a social or military model imposed upon a collection of churches is historically unsustainable. From earliest times, Baptist churches associated for mutual support, to share resources, to establish credibility to be true churches, not merely schismatic groups with an obsession for immersionism. If the pragmatism of the early years explains the origins of association, a theology of translocal ecclesiology soon emerged as an essential component of Baptist identity. By the 1650s, associationalism was intentional and in

---

163. Ibid., 72.
164. Ibid.
165. Wamble, "Beginning of Associationalism," 546.

the Midlands Baptist churches were founded and mutually related in one calculated campaign.

The association of early Baptist churches evidenced a willingness of members to receive as well as to give help and support from the wider constituency. The five articles of action which defined the purposes of association amongst early Calvinistic Baptists suggest relationships of trust and openness between congregations, facilitated by their messengers. Advice about controversial matters, help in alleviating poverty, enabling ministry in churches lacking leaders, partnership in gospel work and evangelistic mission, watch-care and discipline were the business of associational gatherings. Relationships were, in turn, informed by biblical precedent, such as the Council of Jerusalem in Acts 15, and biblical teaching about the body of Christ, which was applied to translocal reality of the church. In addition, associationalism was motivated by a determination to fulfil the dominical command to love one another and to cultivate unity, an ordinance it was believed could not, and should not be limited to the local church. Nor can we ignore the commitment to united prayer as a means of communal discernment for strategic evangelistic decisions and the flourishing of churches. This was a time when Baptist churches looked to one another for counsel and help in order to be the churches, and the people, of which King Jesus approved.

Conclusions

IN THIS ACCOUNT OF the emergence and expansion of the English Calvinistic Baptists, we have traced the primary features of their doctrine of the church. The ecclesiological convictions of the Particular Baptists were forged in a context of political and ecclesiastical revolution. Experimental and distinctive ways of forming the church were possible in this lacuna of authority and governance. We have seen that the historical foundations of the Particular Baptists were in English Puritan separatism of the early seventeenth century and the Puritan element of Baptist ecclesiology accounted for their commitment to biblical primitivism, a determination to re-form the church in strict conformity to the New Testament. Adherence to scripture, as the canon of their ecclesiology, derived from a more foundational devotion, to the person, and rule, of Christ, the personal Lord of each believer, and rightful king of the church.

The outworking of this principle committed Particular Baptists to a separatist policy in contrast to the National Church settlement of the Civil War period. In the earliest phase of their history, through the 1620s and 1630s, separatism was not necessarily an assured position, since Henry Jacob had adopted a modified form of this stance in the formation of his own congregation. Jacob's semi-separatism evidenced a generosity of spirit towards evangelical preaching by godly clergy that suggested a recognition of the National Church which resulted in internal debate and even division within the J-L-J congregation. By the early 1640s, however, the question of the stance toward the National Church was resolved, and Baptists formed independent congregations divorced from the parish system. This arrangement demonstrated the right Baptists claimed to gather under the unmediated authority of Christ. No bishops, priests, synods, or elders, stood between the gathered company of believers, and Christ, the head of the church.

Congregationalism was the settled polity of the Particular Baptists, and this was reinforced by their most characteristic feature, believer's baptism. The rejection of infant baptism came early in their development, initially motivated by the judgment that the Church of England was a false church, and their administration of the sacrament invalid. Having rejected the common mode of baptism, they saw in the precepts of Christ, and practice of the Early Church, a baptism analogous to the pattern of Christ's death and resurrection, offered to those voluntarily professing faith in Jesus Christ. By 1638, Particular Baptists were practicing believer's baptism, and by 1642, baptism by immersion. Labelled by their enemies and detractors "Anabaptists," a terms they themselves rejected, the break with other forms of ecclesiology in England was essentially complete, and irrevocable.

Throughout this study it has been observed that despite their ecclesiological independence, the Calvinistic Baptists remained committed to many elements of the Reformed doctrine of the church as derived from Calvin. They were loyal to the traditional teaching about original sin, total depravity, predestination and election, limited atonement, and the perseverance of the saints. Their adoption of believer's baptism by immersion, however, brought a relinquishment of a central plank of Calvinism, namely the covenant of grace. The continuity between the old and new covenants, typical of Reformed theology, underpinned the inclusion of infants in the church, and their baptism at birth. Baptists regarded this theology and practice as inconsistent, since certainty that a child was among the elect was impossible, and therefore their baptism unwarranted. In Baptist theology and practice, conversion was the basis of covenant, since it was only on profession of faith, and evidence of spiritual fruit, that a judgment regarding election might be made, baptism administered, and inclusion in the visible church confirmed. While early Particular Baptists were unquestionably Calvinistic, their form of Calvinism was modified, showing both continuity and discontinuity with the Reformed heritage.

The basic unit of the church for Particular Baptists was the gathered congregation. The congregation was comprised of those who had undergone spiritual conversion, "living stones" hewn out of the quarry of mankind, as Collier described them.[1] Their primary allegiance was to Christ, and thereafter, to one another. A gathered company of believers, not less than twelve or thirteen in number, were competent to organize worship, appoint their own officers, and exercise discipline toward each other. Their qualifications

---

1. Collier, *Certaine Queries*, 9.

in such matters were not based on education, training, or external authorization, but on the authority Christ bestowed on those gathered in his name. In such circumstances, ministry and worship might easily have become chaotic, and misleading, however, the guard against this was the congregation itself. Baptists insisted, to the consternation of detractors like Daniel Featley, that ministry in the church was derived from the congregation which chose and ordained suitable persons to office, and which might discipline or dispose of their officers. The ministry of officers in the church was to be tested and approved by the congregation, for evidence of the gift of ministry from Christ, the sovereign of the church.

The priority of the congregation in Baptist ecclesiology was tied to their theological commitment to the visible nature of the church. The metaphysical construct of the invisible church, a prominent element in traditional Calvinist teaching about the *ecclesia*, was absent from Calvinistic Baptist thinking about the church. The visible church, comprised of visible saints, was the sole object of their concern. This accounted for the emphasis placed on the manifestation of faith in repentance and good works, especially the spiritual fruit of love.[2] Among Baptists these were the essential *notae* of the church. This accounts for the Baptist emphasis on discipline within their congregations, the practice of keeping the saints in holy and orderly communion.

At the heart of my argument is the claim that early Particular Baptist ecclesiology was rooted in and oriented around the will and purpose of Christ for his people. When Robert Poole asked William Kiffin, "what *warrant* have you to separate from the national Church? and what *warrant* have you to form congregations? And what *warrant* have you to be a minister of a Separate Congregation?" How can you *vindicate* your schism and defection from the reformed Churches? Kiffin's response was, ". . . according to the Rule of Christ."[3] Phrases commonly used by Baptists were that Jesus Christ is the head of the church, he is both Lord and King of the churches, he is King of saints, and of Sion. The power and authority of Christ, was believed to be directly present and available to the church, unmediated by clergy. The systematic application of this principle to the church in the "ten ordinances," by Thomas Collier, was probably the most contrived attempt to make visible the rule of Christ, but the codification of the Rule of Christ was the logical step for Baptists to take. These were, baptism, prayer, praise, preaching, the Lord's Supper, assembling together, discipline, excommuni-

---

2. Collier, *Right Constitution*, 8.

3. The questions and answers are recorded in only one document, Kiffin, *Briefe Remonstrance*, 3 and 6.

cation, providing for the poor, and holiness of life. Derived from the New Testament, these ordinances demonstrated that Baptists did not distinguish between Christ, by his Spirit, present among his people here and now, and Christ accessed through the witness of scripture. It was not conceivable that there could be conflict between these two points of access to the mind and will of Christ. It was, therefore, incumbent upon believers to be people of the Word, to regard scripture highly.[4]

The influence of Henry Jacob in establishing the Christ-centered organization of the church was important for a number of reasons. First, by prioritizing Christ in the ordering of a church Jacob established a link between ecclesiology and soteriology. The proper order of church government and organization was necessary so that Christ be clearly recognized as King, Lord and lawgiver. The right order of the church was the first test of submission to Christ as King. Every element in true worship was ordained by Christ, he asserted. Jacob also bequeathed to Particular Baptists an accommodation to the authority to the magistrate. A church under the Rule of Christ, he argued, must necessarily be free from episcopal jurisdiction in spiritual matters, but in civil matters, due respect should be given to the appointed authorities.[5] In practice, this meant that where possible Baptists were willing to serve the instruments of state, not regarding this as inconsistent with loyalty to King Jesus. Particular Baptists were therefore willing to take oaths, to hold civil office,[6] to serve in the army,[7] and take employment for Cromwell.[8]

In the 1640s, the Christocratic orientation of the church was codified by using the traditional structure of the *munus triplex Christi*, Christ as prophet, priest and King. The threefold office of Christ was determinative for Baptist thinking about the work of salvation, and for the life of God's people corporately. Thomas Collier, in particular, explored this relationship between Christ and his church, expanding the ideas briefly stated in the 1644 London Confession. Collier emphasized that since Christ is the

---

4. Baptists spoke of the Bible as "the rule," the "sure word of truth," and "Christ never teacheth contrary to this scripture." Collier, *Exaltation of Christ*, 87.

5. First London Confession, article XLIX. In Lumpkin, *Baptist Confessions*, 169.

6. Kiffin was M.P. for Middlesex in 1566, Sir Hierome Sankey was M.P. in three Irish constituencies, as well as Marlborough and Woodstock, and Robert Bennett represented Cornwall in the Parliament of the Saints, becoming M.P. for Launceston and Looe in 1654 and for Launcesaton in 1659. See Bebbington, "Baptist M.Ps in the Seventeenth and Eighteenth Centuries," 253-4; and White, "Early Baptist Letters (1)," 148. Kiffin was later made Alderman of the city of London. Orme, *Remarkable Passages*, 87.

7. See "Baptists in the New Model Army," in Whitley, *HBB*, 73–81.

8. Henry Jessey served as one of Cromwell's Triers in 1654. White, "Henry Jessey," 104.

only true priest, all other priestly ministry in the church is secondary and derivative from Christ. The priesthood of all believers, a necessary doctrine in congregational ecclesiology to validate the lay-led worship of the people as true and valid worship, was justified in this manner. As prophet, Christ is the proper teacher of his people, guiding them in true paths without the requirement of university educated clergy. The primary and essential task of the church was to follow the Lamb wherever he goeth. The practical outworking of this principle was the development of the church meeting, where the congregation gathered to exercise communal discernment, seeking the mind of Christ. In one famous instance in 1643, the Jessey church was plunged into a series of conferences as they wrestled with a question put to the congregation by Hanserd Knollys regarding the baptism of his child.[9] Communal discernment was also applied to all matters of excommunication, according to the 1644 London Confession: "Christ has likewise given power to his whole Church to receive in and cast out."[10] The prophetic ministry of Christ in the church was likewise a corporate experience, by which Christ maintained his people in truth and purity.

As King, early Baptists emphasized the temporal priority of Christ's rule "in the hearts" of the saints, as the basis for asserting Christ's Kingly authority over his people. Christ's sovereignty was regarded as a reality to be evidenced in personal loyalty and devotion in each believer, and its visible manifestation was a prerequisite for church membership. The gathered congregation was comprised of those living consciously under the rule of Christ, and, as a "regiment" the church lives in submission to Christ. William Kiffin, captured the central conviction of Baptist ecclesiology when he stated, "this great truth, Christ the king of his church."[11]

The kingly rule of Christ in and over the saints was a doctrine not only of spiritual significance, but eschatological and political consequence. In the first place, the separatist vision of the church positioned their congregations outside State interference, implying they were an *imperium in imperio*. Secondly, despite the insistence of early Baptist Confessions,[12] and the teaching of leaders like Collier, that the kingdom of Christ on earth was a spiritual kingdom,[13] and his rule a spiritual sovereignty, in the late 1640s and throughout the 1650s a political vision of Christ's reign became

---

9. The Stinton mss No. 4, "Debate on Infant Baptism, 1643," 239–45.
10. In Lumpkin, *Baptist Confessions*, 168.
11. Kiffin, "Epistle to the Reader," in Anon., *Glimpse of Sions Glory*.
12. First London Confession, article XIX. In Lumpkin, *Baptist Confessions*, 161.
13. For example, Collier, *Marrow of Christianity*, 90.

an option for radical members of Baptist congregations.[14] This vision was associated with the Fifth Monarchists[15] who predicted the imminent advent of Christ's kingdom on earth, and the rule of the saints[16] over the political kingdoms of the world. A number of Particular Baptists were initially drawn towards this politico-religious enterprise[17] through the teaching of trusted men such as Henry Jessey,[18] and Christopher Feake.[19]

Kiffin's response to what he called the "pretence of the fifth monarchy"[20] was to warn fellow Baptists against supporting an anti-government movement, and to encourage compliance with the political regime.[21] In a letter to Irish Baptists on 20 January 1654, he argued that association with Fifth Monarchist attempts to "throw down potentates and powers" would be utterly ruinous for the Baptist cause.[22] The wiser course, he proposed, was to adopt a "humble and patient waiting for the kingdom of our Lord Jesus."[23]

If it is asked, what would an alliance between Baptists and Fifth Monarchists have meant for the development of Particular Baptist ecclesiology the following points can be made. First, the Fifth Monarchy movement represented a proposal to extend the scope of Christ's kingdom from the sphere of the church to the wider political realm. The Fifth Monarchy Manifesto of

---

14. This is the thesis of Brown, *The Political Activities of the Baptists and Fifth Monarchy Men in England During the Interregnum*. Another early study touching on Baptists and Fifth Monarchists is, Burrage, "Fifth Monarchy Insurrections," 722–47, esp. 724.

15. A contemporary account of the beginnings of Fifth Monarchism is given by Feake, *Beam of Light*, 39–47. Modern studies include Brown, *Political Activities of the Baptists*; Capp, "Extreme Millenarianism," in Peter Toon, *Puritans, the Millennium and the Future of Israel*, 66–90; Capp, *Fifth Monarchy Men*, 27–49; and Liu, *Discord in Zion*, chapter 3.

16. Anon. *Certain Quaeries*, 6.

17. See Capp, "*A Door of Hope* Re-opened," 21; White, "John Pendarves, the Calvinistic Baptists and the Fifth Monarchy," 251–71. Hanserd Knollys, for one, became absorbed with the doctrine of the last things. See Howson, "Hanserd Knollys," in Haykin, *British Particular Baptist*, 1:57f. Also, Woodhouse, *Puritanism and Liberty*, 233–41.

18. See Jessey, *A Calculation for this Present Year*, 1645, n.p. For context see White, "Henry Jessey," 98–110.

19. See Feake, *Beam of Light*, also *The Prophets Malachy and Isaiah*, an anonymous work for which he and John Pendarves wrote extended introductions.

20. Kiffin, "Letter from Mr. Kiffen and Others," in Underhill, *Confessions of Faith*, 324.

21. The response of the General Baptists was quite different and many General Baptists were allied to the Fifth Monarchy cause in the early 1650s. See Bell, *Apocalypse How?* 163–204, especially 172 where a list of prominent General Baptists who were also Fifth Monarchists is given.

22. Kiffin, "Letter from Mr. Kiffen and Others," 325.

23. Ibid., 322.

1654 spoke of Christ as, "King of kings, and of all Nations."[24] In contrast, Baptists preached the rule of Christ in the Church, the dominion of Christ over the saints, and the laws of Christ governing the godly.

Second, the Fifth Monarch movement externalized the kingdom of Christ and regarded the political instruments of power, especially government, legitimate means to establish the reign of Christ over the world.[25] If the first point in their agenda concerned the *scope* of Christ's reign, this element concerned the *medium* of Christ's reign, namely the government. In contrast, Particular Baptists spoke of the internal, spiritual dominion of Christ in the lives of the saints. John Spittlehouse proposed that the reins of government be given to the godly in the army, and Thomas Collier preached,

> Some apprehend that Christ shall come and reign personally, subduing his enemies, and exalting his people, and that this is the new heaven and the new earth; but this is not my apprehension: but that Christ will come in the Spirit, and have a glorious Kingdome in the spirits of his people, and they shall by the power of Christ in them, raign [sic] over the world, and this is the new heavens and the new earth.[26]

He continued on, emphasizing over and over that heaven is God's kingdom, and the kingdom is within the saints. The spiritual nature of Christ's reign meant Baptists argued for separation of Church and State.

Third, following from the previous point, Fifth Monarchists aspired to make the national government conform as closely as possible to the rule of Christ, and justified use of violence against an ungodly government on the basis that they were "preparing the way for the Lord."[27] In contrast, the

---

24. *A Declaration of Several Churches*, 16, transcribed in *TBHS* 3.3 (1913) 143. See also Spittlehouse, *Army Vindicated*, 13–14; Feake, *Beam of Light*, 40. Many Fifth Monarchists evidenced a deep desire to send godly youths to all nations to spread the gospel and prepare the way for Christ. See Capp, *Fifth Monarchy men*, 189–90. The millenarian Robert Eburne argued it was sinful not to colonize America since the Gospel must be preached throughout the world before Christ returns. See Hill, *English Bible and the Seventeenth Century*, 300.

25. Spittlehouse, *Army Vindicated*, 6-10.

26. Thomas Collier, "Discovery of the New Creation," 8, see also 32. See also Collier, *Marrow of Christianity*, 151–68. Land, *Doctrinal Controversies*, 250–51, observes a change of emphasis towards a more literal personal appearing and reign of Christ in *The Personal Appearing of Christs Kingdom and Reign Upon the Earth*. While this is true, Collier's theological adjustment appears to have had no noticeable impact on Particular Baptist millenarianism, or their policy towards the Fifth Monarchists. Kiffin remained the dominant opinion former among the Baptists on this subject.

27. See Feake's preface to Anon., *Prophets Malachy and Isaiah*, 16. See also Solt, "Fifth Monarchy Men," 318. See also, Thurloe *State Papers*, 1:441.

majority of Baptists considered it to be Christ's prerogative to set the time for the establishing of his kingdom, and they would wait patiently for that event. The Midland Association assembly of 15 October 1656 stated:

> When the Lord shall make his people a smiting people will hee not first clearely put a just and lawfull power and authoritie into their hands or cause such a power to be [at] their sides and to commande them as that in the exercise thereof or in yielding obedience thereunto their actions shall be clearely just and goode. . . . Wee offer it to the searious consideration whether it be not implied in Ro. 11.12,15 that the Gentile churches be in a low condition till the calling of the Jewes and whether it may not be gathered from Mic. 4.8, that the Jewish Church shall have the kingdom and the first dominion, Japhet being to dwell in the tents of Shem, Gen 9.27. If so, then whether it doth not behove us with patience and quietness to wait for the time.[28]

Such a policy of quietism towards the State distanced Baptists from the violent methods of Fifth Monarchists. Not all Baptists were agreeable to the policy of accommodation, as was evident from the *Declaration of Several of the People Called Anabaptists*, in 1659, but the influence of London leaders, particularly William Kiffin and Samuel Richardson, was decisive.[29] Thus it can be said that although the Particular Baptists were not untouched by the radical wing of Fifth Monarchism they rejected violent engagement with the authorities and maintained their commitment to the spiritual nature of Christ's kingdom, and the spiritual preparation to be made by the saints awaiting its arrival.

The importance of the spiritual preparation of the saints was discussed in chapter four, and consisted of holiness of life, enforced through a formal system of church discipline. Theologically, discipline was grounded in God's eternal purposes for humanity that there be a godly people possessing the moral perfection of God himself. Sin has disrupted the purpose of God, to which the redemptive activity of God in Christ is the response. Following the traditional Calvinist schema, Particular Baptists understood the nature and purpose of the church to reside, theologically, within the redemptive purposes of God, and for this reason church discipline was regarded as an essential mark of a true church. A true church is comprised of "saints," those made pure from sin, living in obedience to God's word, under the heavenly

---

28. *ARPB*, 30.

29. On Richardson's defense of the Protectorate parliament see Brown, *Political Activities of the Baptists*, 99.

government of Christ, separated from the "world," and Baptists were determined to play their part in bringing this to fruition.

This was an ideal vision of the church, as defined in the 1644 London Confession, and other writings. The reality of early Baptist congregational life, however, was reflected in the *Association Records*, in which instances of improper behavior are recorded together with their remedy even to the point of excommunication in the name of Christ, according to 1 Cor 5:4.

The importance of discipline in Baptist congregations was the significance it help for the doctrine of the rule of Christ. The church being the spiritual kingdom of Christ, evil doers were an affront to the crown rights, and dignity of King Jesus.[30] As a secondary issue, the "right walking" of members also served to justify the decision of Baptists to separate from the National Church, and any compromise in the lives of saints undermined the validity of the ecclesiastical enterprise undertaken by the Particular Baptists.

One criticism which might be levelled at early Baptist ecclesiology, and the disciplinary practice which flowed from it, is that in effect it unchurched the reprobate masses by restricting membership of the church, and the receiving of the ordinances, to the elect suitably identified and baptized.[31] The alternative, Presbyterian model of the church, was inclusive of both elect and reprobate, assuming that all members of society were members of the church, and using discipline and suspension from the sacraments, to reform the worldly and make them into the godly. This difference in approach was not simply a matter of two alternative ways of organizing the visible church, but represented two different views of the nature and basis of the church. Baptists did not feel responsible for the masses outside the church beyond the responsibility to preach and evangelize. They regarded the National Church arrangement as beginning at the wrong point, namely with a *corpus permixtum*, needing to be disciplined and reformed. A true ecclesial policy began with the Christocratic orientation of the church, seeking to work out all other matters from that point.

The policy of a godly membership was of importance for Baptists in relation to the organization of its ministry. The unmediated presence of Christ to the congregation meant that each congregation was obliged to choose from their own number "meet persons" to the offices of pastor, teacher, elder, and deacon.[32] Ministers did not come from without, and were not above, the congregation, but from within, and among the congregation. This practice was unthinkable in a *corpus permixtum* ecclesiology.

30. ARPB, 93–94.
31. See Tolmie, *Saints*, 101.
32. 1644 London Confessions, article XXXVI.

In formulating their theology and practice of ministry, Baptists again exploited the pattern of Christ's life and work. As previously noted, the primary ministry in the church was that of Christ, Prophet, Priest and King. Ministry in the church was, therefore, derivative from Christ, and in no sense substitutionary, or even representative, of Christ. Baptists believed that every member of the church was ordained to ministry on account of their baptism. Every member was enrolled in the service of Christ, though some service had significant public responsibility and therefore required extraordinary validation. This was the justification for ordination of those called to oversight of a congregation. To be a minister was to hold an office, and as holder of an office, to perform a function. The office was co-extensive with the function, so that if one no longer functioned in ministry, it followed that the office would be vacated. Likewise, if one were deprived of office, the officer would return to membership of the congregation, seeking service in some other capacity.

Throughout the 1650s, Calvinistic Baptists consolidated a corporate ecclesiological identity in the formation of Associations. The reasons for gathering in this manner were practical, since they allowed for the common resourcing of congregations financially and, or, ministerially impoverished. Wisdom was also a shared commodity, as congregations discussed questions of mutual concern in the attempt to fashion churches strictly conformed to the will of Christ. Matters relating to singing in worship, fasting, dress code, remuneration of ministers, closed and open membership, discipline, and authority, drew them together for the purposes of counsel and help.

The question of the origins of Associational relations was briefly considered, and the theological concept of most significance to the trans-local network of churches was again Christological. Associations regarded themselves as the natural extension of the "body of Christ" metaphor which shaped their understanding of the local congregation. This was codified in the 1644 London Confession[33] which upheld the independency of each congregation, within a theology of "one body," in common faith, under Christ the head.[34] As in the local church, where individual members are bound together in Christ, and comprise the body of Christ, congregations united in Association constituted a translocal expression of the body of Christ. From the Irish Baptist churches, Baptists also learnt the language of family, to describe their inter-relationality. Here also, it is Christ who determines the appropriateness of this image, since churches are "nere relation[s] in Christ."[35]

33. Article XLVII.
34. In Lumpkin, *Baptist Confessions*, 168–69.
35. *ARPB*, 117–18.

One of the primary functions of Associational gatherings was the task of enquiring of the Lord what Christ legislated for his church.[36] Underlying this commitment to communal discernment was the conviction that Christ, the head of the body, would not leave his people ignorant of his intentions for the church. This conviction had possessed Henry Jacob in 1605 when writing *Principles and Foundations of the Christian Religion*, and determined his commitment to the formation of a church conformed to the will of Christ as King. This theological principle he bequeathed to the churches which emerged from his congregational innovation in 1616, and became the *norma normans* of the ecclesiology of the English Calvinistic Baptists in the period 1640–1660.

While a number of scholars have undertaken to write the history of the seventeenth century Calvinistic Baptists it is to be hoped that this work makes a contribution to the theological interpretation of their congregational organization, and highlights the contribution of the early Calvinistic Baptists to the ecclesiological controversies of the period.

36. Ibid., 131.

Bibliography

Abbot W. C. ed. *The Writings and Speeches of Oliver Cromwell*. 4 vols. Cambridge, MA: Clarendon, 1937–47.
Acheson, R. J. *Radical Puritans in England 1550–1660*. London: Longman, 1990.
Adis, H. "Baptist Literature till 1688." *Transactions of the Baptist Historical Society* 1 (1908) 114–20.
Ames, W. *The Marrow of Sacred Divinity, Drawne Ovt of the Holy Scriptures therof, and brought into Method*. London: Edward Griffin, 1643.
Anon. "Baptist Churches Before 1660." *Transactions of the Baptist Historical Society* 2 (1910) 236–54.
———. "The Baptist Doctrine of the Church." *Baptist Quarterly* 12 (1946) 440–48.
———. *Certain Quaeries Humbly Presented In Way of Petition*. London: n.p., 1648.
———. *The Complaining Testimony of Some . . . of Sions Children*. London: n.p., 1656.
———. *A Declaration by Congregational Societies*. London: M. Simmons, 1647.
———. *A Declaration of Divers Elders and Brethren of Congregationall Societies, in and about the City of London*. London: M. Simmons, 1651.
———. *The Humble Petition and Representation of Several Churches of God in London, commonly (though falsly) called Anabaptists*. London: Francis Tyton and John Playford, 1649.
———. "London Baptists in 1638." *Baptist Quarterly* 6 (1932) 149.
———. "Rise of the Particular Baptists in London, 1633–1644." *Transactions of the Baptist Historical Society* 1 (1908) 226–36.
Avis, P. D. L. *The Church in the Theology of the Reformers*. London: Marshall, Morgan and Scott, 1981.
———. "'The True Church' in Reformation Theology." *Scottish Journal of Theology* 30.4 (1977) 319–45.
Backhouse, J. *Memoirs of Francis Howgill with Extracts from his Writings*. York: n.p., 1828.
Baillie, R. *Anabaptism the True Fountaine of . . . Errors*. London: n.p., 1647.
———. *The Letters and Journals of Robert Baillie*. 3 vols. Edinburgh: Alex Lawrie, 1841–42.
Bakewell, T. *A Confutation of the Anabaptists and All Others Who Affect Not Civill Government*. London: Printed by M.O. for T. Bankes, 1644.
Bakker, H. "Baptists in Amsterdam." *Baptist Quarterly* 43.4 (2009) 229–34.

Ballamie, R. *The Leper Clensed, or the Reduction of an erring Christian*. London: n.p., 1657.

Bannerman, J. *The Church of Christ vol.1*. Edinburgh: Banner of Truth Trust, 1960.

Barnard, J. "London Publishing, 1640–1660: Crisis, Continuity, and Innovation." *Book History* 4 (2001) 1–16.

Barrowe, H. *A Brief Discoverie of the False Church*. London: n.p., 1590.

Bastwick J. *The Utter Routing of the Whole Army of all the Independents and Sectaries, with the Total Overthrow of the Hierarchy that New Babel, more groundless than that of the Prelates*. London: John Macock, 1646.

Bebbington, D. "Baptist M.P.s in the Seventeenth and Eighteenth Centuries." *Baptist Quarterly* 28 (1980), 245–62.

Beeke, J. R. and Jones, M. *A Puritan Theology*. Grand Rapids: Reformation Heritage, 2012.

Belcher, R. P. and Mattia, T. *A Discussion of Seventeenth Century Baptist Confessions of Faith*. Columbia: Richbarry, 1983.

Bell, M. *Apocalypse How? Baptist Movements during the English Revolution*. Macon, GA: Mercer University Press, 2000.

———. "Freedom to Form: The Development of Baptist Movements during the English Revolution." In *Religion in Revolutionary England*, edited by Christopher Durston and Judith Maltby, 181–201. Manchester: Manchester University Press, 2006.

Belyea, G.L. "Origins of the Particular Baptists." *Themelios* 32.3 (2007) 40–66.

Birch, I. "The Counsel and Help of One Another." *BQ* 45.1 (2013) 4–29.

———. "Particular Baptists in the 1640s through the Eyes of their Enemies." In *Mirrors and Microscopes*, edited by C. Douglas Weaver, 25–38. Milton Keynes: Paternoster, 2015.

Birch, T., ed. *A Collection of the State Papers of John Thurloe*. 7 vols. London: n.p., 1742.

Black, J. W. "From Martin Bucer to Richard Baxter: "Discipline" and Reformation in Sixteenth and Seventeenth-Century England." *Church History* 70.4 (2001) 644–73.

Burroughes, J. *A Vindication of Mr. Borroughes*. London: n.p., 1646.

Bouwsma, W. J. *John Calvin: A Sixteenth Century Portrait*. Oxford: Oxford University Press, 1988.

Brachlow, S. *The Communion of Saints: Radical Puritan and Separatist Ecclesiology 1570-1625*. Oxford: Oxford University Press, 1988.

———. "The Elizabethan Roots of Henry Jacob's Churchmanship: Refocusing the Historiographical Lens." *The Journal of Ecclesiastical History* 36.2 (1985) 228–54.

———. "Puritan Theology and General Baptist Origins." *Baptist Quarterly* 31.4 (1985) 179–94.

Brackney, W. H. *A Genetic History of Baptist Thought*. Macon, GA: Mercer University Press, 2004.

Bradstock, A. *Radical Religion in Cromwell's England*. London: I.B. Taurus, 2011.

Brailsford, H. N. *The Levellers and the English Revolution*. London: Cresset, 1961.

Bray, G. "The 1552 Reform of English Church Discipline." *Churchman* 116.3 (2002) 201–19.

Briggs, J. "The Influence of Calvinism on Seventeenth-Century English Baptists." *Baptist History and Heritage* (2004) 8–25.

———."She-Preachers, Widows and Other Women: The Feminine Dimension in Baptist Life since 1600." *Baptist Quarterly* 31.7 (1986) 337–52.

Brookes, T. *God's Delight in the Progress of the Upright*. London: n.p., 1649.

Brown, D. "Christopher Blackwood: Portrait of a Seventeenth-Century Baptist." *Baptist Quarterly* 30.1 (1987) 28–38.
Brown, L. F. *The Political Activities of the Baptists and Fifth Monarchy Men in England During the Interregnum*. Washington: American Historical Society, 1912.
Brown, Raymond E., et al., eds. *The Jerome Biblical Commentary*. London: Geoffrey Chapman, 1968.
Bunyan, J. *A Case of Conscience Resolved*. London: Benjamin Alsop, 1683.
———. *Some Gospel-truths Opened*. London: n.p., 1656.
Burrage, C. *The Early English Dissenters in the Light of Recent Research (1550-1641)*. 2 vols. Cambridge: Cambridge University Press, 1912.
———. "The Fifth Monarchy Insurrections." *English Historical Review* 25.100 (1910) 722–47.
Burgess, W. "James Toppe and the Tiverton Anabaptists." *TBHS* 3.4 (1913) 193–211.
Bustin, D. "Hanserd Knollys and the Formation of Particular Baptist Identity in Seventeenth-Century London." In *Baptist Identities*, edited by I. M. Randall, T. Pilli, and A. Cross, 3–21. Milton Keynes: Paternoster, 2006.
Butterfield, R. "'The Royal Commission of King Jesus.' General Baptist Expansion and Growth 1640–1660." *Baptist Quarterly* 35.2 (1993) 56–80.
Calamy, E. *An Indictment Against England Because of Her Selfe-Murdering Divisions*. London: n.p., 1645.
Cameron, E. *The European Reformation*. Oxford: Oxford University Press, 1991.
Calvin, J. *Commentaries*. 22 vols. Grand Rapids: Baker, 1979.
———. *Institutes of the Christian Religion*. 2 vols. Edited by J. T. McNeill. Philadelphia: Westminster, 1960.
———. *Letters*. Vols. 1–4. Eugene: Wipf and Stock, 2007.
Canipe, L. "'That Most Damnable Heresie': John Smyth, Thomas Helwys, and Baptist ideas of Freedom." *Baptist Quarterly* 40.7 (2004) 389–411.
Capp, B. S. "The Cry of a Stone, by Anna Trapnel." *English Historical Review* 118.475 (2003) 223–24.
———. *The Fifth Monarchy Men*. London: n.p., 1972.
———. "A Door of Hope Re-opened: The Fifth Monarchy, King Charles and King Jesus." *Journal of Religious History* 32.1 (2008) 16–30.
Carroll, K. "Early Quakers and 'Going Naked as a Sign.'" *Quaker History* 67.2 (1978) 69–87.
Carruthers, S. W. *The Everyday Work of the Westminster Assembly*. Philadelphia: Presbyterian Historical Society, 1943.
Chadwick, O. *The Early Reformation on the Continent*. Oxford: Oxford University Press, 2001.
Child, R. L. "The Priesthood of All Believers." *Baptist Quarterly* 16.2 (1955) 99–108.
Chidley K. *The Justification of Independent Churches*. London: n.p., 1641.
Chown, J. L. "Baptists in the State Papers, 1632–1636." *Transactions of the Baptist Historical Society* 5 (1916) 144–53.
Clarke E. "The Legacy of Mothers and Others: Women's Theological Writing, 1640–60." In *Religion in Revolutionary England*, edited by Christopher Durston and Judith Maltby, 69–90. Manchester: Manchester University Press, 2006.
Claxton, L. *The Lost Sheep Found*. London: n.p., 1660.
Clouse, R. "The Apocalyptic Interpretation of Thomas Brightman and Joseph Meade." *Bulletin of the Evangelical Theological Society* 11.4 (1968) 181–93.

Coffey, J. *John Goodwin and the Puritan Revolution: Religion and Intellectual Change in 17th-Century England*. Suffolk: Boydell, 2006.

———. *Persecution and Toleration in Protestant England 1558–1689*. Essex: Pearson, 2000.

———. *Politics, Religion and the British Revolutions: The Mind of Samuel Rutherford*. Cambridge: Cambridge University Press, 1997.

———. "The Toleration Controversy During the English Revolution." In *Religion in Revolutionary England*, edited by Christopher Durston and Judith Maltby, 42–68. Manchester: Manchester University Press, 2006.

Coffey, J. and P. Lim. *The Cambridge Companion to Puritanism*. Cambridge: Cambridge University Press, 2008.

Coggins, J. R. *John Smyth's Congregation: English Separatism, Mennonite Influence, and the Elect Nation*. Waterloo, ON: Herald, 1991.

———. "The Theological Positions of John Smyth." *Baptist Quarterly* 30.6 (1984) 247–64.

Coker, J. L. "'Cast Out From Among the Saints': Church Discipline among Anabaptists and English Separatists in Holland, 1590–1620." *Reformation* 11.1 (2006) 1–27.

Collier, J. T. "The Sources Behind the First London Confession." *American Baptist Quarterly* 21.2 (2002) 197–214.

Collier, T. *Certain Queries or, Points in Controvery now Examined*. London: n.p., 1645.

———. "A Discovery of the New Creation, A Sermon at Putney." In *Puritanism and Liberty: Being the Army Debates (1647)*, edited by A. S. P. Woodhouse, 390–96. London: Dent, 1938.

———. *The Exaltation of Christ, The Alone High-Priest of SAINTS*. 2nd ed. London: Giles Calvert, 1647.

———. *First General Epistle to the Saints*. London: n.p., 1648.

———. *The Marrow of Christianity*. London: n.p., 1647.

———. *The Pulpit-Guard Routed in Its Twenty Strongholds*. London: Giles Calvert, 1651.

———. *The Right Constitution and True Subjects of the Visible Church of Christ*. London: Henry Hills, 1654.

———. *A Sober and Moderate Answer to Nehemiah Coxe's Invective (pretended) Refutation (as He Saith) of the Gross Errors and Heresies Asserted by Thomas Collier, In His Additional Word, Wherein His Refutation is Examined and Found too Light*. London: n.p., 1677.

Collins, H. *Believers Baptism From Heaven and of Divine Institution*. London: J. Hancock, 1691.

Collins, J. R. "The Church Settlement of Oliver Cromwell." *History* 87.285 (2002) 18–40.

Collins, W. J. "The General Baptists and the Friends." *Transactions of the Baptist Historical Society* 5 (1916) 65–73.

Collinson, P. *The Elizabethan Puritan Movement*. Oxford: Clarendon, 1967.

———. *From Cranmer to Sancroft*. London: Continuum, 2006.

Copson, S. "Advocate of the Reformed Protestant Religion: The Writings (1645–58) of William Kaye, Yorkshire Puritan." *Baptist Quarterly* 35.6 (1994), 279–93.

Cotton, J. *The Keyes of the Kingdom of Heaven*. London: M. Simmons for Henry Overton, 1644.

Couenhoven, J. "St. Augustine's Doctrine of Original Sin." *Augustinian Studies* 36.2 (2005) 359–96.

Coward, B. *The Stuart Age: England 1603-1714*. 2nd ed. London: Longman, 1994.
———, ed. *A Companion to Stuart Britain*. Oxford: Blackwell, 2003.
Coxe, Benjamin, et al. *A Declaration Concerning the Publike Dispute*. London: n.p., 1645.
Coxe, N. *Vindiciae Veritatis*. London: n.p., 1677.
Crosby, T. *The History of the English Baptists, from the Reformation to the Beginning of the Reign of King George I*. 4 vols. London: n.p., 1738–40.
Cross, A. R., and N. J. Wood. *Exploring Baptist Origins*. Oxford: Regents Park College, 2010.
Cross, C. "The Church in England 1646–1660." In *The Interregnum: The Quest for Settlement 1646-1660*, edited by G. E. Aylmer, 99–120. London: Macmillan, 1974.
———. *Church and People: England 1450-1660* 2nd ed. Oxford: Blackwell, 1999.
———. "'He-Goats Before the Flocks': A Note on the Part Played by Women in the Founding of some Civil War Churches." *Studies in Church History* 8 (1972) 195–202.
Dailey, B. R. "The Visitation of Sarah Wight: Holy Carnival and the Revolution of the Saints in Civil War London." *Church History* 55.4 (1986) 438–55.
Dale, R. W. *History of English Congregationalism*. London: Hodder and Stoughton, 1907.
Danker, F. W., ed. *A Greek English Lexicon of the New Testament and Other Early Christian Literature*. Chicago: Chicago University Press, 2000.
Davies, H. *Worship and Theology in England: From Cranmer to Baxter and Fox, 1534-1690*. 5 vols. Grand Rapids: Eerdmanns, 1996.
Davies, W. D. and D. C. Allison. *Matthew* vol. 2. Edinburgh: T. & T. Clark, 1991.
Dell, W. *Right Reformation: Or, the Reformation of the Church of the New Testament represented in Gospel-Light*. London: n.p., 1646.
Dellar, H. "The Influence of Martin Bucer on the English Reformation." *Churchman* 106.4 (1992) 351–56.
Dickens, A. G. *The English Reformation*2 (1989).
Doran, S., and C. Durston. *Princes, Pastors and People: The Church and Religion in England, 1500–1700*. London: Routledge, 2003.
Dowley, T.E. "Baptists and Discipline in the Seventeenth Century." *Baptist Quarterly* 24.4 (1971) 157–66.
———. "A London Congregation during the Great Persecution: Petty France Particular Baptist Church, 1641–1688." *Baptist Quarterly* 27.5 (1978), 233–39.
Downame, J. et al. *A Testimony to the Truth of Jesus Christ and to our Solemn League and Covenant*. London: n.p., 1647.
Duesing, J. "Henry Jacob (1563–1624) Pastoral Theology and Congregational Ecclesiology." *Baptist Quarterly* 43.5 (2010) 284–301.
Durnbaugh, D. "Baptists and Quakers—Left Wing Puritans?" *Quaker History* 62.2 (1973) 67–82.
Durso, P. "Baptists and the Turn Toward Baptist Women in Ministry." In *Turning Points in Baptist History*, edited by M. E. Williams and W. B. Shurden, 275–87. Macon, GA: Mercer University Press, 2008.
Durston, C., and J. Maltby, eds. *Religion in Revolutionary England*. Manchester: Manchester University Press, 2006.
Dynes, R. "Church-Sect Typology and Socio-Economic Status." *American Sociological Review* 20 (1955) 555–60.

Eastwood, C. *The Priesthood of All Believers*. Reprint. Eugene, OR: Wipf and Stock, 1960.

———. *The Royal Priesthood of the Faithful*. Reprint. Eugene, OR: Wipf and Stock, 1963.

Edwards, T. *Antapologia*. London: n.p., 1644.

———. *Gangraena*. 3 parts. London: n.p., 1646.

———. *Reasons Against the Independent Government of Particular Congregations*. London: n.p., 1641.

Estep, W. R. "The Nature and Use of Biblical Authority in Baptist Confessions of Faith, 1610–1963." *Baptist History and Heritage* 22.4 (1987) 3–16.

———. *The Anabaptist Story*. Grand Rapids: Eerdmans, 1996.

Evans, G. R. *John Wyclif*. Oxford: Lion, 2005.

Farrar, A. J. D. "Cromwell as Dictator." *Baptist Quarterly* 7 (1934) 193–201.

———. "The Fifth Monarchy Movement." *TBHS* 2.3 (1911) 166–81.

Feake, C. *A Beam of Light Shining in the Midst*. London: n.p., 1659.

Featly, D. *The Dippers Dipt*. London: n.p., 1645.

Fiddes, P. "Church and Sect: Cross-Currents in Early Baptist Life." In *Exploring Baptist Origins*, edited by A. R. Cross and N. J. Wood, 33–57. Oxford: Regent's Park College, 2010.

———. *Tracks and Traces: Baptist Identity in Church and Theology*. Milton Keynes: Paternoster, 2003.

———. *Under the Rule of Christ*. Oxford: Regents Park College, 2008.

Fincham, K. C. "Ramifications of the Hampton Court Conference in the Dioceses, 1603–1609." *The Journal of Ecclesiastical History* 36.2 (1985) 208–27.

———, ed. *The Early Stuart Church*. Basingstoke: Macmillan, 1993.

Firth, C. H. "Cromwell and the Expulsion of the Long Parliament in 1653." *English Historical Review* 8.31 (1893) 526–34.

———. *The Clarke Papers*. London: The Historical Society, 1992.

Ford, J. "A Seventeenth Century Baptist Church: Bromsgrove." *Transactions of the Baptist Historical Society* 1 (1908) 100–6.

Foster, H. D. "Geneva Before Calvin." *American Historical Review* 8 (1902) 217–40.

Freeman, C. "Visionary Women Among Early Baptists." *Baptist Quarterly* 43.5 (2010) 260–83.

———, ed. *A Company of Women Preachers: Baptist Prophetesses in Seventeenth Century England*. Waco: Baylor University Press, 2011.

Gardiner, S. R., ed. *The Constitutional Documents of the Puritan Revolution, 1625–1660*. 3rd ed. Oxford: Clarendon, 1906.

Gentles, I. "London Levellers in the English Revolution: the Chidleys and Their Circle." *The Journal of Ecclesiastical History* 29.3 (1978) 281–309.

———. "Chidley, Katherine (fl. 1616–1653)." In *Oxford Dictionary of National Biography*, edited by H. C. G. Matthew and Brian Harrison. Oxford: OUP, 2004.

George, T. *John Robinson and the English Separatist Tradition*. Macon: Mercer University Press, 2005.

———. *Theology of the Reformers*. Nashville: Broadman, 1988.

Gerrish, B. "The Place of Calvin in Christian Theology." In *The Cambridge Companion to John Calvin*, edited by Donald McKim, 289–304. Cambridge: CUP, 2004.

Gillespie, K. *Domesticity and Dissent in the Seventeenth Century: English Women's Writing and the Public Sphere*. Cambridge: Cambridge University Press, 2004.

Goertz, Hans-Jurgen. *The Anabaptists*. London: Routledge, 1988.
Goodwin, T, et al. *An Apologeticall Narration, Humbly Submitted to the Honourable Houses of Parliament*. London: Robert Dawlman, 1643.
———. *The Government of the Churches of Christ*, in *The Works of Thomas Goodwin* Vol. 6. Edinburgh: James Nichol, 1865.
———. "Memoir of Dr, Thomas Goodwin." In *The Works of Thomas Goodwin, D. D.*, Vol. 2. Edinburgh: James Nichol, 1861.
Gould, G. P. "The Origins of the Modern Baptist Denomination." *Transactions of the Baptist Historical Society* 2 (1910) 193–212.
Gouldbourne, R. "'This Sad Work': Scandal in Broadmead." *Baptist Quarterly* 39.3 (2001) 146–52.
Greaves, R. L. "Hobson, Paul (d. 1666)." In *Oxford Dictionary of National Biography*, edited by H. C. G. Matthew and Brian Harrison. Oxford: OUP, 2004. Online ed.,
———. "John Bunyan's "Holy War" and London Nonconformity." *Baptist Quarterly* 26.4 (1975) 158–68.
———."The Ordination Controversy and the Spirit of Reform in Puritan England." *The Journal of Ecclesiastical History* 21.3 (1970) 225–41.
———. "Patient, Thomas (d. 1666)." In *Oxford Dictionary of National Biography*, edited by H. C. G. Matthew and Brian Harrison. Oxford: OUP, 2004.
Green, S. W. "To Sions Virgins, 1644." *Transactions of the Baptist Historical Society* 4 (1914) 162–72.
Ha, P. *English Presbyterianism, 1590–1640*. Stanford: Stanford University Press, 2011.
Haigh, C., ed. *The English Reformation Revised*. Cambridge: Cambridge University Press, 1987.
Hall, D. D. *The Faithful Shepherd: A History of the New England Ministry in the Seventeenth Century*. Chapel Hill: The University of North Carolina Press, 1972.
Haller, W. and G. Davies, eds. *The Leveller Tracts 1647–1653*. New York: Columbia University Press, 1944.
Haller, W. *Foxe's Book of Martyrs and the Elect Nation*. London: Jonathan Cape, 1963.
Hardacre, P. N. "William Allen, Cromwellian Agitator and 'Fanatic.'" *Baptist Quarterly* 19.7 (1962) 292–308.
Harmon, S. R. "Baptist Confessions of Faith and the Patristic Tradition." *Perspectives in Religious Studies* 29.4 (2002) 349–58.
Harrison, W. "The Renewal of the Practice of Adult Baptism by Immersion During the Reformation Era, 1525–1700." *Restoration Quarterly* 43.2 (2001) 95–112.
Hayden, R. "The Particular Baptist Confession 1689 and Baptists Today." *Baptist Quarterly* 32.8 (1988) 403–17.
Haykin, M. A. G. *Kiffin, Knollys and Keach*. Leeds: Reformation Trust Today, 1996.
Haykin, M. A. G., and M. Jones. *Drawn Into Controversie: Reformed Theological Diversity and Debates Within Seventeenth-Century British Puritanism*. Oakville: Vandenhoeck & Ruprecht, 2011.
Haymes, B., et al., *On Being the Church*. Milton Keynes: Paternoster, 2008.
Hedger, V. "Some Experiences of a Woman Minister." *Baptist Quarterly* 10 (1940) 243–53.
Hendel, K. "The Doctrine of the Ministry: The Reformation Heritage." *Currents in Theology and Mission* 17.1 (1990) 23–33.
Heron, A., ed. *The Westminster Confession in the Church Today*. Edinburgh: Saint Andrew, 1982.

Bibliography

Hill, C. *The Century of Revolution*. London: Routledge, 1980.

———. *The English Bible and the Seventeenth Century Revolution*. London: Penguin, 1993.

———. *God's Englishman: Oliver Cromwell and the English Revolution*. London: Penguin, 2000.

———. "History and Denominational History." *Baptist Quarterly* 22 (1967) 65–71.

———. *Society and Puritanism in Pre-Revolutionary England*. London: Secker and Warburg, 1964.

———. *A Turbulent, Seditious, and Factious People: John Bunyan and His Church*. Oxford: Oxford University Press, 1988.

———. *The World Turned Upside Down: Radical Ideas During the English Revolution*. London: Penguin, 1991.

Hill, R. "The Theory and Practice of Excommunication in Mediaeval England." *History* 42.144 (1957) 1–11.

Hillerbrand, H., ed. *Oxford Encyclopedia of the Reformation*. Vol. 1. Oxford: Oxford University Press, 1996.

Himbury, D. M. "The Religious Beliefs of the Levellers." *Baptist Quarterly* 15.6 (1954) 269–76.

Hobson, P. *Christ the Effect not the Cause of the Love of God*. London: n.p., 1645.

———. *The Fallacy of Infants Baptisme Discovered*. London: n.p., 1646.

———. *Fourteen Queries and ten Absurdities about the extent of Christ's Death*. London: 1655.

———. *Innocency, though Under a Cloud, Cleared*. London: n.p., 1664.

Hoile, D. "The Levellers: Libertarian Radicalism and the English Civil War." *Libertarian Heritage* 5 (1992) 2–15.

Holmes, C. *The Eastern Association in the English Civil War*. Cambridge: Cambridge University Press, 1974.

Höpfl, H. *The Christian Polity of John Calvin*. Cambridge: Cambridge University Press, 1982.

Horning, E. B. "The Rule of Christ: An Exposition of Matthew 18:15–20." *Brethren Life and Thought* 38.2 (1993) 69–107.

Horsch, J. "Did Menno Simons Practice Baptism by Immersion." *Mennonite Quarterly Review* 1.1 (1927) 54–56.

How, S. *The Sufficiencie of the Spirits Teaching without Humane Learning*. Amsterdam, 1640.

Howard, L. *A Looking-Glass for Baptists*. London: n.p., 1672.

Howson, Barry, H. *Erroneous and Schismatical Opinions: The Question of Orthodoxy Regarding the Theology of Hanserd Knollys (c. 1599–1691)*. Leiden: Brill, 2001.

Hubberthorn, R. *An Answer to a Declaration put forth by the general Consent, of the People called Ananbaptists In and about the City of London*. London: Thomas Simmons, 1659.

Hughes, A. *Seventeenth-Century England: A Changing Culture*. vol. 1. Primary Sources. London: The Open University, 1980.

———. "The Pulpit Guarded: Confrontations between Orthodox and Radicals in Revolutionary England." In *John Bunyan and His England 1628–88*, edited by Anne Laurence, W. R. Owens, Stuart Sim, 31–50. London: Hambledon, 1990.

———. "'The Public Profession of these Nations': The National Church in Interregnum England." In *Religion in Revolutionary England*, edited by Christopher Durston and Judith Maltby, 93–114. Manchester: Manchester University Press, 2006.

———. *Gangraena and the Struggle for the English Revolution*. Oxford: Oxford University Press, 2004.

Hutchinson, E. *A Treatise Concerning the Covenant and Baptism*. London: 1676.

Hutchinson, L. *Memoirs of the Life of Colonel Hutchinson*. London: Keegan Paul, 1904.

Ivimey, J. *A History of the English Baptists*. 4 vols. London: n.p., 1811.

Jacob, H. *An Attestation of Many Learned, Godly, and Famous Divines, Lightes of Religion, and Pillars of the Gospell Iustifying This Doctrine, Viz. That the Church-Governement Ought to Bee Always with the Peoples Free Consent. Also This; That a True Church Vnder the Gospell Contayneth No More Ordinary Congregations but One*. Middelburg: G. Thorp, 1613.

———. *A Confession and Protestation of the Faith of Certaine Christians*. Middelburg: G. Thorp, 1616.

———. *A Declaration and Plainer Opening of Certain Points with a Sound Confirmation of some other, contained in a treatise intituled. The Divince Beginning and Institution of Christes true visible and ministeriall Church*. Middelburg: G. Thorp, 1611.

———. *The Divine Beginning and Institution of Christ's True Visible and Ministeriall Church*. Leyden: Henry Hastings, 1610.

Jansen, J. F. *Calvin's Doctrine of the Work of Christ*. London: James Clarke, 1956.

Jessey, H. *A Calculation for this Present Year, 1645*. London: n.p., 1645.

———. *Exceeding Riches of Grace Advanced by the Spirit of Grace, in an Empty Nothing Creature*. London: Matthew Simmons, 1647.

———. *A Storehouse of Provision*. London: n.p., 1650.

Jewson, C. B. "General and Particular Churches." *Baptist Quarterly* 9 (1938) 432.

———. "St Mary's Norwich." *Baptist Quarterly* 10.2 (1940) 108–17.

Johnson, A. F. "The Exiled English Church at Amsterdam and its Press." *The Library* 5.4 (1951) 219–42.

Johnson, B. "On Church and Sect." *American Sociological Review* 28.4 (1963) 539–49.

Johnson, S. "'The Sinews of the Body of Christ' Calvin's Concept of Church Discipline." *Westminster Theological Journal* 59 (1997) 87–100.

Jones, M. "Why Heaven Kissed Earth: The Christology of Thomas Goodwin (1600–1680)." PhD diss., University of Leiden, 1980.

Jones R. M., ed. *The Journal of George Fox*. Indiana: Friends United, 2006.

Jones, S. R. "The Invisible Church of the Westminster Confession of Faith." *Westminster Theological Journal* 59 (1997) 71–85.

Jordan, W. K. *Development of Religious Toleration in England*, 4 vols. London: George Allen & Unwin, 1932–40.

Jue, J. K. "Puritan Millenarianism in Old and New England." In *The Cambridge Companion to Puritanism*, edited by John Coffey and Paul Lim, 259–76. Cambridge: Cambridge University Press, 2008.

Kaplan, L. "Presbyterians and Independents in 1643." *The English Historical Review* 84.331 (1969) 244–56.

Keeble, N. H. *The Cambridge Companion to Writing of the English Revolution*. Cambridge: Cambridge University Press, 2001.

Kendal, R. T. *Calvin and English Calvinism to 1649*. Oxford: Oxford University Press, 1979.

Bibliography

Kenyon, J. P. *The Stuart Constitution 1603-1688: Documents and Commentary.* Cambridge: Cambridge University Press, 1966.

Kiffin, W. *A Briefe Remonstrance of the Reasons and Grounds of those People commonly Called Anabaptists, for their Seperation, &c.* London: n.p., 1645.

———. *The Life and Death of . . . Mr Hanserd Knollys.* London: 1692.

Killcop, T. *The Unlimitted Authority of Christ's Disciples Cleared, or The Present Church or Ministry Vindicated.* London: n.p., 1651.

King, D. *A Way to Sion Sought out, and Found for Believers to Walke in.* London: n.p., 1649.

Kingdon, R. "The Control of Morals in Calvin's Geneva." In *The Social History of the Reformation*, edited by Lawrence P. Buck and Jonathan W. Zophy, 3-16. Columbus: Ohio State University Press, 1972.

Kingsley, G. "Opposition to Early Baptists (1638-1645)." *Baptist History and Heritage*, 4.1 (1969).

Kirby, E. W. "The English Presbyterians in the Westminster Assembly." *Church History* 33.4 (1964) 418-28.

Kirkland, T. "This Sad Work: The Case of Mary Smith of Broadmead: A Rejoinder." *Baptist Quarterly* 39.4 (2001) 199-203.

Knollys, H. *A Moderate Answer unto Dr. Bastwicks Book Called "Independecy Not God's Ordinance."* London: Jane Coe, 1645.

———. *The Shining of a Flaming Fire in Zion. Or a Clear Answer unto 13 Exceptions Against the Grounds of New Baptism (So Called in Mr. Saltmarsh His Book Intituled, The Smoke in the Temple).* London: Jane Coe, 1646.

Kreitzer, L. J. "1653 or 1656: When did Oxford Baptists Join the Abingdon Association." In *Researching the Past or History? Studies in Baptist Historiography and Myths*, edited by Philip E. Thompson and Anthony R. Cross, 207-19. Milton Keynes: Paternoster, 2005.

———. "The Fifth Monarchist John Pendarves (d. 1656): A Victim of "Studious Bastard Consumption"?" In *Researching the Past or History? Studies in Baptist Historiography and Myths*, edited by Philip E. Thompson and Anthony R. Cross, 220-30. Milton Keynes: Paternoster, 2005.

———. "The Fifth Monarchist John Pendarves: Chaplain to Colonel Thomas Rainborowe's Regiment of Foot (1645-47)." *Baptist Quarterly* 43.2 (2009) 112-22.

———. "A Letter of John Pendarves from 1656." *Baptist Quarterly* 43.2 (2009) 49-55.

———. *William Kiffen and his World (Part 1 and Part 2).* Oxford: Regent's Park College, 2010.

Lake, P. "Calvinism and the English Church 1570-1635." *Past & Present* 114 (1987) 32-76.

———. "The Laudian Style." In *The Early Stuart Church*, edited by Kenneth Fincham, 161-85. Basingstoke: n.p., 1993.

———. *Moderate Puritans and the Elizabethan Church.* Cambridge: CUP, 1982.

———. "The Significance of the Elizabethan Identification of the Pope as Antichrist." *The Journal of Ecclesiastical History* 31.2 (1980) 161-78.

———. "William Bradshaw, Antichrist and the Community of the Godly." *The Journal of Ecclesiastical History* 36.4 (1985) 570-89.

Lamont, W. *Godly Rule: Politics and Religion 1603-60.* London: n.p., 1969.

———. *Richard Baxter and the Millennium.* London: Croom Helm, 1979.

Land, R. D. "Doctrinal Controversies of English Particular Baptists (1644-1691) as Illustrated by the Career and Writings of Thomas Collier." D.Phil diss., Oxford University, 1980.

Langley, A.S. "Seventeenth Century Baptist Disputations." *Transactions of the Baptist Historical Society* 6 (1918) 216-43.

———. "John Tombes as a Correspondent." *Transactions of the Baptist Historical Society* 7 (1920) 13-18.

Laurence, A., et al. *John Bunyan and his England 1628-88*. London: Hambledon, 1990.

Laurence, A. "A Priesthood of She-Believers: Women and Congregations in Mid-Seventeenth Century England." *Studies in Church History* 27 (1990) 345-63.

Lilburne, J. *An Impeachment of High Treason Against Oliver Cromwell*. London: 1649.

Lindberg, C. *The European Reformations*. Oxford: Blackwell, 1996.

Liu, T. *Discord in Zion: The Puritan Divines and the Puritan Revolution 1640-1660*. The Hague: Martinus Nijhoff, 1973.

Loader, C., and Alexander, J. C. "Max Weber on Churches and Sects in North America: An Alternative Path Toward Rationalization." *Sociological Theory* 3.1 (1985) 1-6.

Lockyer, R. *The Early Stuarts: A Political History of England 1603-1642*. London: Longman, 1989.

Loewenstein, D. "Scriptural Exegesis, Female Prophecy and Radical Prophecy in Mary Cary." *Studies in English Literature 1500-1900* 46.1 (2006) 133-53.

Long, J. "William Perkins: 'Apostle of Practical Divinity.'" *Churchman* 103.1 (1989) 53-59.

Love, C. *Short and Plaine Animadversions on Some Passages in Mr. Del's Sermon*. London: n.p., 1646.

Lumpkin, W. L. *Baptist Confessions of Faith*. Valley Forge: Judson, 1969.

———. "The Nature and Authority of Baptist Confessions of Faith." *Review and Expositor* 76.1 (1979) 17-28.

———. "The Bible in Early Baptist Confessions of Faith." *Baptist History and Heritage* 19.3 (1984) 33-41.

Luomanen, P. "Corpus Mixtum: An Appropriate Description of Matthew's Community?" *JBL* 117.3 (1998) 469-80.

Luther, M. *Works*. Edited by James Atkinson. Philadelphia: Fortress, 1966.

Luz, U. *Matthew 8-20*. Minneapolis: Fortress, 2001.

MacLear, J. F. "The Making of the Lay Tradition." *The Journal of Religion* 33.2 (1953) 113-36.

———, J. F. "Popular Anticlericalism in the Puritan Revolution." *Journal of the History of Ideas* 17.4 (1956) 443-70.

Mack, P. *Visionary Women: Ecstatic Prophecy in Seventeenth Century England*. Berkeley: University of California Press, 1992.

Mackenzie, J. "1689 and all that: An Exploration of the Function and Form of the Second London Baptist Confession of Faith." *Baptist Quarterly* 42.1 (2008) 555-68.

Maltby, J. *Prayer Book and People in Elizabethan and Early Stuart England*. Cambridge: Cambridge University Press, 1998.

Mansel, J. *Welsh Baptists Studies*. South Wales: South Wales Baptist College, 1976.

Marshall, S. *A Sermon of the Baptizing of Infants*. London: Richard Cotes for Stephen Bowtell, 1644.

Mayer, F. E. "The Proper Distinction Between Law and Gospel and the Terminology Visible and Invisible Church." *Concordia Theological Monthly* 25.3 (1954) 177-98.

Mayfield, N. H. *Puritans and Regicides: Presbyterian-Independent Differences over the Trial and Execution of Charles (I) Stuart.* Maryland: Rowman & Littlefield, 1988.

McBeth, H. L. *The Baptist Heritage: Four Centuries of Baptist Witness.* Nashville: Broadman, 1987.

McCulloh, G. W. *Christ's Person and Life-Work in the Theology of Albrecht Ritschl with Special Attention to Munus Triplex.* Maryland: University Press of America, 1990.

McGlothlin, W. J. "Dr. Daniel Featley and the First Calvinistic Baptist Confession." *The Review and Expositor* 6.4 (1909) 579–89.

———. *Baptist Confessions of Faith.* Philadelphia: American Baptist Publication Society, 1911.

McGregor, J. F. "The Baptists: Fount of All Heresy." In *Radical Religion in the English Revolution,* edited by J. F. McGregor and B. Reay, 23–63. Oxford: Oxford University Press, 1984.

McGregor, J. F., and B. Reay, eds. *Radical Religion in the English Revolution.* Oxford: Oxford University Press, 1984.

McKim, D., ed. *The Cambridge Companion to John Calvin.* Cambridge: CUP, 2004.

Metzger, B. *A Textual Commentary on the Greek New Testament.* London: United Bible Societies, 1975.

Mikolaski, Samuel J. "The Contemporary Relevance of the Priesthood of all Christians." *Southwestern Journal of Theology* 30.2 (1988) 6–14.

Miles, J. *An Antidote Against the Infection of the Times.* London: T. Brewster, 1656.

Milner, B. C. *Calvin's Doctrine of the Church.* Leiden: E. J. Brill, 1970.

Morgan, D. "John Myles (1621–83) and the Future of Ilston's Past." *Baptist Quarterly* 38.4 (1999) 176–84.

Morrill, J., ed. *Reactions to the English Civil War.* London: Macmillan, 1982.

———. "The Church in England, 1642–9." In *Reactions to the English Civil War,* edited by J. Morrill, 89–114. London: Macmillan, 1982.

Nagel, N. "Luther and the Priesthood of All Believers." *Concordia Theological Quarterly* 61.4 (1997) 277–98.

Naphy, W. G. *Calvin and the Consolidation of the Genevan Reformation.* Manchester: Manchester University Press, 1994.

Nelson, S. A. "Reflecting on Baptist Origins: The London Confession of Faith of 1644." *Baptist History and Heritage* 29 (1994) 33–46.

Nevitt, M. "Elizabeth Poole Writes the Regicide." *Women's Writing* 9.2 (2002) 233–48.

Niebuhr, H. Richard. *The Social Sources of Denominationalism.* New York: Meridian, 1957.

Nuttall, G. F. "Abingdon Revisited 1656–1675." *Baptist Quarterly* 36.2 (1995) 96–103.

———. "Association Records of the Particular Baptists." *Baptist Quarterly* 26.1 (1975) 14–25.

———. "The Baptist Western Association 1653–1658." *Journal of Ecclesiastical History* 11 (1960) 213–18.

———. "Calvinism in Free Church History." *Baptist Quarterly* 22.8 (1968) 418–28.

———. *The Holy Spirit in Puritan Faith and Experience.* Chicago: University of Chicago Press, 1992.

———. "Thomas Collier—An Unrecorded Tract." *Baptist Quarterly* 28.1 (1979) 40–41.

———. *Visible Saints: The Congregational Way 1640–1660.* Oxford: Blackwell, 1957.

———. *The Welsh Saints 1640–1660.* Cardiff: University of Wales, 1957.

Orme, W. *Remarkable Passages in the Life of William Kiffin*. London: Burton and Smith, 1823.
Outhwaite, R. B. *The Rise and Fall of the English Ecclesiastical Courts, 1500-1860*. Cambridge: Cambridge University Press, 2006.
Overton, R. *An Arrow Against All Tyrants and Tyrany*. London: n.p., 1646.
———. *A Remonstrance of Many Thousand Citizens*. London: n.p., 1646.
———. *Vox Plebis*. London: n.p., 1646.
Owen, J. *The Works of John Owen*. Vol. 21. London: Richard Baynes, 1826.
Owens, B.G. "An Early Letter from the Church at Netherton, Gloucestershire, to the Church at Hay-on-Wye, Powys, 20 December 1650." *Baptist Quarterly* 35.8 (1994) 407-9.
———. *The Ilston Book*. Aberystwyth: The National Library of Wales, 1996.
Partee, C. *The Theology of John Calvin*. Louisville: John Knox, 2008.
Paul, R. S. *The Assembly of the Lord: Politics and Religion in the Westminster Assembly and the "Grand Debate."* Edinburgh: T. & T. Clark, 1985.
———. "Henry Jacob and Seventeenth-Century Puritanism." *The Hartford Quarterly* 7.3 (1967) 92-113.
Payne, E. A. "The Glass Yard Minute Book, 1682-1740." *Baptist Quarterly* 7.7 (1935) 321-24.
———. *The Free Churches*. London: SCM, 1944.
Pearson, S.C. "Reluctant Radicals: The Independents at the Westminster Assembly." *Journal of Church and State* 11 (1969) 473-86.
Peel, A. and L. H. Carlson, eds. *The Writings of Robert Harrison and Robert Browne*. London: George Allen and Unwin, 1953.
Pelikan, J. *The Christian Tradition*. Vol. 4. Chicago: The University of Chicago Press, 1984.
Pelikan, J., and V. Hotchkiss, eds. *Creeds and Confessions of Faith in the Christian Tradition Volumes I-IV*. New Haven: Yale University Press, 2003.
Perkins, W. *A Golden Chaine: or, The Description of Theologie, Containing the Order of the Causes of Salvation and Damnantion, according to Gods Word*. London: John Legatt, 1623.
Pettegree, A., ed. *The Reformation World*. London: Routledge, 2000.
Petto, S. *Infant Baptism of Christ's Appointment, or A Discovery of Infants Interest in the Covenant with Abraham, Shewing Who Are the Spiritual Seed and Who the Fleshly Seed*. London: Edward Giles, 1687.
Polizzotto, C. "Liberty of Conscience and the Whitehall Debates of 1648-49." *Journal of Ecclesiastical History* 26.1 (1975) 69-82.
———. "The Campaign against The Humble Proposals of 1652." *Journal of Ecclesiastical History* 38.4 (1987) 569-81.
Poole, E. *An Alarum of War, Given to the Army*. London: n.p., 1649.
Pooley, R. "Dell, William (d. 1669)." *Oxford Dictionary of National Biography* Oxford: Oxford University Press, 2004.
Powell, H. "October 1643: The Dissenting Brethren and the *Proton Dektikon*." In *Drawn Into Controversie: Reformed Theological Diversity and Debates Within Seventeenth-Century British Puritanism*, edited by M. A. G. Haykin, and M. Jones, 52-82. Oakville: Vandenhoeck & Ruprecht, 2011.
Powicke, F. J. *Henry Barrow Separatist (1550-1593) and the Exiled Church of Amsterdam (1593-1622)*. London: James Clarke, 1900.

———. "John Robinson and the Beginning of the Pilgrim Movement." *The Harvard Theological Review* 13.3 (1920) 252–89.
Powicke, F. T. "Richard Baxter's Relation to the Baptists, and His Proposed Terms of Communion." *Transactions of the Baptist Historical Society* 6 (1918) 193–215.
Provincial Assembly of London. *Jus Divinum Ministerii Evangelici. Or The Divine Right of the Gospel-Ministry: Divided into Two Parts*. London: G. Latham, J. Rothwell, S. Gellibrand, T. Underhill, and J. Cranford, 1654.
Prynne, W. *A Fresh Discovery of Some Prodigious New Wandring-Blazing-Stars, & Firebrands, Stiling Themselves New-Lights*. London: John Macock, 1645.
———. *The Sword of Christian Magistracy Supported*. London: 1647.
Randall, I. M. "'Counsel and Help': European Baptists and the Wider Baptist Fellowship." *Journal of European Baptist Studies* 11.1 (2010).
"Records of the Jacob-Lathorp-Jessey Church, 1616–1641." *Transactions of the Baptist Historical Society* 1 (1908) 203–25.
Reid, A. A. "Benjamin Keach, 1640." *Baptist Quarterly* 10 (1940) 67–78.
Renihan, J. M. "*Edification and Beauty: The Practical Ecclesiology of the Particular Baptists 1675–1705*. Eugene: Wipf & Stock, 2008.
———. An Examination of the Possible Influence of Menno Simons' *Foundation Book* upon the Particular Baptist Confession of 1644." *American Baptist Quarterly* 15.3 (1996) 190–207.
Rich, A. D. "Thomas Helwys' First Confession of Faith, 1610." *Baptist Quarterly* 43.4 (2009) 235–41.
Thomas Richards, "John Miles in Wales." *Baptist Quarterly* 5.8 (1931) 362–65.
Richardson, S. *Justification by Christ Alone*. London: n.p., 1647.
———. *Some Brief Considerations On Doctor* Featley *his Book Intituled, The Dipper Dipt*. London: n.p., 1645.
———. *The Necessity of Toleration in matters of Religion*. London: n.p., 1647.
Ricraft, J. *A Looking Glass for the Anabaptists and the Rest of the Separatists*. London: n.p., 1645.
Robinson, H. W. "Baptist Church Discipline 1689-1699." *Baptist Quarterly* 1.3 (1922) 112–28, 179–85.
———. "Faith and Creed." *Baptist Quarterly* 2 (1924) 348–57.
———. "The Works of John Smyth, 1603–1612." *Transactions of the Baptist Historical Society* 5 (1916) 1–7.
Rohr, J von. "*Extra Ecclesium Nulla Salus*. An Early Congregational Version." *Church History* 36.2 (1967) 107–21.
Richardson, S. *Certain Questions Propounded to the Assembly, to Answer by the Scriptures: Whether Corporall Punishments May be Inflicted upon Such as Hold Errours in Religion*. London: n.p., 1646.
Rupp, G. "Luther and the Doctrine of the Church." *Scottish Journal of Theology* 9.4 (1956) 384–92.
Russell, C., ed. *The Origins of the English Civil War*. London: Macmillan, 1975.
Russel, W. *Quakerism is Paganism*. London: n.p., 1674.
Saltmarsh, J. *Smoke in the Temple, Wherein is a Design for Peace and Reconciliation of Believers of the Several Opinions of these Times about Ordinances, to a Forbearance of each other in Love, and Meeknesse, and Humility*. London: n.p., 1646.
Schaff, P. *Bibliotheca Symbolica Ecclesiae Universalis, The Creeds of Christendom, with a History and Critical Notes*. New York: Harper and Brothers, 1877.

Schnackenburg, R. *The Gospel of Matthew*. Grand Rapids: Eerdmans, 2002.
Scott, J. *England's Troubles: Seventeenth-Century English Political Stability in European Context*. Cambridge: Cambridge University Press, 2000.
Seaman, L. *Solomons Choice*. London: n.p., 1644.
Sellars, I. "Edwardians, Anabaptists and the Problem of Baptist Origins." *Baptist Quarterly* 29.3 (1981) 97–112.
Shakespeare, J. H. *Baptist and Congregational Pioneers*.London: Kingsgate, 1906.
Sharpe, J. A. "Crime and Deliquancy in an Essex Parish 1600-1640." In *Crime in England 1550-1800*, edited by J. S. Cockburn, 90–109. London: Methuen, 1977.
Sharpe, K. "Archbishop Laud." In *Reformation to Revolution: Politics and Religion in Early Modern England*, edited by M. Todd, 71–77. London: Routledge, 1995.
Shaw, W. *A History of the English Church During the Civil Wars and Under the Commonwealth 1640-1660*, 2 vols. London: Longmans, Green, and Co., 1900.
Shriver, F. "Hampton Court Re-visited: James I and the Puritans." *The Journal of Ecclesiastical History* 33.1 (1982) 48–71.
Shurden, W. *The Doctrine of the Priesthood of Believers*. Nashville: Convention, 1987.
———, ed. *Proclaiming the Baptist Vision: The Priesthood of All Believers*. Macon, GA: Smyth & Helwys, 1993.
Spilsberie, J. *God's Ordinance, The Saints Priviledge*. London: M. Simmons, 1646.[1]
Spilsbery, J. *A Treatise Concerning the Lawfull Subiect of Baptisme*. London: n.p. 1643.
Spittlehouse, J. *The Army Vindicated in their late Dissolution of the Parliament*. London: 1653.
Sprunger, K. L. "William Ames, A Seventeenth Century Puritan, Looks at the Anabaptists." *Mennonite Quarterly Review* 39.1 (1965) 72–74.
———. "Archbishop Laud's Campaign Against Puritanism at The Hague." *Church History* 44 (1975) 308–20.
———. *Dutch Puritanism: A History of English and Scottish Churches of the Netherlands in the Sixteenth and Seventeenth Centuries*. Leiden: E. J. Brill, 1982.
Spurstowe, W. *Englands Eminent Judgements Caus'd by the Abuse of Gods Eminent Mercies*. London: n.p., 1644.
Stark, W. *The Sociology of Religion*. Vols. 1–5. London: Routledge, 1961–72.
Stassen, G.H. "Anabaptist Influences in the Origin of the Particular Baptists." *Mennonite Quarterly Review* 36.4 (1962) 322–48.
———. "Opening Menno Simons's Foundation-Book and Finding the Father of Baptist Origins Alongside the Mother-Calvinist Congregationalism." *Baptists History and Heritage* 33.2 (1998) 34–44.
———. "Revisioning Baptist Identity by Naming our Origin and Character Rightly." *Baptist History and Heritage* (1999) 45–54.
Stearns, R.P. "The New England Way in Holland." *The New England Quarterly* 6.4 (1933) 747–92.
Steeman, Theodore M. "Church, Sect, Mysticism, Denomination: Periodological Aspects of Troeltsch's Types." *Sociological Analysis* 36.3 (1975) 181–204.
Stinton, B. *A Repository of Diverse Historical Matters Relating to the English Antipedobaptists*. Handwritten manuscript held in the Angus Library, Oxford, 1712.

---

1. The alternative spellings of the name Spilbsery/Spilsberie follow the front, or inside, of the book.

Sunshine, G. S. "Discipline as the Third Mark of the Church: Three Views." *Calvin Theological Journal* 33 (1998) 469–80.
Taylor, J. *New Preachers, New.* London: n.p., 1641.
Terry, D. "Mark Lucar: Particular Baptist Pioneer." *Baptist History and Heritage* 25.1 (1990) 43–49.
Thatcher,[2] Anthony. *A Christian Reprofe Against Contention.* London: n.p., 1631.
The Confession of Faith. Glasgow: Free Presbyterian, 1973.
The Grand Remonstrance. London: n.p., 1641.
The Manner of the Deposition of Charles Stewart, King of England, by the Parliament, and the Generall Councell of the Armie. London: n.p., 1649.
Thomas, J. *A History of the Baptist Association in Wales, from the Year 1650 to the Year 1790.* London: n.p., 1795.
Thomas, K. "Women and the Civil War Sects." In *Crisis in Europe 1560-1660*, edited by Trevor Aston, 317–40. London: Routledge & Kegan Paul, 1965.
Thomas, W. H. G. *The Principles of Theology: An Introduction to the Thirty-Nine Articles.* London: Church Book Room, 1963.
Thompson, M. *Outside the Camp: John Spilsbury, the Pioneer of English Particular Baptists.* Texas: Charis, 2011.
Thompson, P.E. "Seventeenth-Century Baptist Confessions in Context." *Perspectives in Religious Studies* 29.4 (2002) 335–48.
Thorowgood, T. *Moderation Justified, and the Lords Being at Hand Emproved.* London: n.p., 1644.
Tichborne, R. *The Rest of Faith.* London: n.p., 1649.
Tolmie, M. "Thomas Lambe, Soapboiler, and Thomas Lambe, Merchant, General Baptists." *Baptist Quarterly* 27.1 (1977) 4–13.
———. *The Triumph of the Saints: The Separate Churches of London, 1616-1649.* Cambridge: Cambridge University Press, 1977.
Tombes, J. *An Examen of the Sermon of Mr. Stephen Marshall About Infant Baptisme, in a Letter Sent to Him.* London: R.W. for George Whitington, 1645.
Toon, P. *Puritans, the Millennium and the Future of Israel: Puritan Eschatology 1600 to 1660.* Cambridge: James Clarke & Co., 1970.
Torbet, R.G. *A History of the Baptists.* Valley Forge: Judson, 1950.
Torrance I. R. "*Mysterium Christi* and *Mysterium Ecclesiae*: The Christological Ecclesiology of John Calvin." *The Greek Orthodox Theological Review* 43.1-4 (1998) 459–67.
Troeltsch, E. *The Social Teaching of the Christian Churches.* London: George Allen & Unwin, 1931.
Tucker, A. "Salisbury and Tiverton about 1630." *TBHS* 3.1 (1912) 1–7.
Turner, J. *Choice Experiences of the Kind Dealings of God Before, In, and After Conversion.* London: n.p, 1653.
Tyacke, N. "Archbishop Laud." In *The Early Stuart Church, 1603-1642*, edited by K. Fincham, 51–70. Basingstoke: Macmillan, 1993.
———. "Puritanism, Arminianism and Counter-Revolution." In *The Origins of the English Civil War*, edited by Conrad Russell, 119–43. London: Macmillan, 1973.
John Udall, *A Demonstration of Discipline.* East Molesey: R. Waldegrave, 1588.

---

2. The names are suggested by Champlin Burrage, *EED* 1, 176.

Underhill, E. B. *Confessions of Faith and Other Public Documents Illustrative of the Baptist Churches of England in the 17th Century*. London: Haddon, Brothers and Co., 1854.

———, ed. *The Records of a Church of Christ, Meeting in Broadmead, Bristol. 1640–1687*. London: J. Haddon, 1647.

———, ed. *Records of the Churches of Christ Gathered at Fenstanton, Warboys and Hexam, 1644–1720*. London: Haddon, Brothers and Co., 1854.

Underwood, A. C. *A History of the English Baptists*. London: Carey Kingsgate, 1947.

Underwood, T. L. *Primitivism, Radicalism, and the Lamb's War: The Baptist-Quaker Conflict in Seventeenth-Century England*. New York: Oxford University Press, 1997.

Vernon, E. "A Ministry of the Gospel: the Presbyterians during the English Revolution." In *Religion in Revolutionary England*, edited by Christopher Durston and Judith Maltby, 115–36. Manchester: Manchester University Press, 2006.

Vos, G. "The Biblical Importance of the Doctrine of Preterition." *The Presbyterian* 70 (1900) 9–10.

Vos, Johannes G. "The Visible Church: Its Nature Unity and Witness." *Westminster Theological Journal* 9.2 (1947) 147–80.

Waldron, S. E. *A Modern Exposition of the 1689 Baptist Confession of Faith*. Durham: Evangelical, 1989.

Walker, J. "Dissent and Republicanism after the Restoration." *Baptist Quarterly* 8 (1936) 263–80.

Walker, M. J. "The Relation of Infants to Church, Baptism and Gospel in Seventeenth Century Baptist Theology." *Baptist Quarterly* 26.1 (1965) 242–62.

Walker, W. *The Creeds and Platforms of Congregationalism*. New York: Charles Scribner's Sons, 1893.

Walwyn, W. *The Compassionate Samaritane*. London: n.p., 1644.

Wamble, H. "The Beginning of Associationalism Among English Baptists." *Review and Expositor* 54.4 (1957) 544–59.

Ward, S.R. "Authority." *Baptist Quarterly* 4 (1928) 348–54.

Warde, H. "Two Association Meetings in Kent. 1657." *Transactions of the Baptist Historical Society* 3 (1912) 247–50.

Watner, C. "'Come What, Come Will!' Richard Overton, Libertarian Leveller." *The Journal of Libertarian Studies* 4.4 (1980) 405–32.

Watts, M. *The Dissenters I: From the Reformation to the French Revolution*. Oxford: Clarendon, 1978.

Weber, M. "'Churches' and 'Sects' in North America: An Ecclesiastical Socio-Political Sketch." Translated by Colin Loader. *Sociological Theory* 3.1 (1895) 7–13.

———. *The Sociology of Religion*. Boston: Beacon, 1963.

Wendel, F. *Calvin: The Origins and Development of his Religious Thought*. London: Collins, 1963.

Wengert, T. "The Priesthood of All Believers and Other Pious Myths." Online: http://www.valpo.edu/ils/assets/pdfs/05wengert.pdf.

Westlake, A. J. "Some Rare Seventeenth Century Pamphlets." *Baptist Quarterly* 13.3 (1949) 109–15.

White, B. R., ed. *Association Records of the Particular Baptists of England, Wales and Ireland to 1660*, 3 volumes and index. London: The Baptist Historical Society, 1971–77.

———. "Baptist Beginnings and the Kiffin Manuscript." *Baptist History and Heritage* 2.1 (1967) 27–37.
———. "The Baptists of Reading 1652–1715." *Baptist Quarterly* 22.5 (1968) 249–70.
———. "The Doctrine of the Church in the Particular Baptist Confession of 1644." *The Journal of Theological Studies* 19.2 (1968) 570–90.
———. *The English Separatist Tradition, From the Marian Martyrs to the Pilgrim Fathers*. London: Oxford University Press, 1971.
———. "Henry Jessey: A Pastor in Politics." *Baptist Quarterly* 25.3 (1973) 98–110.
———. "How Did William Kiffin Join the Baptists?" *Baptist Quarterly* 23.5 (1970) 201–7.
———. "John Pendarves, Calvinistic Baptists and the Fifth Monarchy." *Baptist Quarterly* 25 (1973) 251–71.
———. "The Organisation of the Particular Baptists, 1644–1660." *Journal of Ecclesiastical History* 17.2 (1966) 209–26.
———. "Samuel Eaton (d. 1639) Particular Baptist Pioneer." *Baptist Quarterly* 24.1 (1971) 10–21.
———. "Thomas Collier and Gangraena Edwards." *Baptist Quarterly* 24.3 (1971) 99–110.
———. "Two Early Propagandists for Believer's Baptism." *Baptist Quarterly* 24 (1971) 167–70.
———. "Who Really Wrote the Kiffin Manuscript?" *Baptist History and Heritage* 1.3 (1966) 3–10, 14.
———. "William Kiffin—Baptist Pioneer and Citizen of London." *Baptist History and Heritage* 2.2 (1967) 91–103.
White, R. B.[3] *Authority: A Baptist View*. London: Baptist Union, 1976.
———. "Baptist Beginnings in Watford." *Baptist Quarterly* 26.6 (1976) 205–8.
———. "Early Baptist Letters (1)." *Baptist Quarterly* 27.4 (1977).
———. *The English Baptists of the Seventeenth Century*. Didcot: The Baptist Historical Society, 1996.
———. "The English Particular Baptists and the Great Rebellion, 1640–1660." *Baptist History and Heritage* 9.1 (1974) 16–29.
———. "John Bunyan and the Context of Persecution, 1660–1688." In *John Bunyan and His England 1628–88*, edited by A. Laurence, W. R. Owens, S. Sim, 51–62 London: Hambledon, 1990.
———. "John Miles and the Structures of the Calvinistic Baptist Mission to South Wales 1649–1660." In *Welsh Baptists Studies*, edited by J. Mansel, 35–76. South Wales: South Wales Baptist College, 1976.
———. "The Origins and Convictions of the First Calvinistic Baptists." *Baptist History and Heritage* 25.4 (1990) 39–47.
White, P. "The Rise of Arminianism Reconsidered." *Past and Present* 101 (1983) 34–54.
Whitely, J. B. "Church Discipline in Loughwood Records." *Baptist Quarterly* 31.1 (1986) 288–94.
———, ed. *From Backwoods to Beacon: Kilmington Baptist Church: The First 350 Years* (2000).
Whitley, W. T. *A Baptist Bibliography*. 2 vols. London: Kingsgate, 1916.
———. *The Baptists of London 1612–1928*. London: The Kingsgate, 1928.
———. "Benjamin Cox." *Transactions of the Baptist Historical Society* 6 (1918) 50–59.

3. The initials are incorrect in the document and should be B. R.

———."Benjamin Stinton and His Baptist Friends." *Transactions of the Baptist Historical Society* 1 (1908) 193–96.
———. "Church Covenants." *Baptist Quarterly* 7 (1934) 227–34.
———. "Continental Anabaptists and Early English Baptists." *Baptist Quarterly* 2.1 (1924) 24–0.
———. "Dissent in Worcestershire during the Seventeenth Century." *Transactions of the Baptist Historical Society* 7 (1920) 1–12.
———. *A History of the British Baptists*. London: The Kingsgate, 1932.
———. "London Churches in 1682." *Baptist Quarterly* I (1922-1923), 82-87.
———. "Loughwood and Honiton, 1650–1800." *Transactions of the Baptist Historical Society* 4 (1914) 129–44.
———. "Militant Baptists, 1660–1672." *Transactions of the Baptist Historical Society* I (1908-1909), 148–155.
———. "The Plantation of Ireland and the Early Baptist Churches." *Baptist Quarterly* 1.6 (1923) 276–81.
———. "Records of the Jacob-Jessey Church, 1616–1641." *Transactions of the Baptist Historical Society* 1 (1908) 203–25.
———. "The Rev. Colonel Paul Hobson, Fellow of Eaton." *Baptist Quarterly* 9 (1938) 307–10.
———. "The Revival of Immersion in Holland and England." *Transactions of the Baptist Historical Society* 3.1 (1912) 31-35.
———. "Sandhurst Bicentenary." *Baptist Quarterly* 5 (1930) 322–33.
———. "Seventh Day Baptists in England." *Baptist Quarterly* 12.8 (October 1947) 252–58.
———. "Stinton's Historical Researches." *Transactions of the Baptist Historical Society* 1 (1908) 197–202.
———. "Story of the Jacob-Jessey Church, 1616–1678." *Transactions of the Baptist Historical Society* 1 (1908) 246–56.
———. "Rise of the Particular Baptists in London, 1633–1644." *Transactions of the Baptist Historical Society* 1 (1908), 226–36.
———. *The Works of John Smyth*. Vols 1–2. Cambridge: Cambridge University Press, 1915.
Wigan, J. *Antichrist's Strongest Hold Overturned*. London: n.p., 1665.
Willen, D. "Godly Women in Early Modern England: Puritanism and Gender." *The Journal of Ecclesiastical History* 43.4 (1992) 561–80.
Williams, E. M. "Women Preachers in the Civil War." *The Journal of Modern History* 1.4 (1929) 561–69.
Williams, G. H. *The Radical Reformation*. London: Weidenfeld and Nicolson, 1962.
Williams, M. E. and W. B. Shurden. *Turning Points in Baptist History*. Macon: Mercer University Press, 2008.
Woodhouse, A. S. P., ed. *Puritanism and Liberty: Being the Army Debates (1647–49)*. London: Dent, 1938.
Worden, B. "The Bill for a New Representative: the dissolution of the Long Parliament, April 1653." *English Historical Review* 86.340 (1971) 473–96.
Wright, D. F., ed. *Martin Bucer, Reforming Church and Community*. Cambridge: Cambridge University Press, 1994.
Wright, S. "Baptist Alignments and the Restoration of Immersion 1638–1644." Part 1, *Baptist Quarterly* 40.5 (2004) 261–83.

———. "Baptist Alignments and the Restoration of Immersion 1638–1644." Part 2, *Baptist Quarterly* 40.6 (2004) 346–68.

———. *The Early English Baptists, 1603–1649*. Woodbridge: Boydell, 2006.

———. "Edward Barber (c. 1595–1663) and his Friends, part 1." *Baptist Quarterly* 41.6 (2006) 355–70.

———. "Edward Barber (c. 1595–1663) and his Friends, part 2." *Baptist Quarterly* 41.7 (2006) 428–38.

———. "Jessey, Henry (1601–1663)." In *Oxford Dictionary of National Biography*, edited by H. C. G. Matthew and Brian Harrison. Oxford: OUP, 2004.

Yarbrough, S. A. "The Ecclesiastical Development in Theory and Practice of John Robinson and Henry Jacob." *Perspectives in Religious Studies* 5.3 (1978) 183–97.

———. "The Origin of Baptist Associations Among the English Particular Baptists." *Baptist History and Heritage* 23.2 (1988) 14–24.

Yrjönsuuri, M. "Disputations, Obligations and Logical Coherence." *Theoria* 66.2 (2008) 205–23.

Index

A

Abergavenny church, 150, 164, 165
Abingdon Association, 167
Abingdon Baptist church, 19, 66, 167
Act for the better propagation and
 preaching of the Gospel in
 Wales, 150
Ames, William, 71, 74, 156
Ancient Church, 3, 4
Andover church, 111, 169
Apostolic succession, 156
associationalism, Particular Baptists
 view of, 188
associations, origins, 161–75

B

Baillie, Robert, 139, 15
baptism, 12–14, 39–48
baptists
 Christology of, 71–77
 expansion of, 14–18
Barebone[s], Praisegod, 8, 20
Barrowe, Henry, 67, 105
Bastwick, John, 58
Batten, Jan, 11
Bedford church, 111, 169
believers' baptism, 1, 5–6, 14
 London Confession of 1644 and, 39
Blacklock, Samuel, 11–12, 14
Blackwood, Christopher, 17

Blunt, Richard, 8–9, 11–12, 14
Bunyan, John, 23, 24

C

Calamy, Edmund, 25
Calvin, John, 104, 135
Canne, John, 10
Canons of Dort, 100
Carmarthen church, 28–29, 150, 164
Carrick Fergus church, 169
Cheriton church, 181
Chidley, Daniel, 5
Chillenden, Edmund, 132
Christ
 kingship, 83–94
 munus triplex, 196
 as priest, 79–80
 as prophet, 80–83
 Rule of, 31, 32–36, 103, 128, 197–98
church, 36–39, 48–54, 60–64
Church at Chard, 29
Church of England, 5, 23
Civil War, 8, 20, 135, 162, 193
Collier, Thomas, 27, 30, 77, 186
communion, 47, 181
congregationalism, 54, 106, 185–86
Copp, Richard of Axminister, 111, 121
covenant of grace, 41–43, 46, 58, 73
Cox, Benjamin, 17, 26, 36, 125
Cromwell, Oliver, 17, 160, 162, 196

225

D

deacons, 56, 91, 201
    appointment; 186
    women assisting, 143
discipline, 109–123
disputations, 22–26
Duppa, John, 5–6, 13
Dutch English classis, 162

E

Eaton, Samuel, 7, 13, 24
Edwards, Thomas, 16, 34, 131
elders, 91, 132, 145, 148, 153, 186, 201
Elizabethan Puritans. *See* Puritans
Eucharist. *See* Lord's Supper
evangelism, missionary, 26–29
excommunication, 101, 106, 117, 124

F

Feake, Christopher, Christ's kingdom on earth and, 198
Featley, Daniel, 24–25, 130, 136–37, 195
Fifth Monarchists, 85–86, 95, 197–200
First London Confession, 1, 13, 14, 66, 71, 75

G

Galloway church, 144, 169
Gelligaer church, 28
General Assembly of Particular Baptists, 187
General Baptists, 9
Gillespie, George, 89
Glamorgan church, 28
Glasshouse church, 170
Glazers Hall, 150
Goodwin, John, 133–35, 139
Green, John, 12, 14, 20

H

Harrison, Richard, 150–51
Hay church, 28, 150, 164, 165
Heidelberg Catechism, 41
Hexham church, 111

Hobson, Paul, 22, 30, 43–44
homosexuality, 112
Hook Norton church, 173
How, Samuel, 6, 137–39
Howard, Luke, 24, 27
Hutchinson, Edward, 10–11

I

Ilston church, 28–29, 164
independent Puritans, 2
infant baptism, 8, 12, 39–48
    John Tombes and, 40, 45–46
    Paul Hobson and, 45
    Stephen Marshall and, 40–43, 46
Ireland, 16, 144, 169, 170, 198
Ivimey, Joseph, 157–58

J

Jacob, Henry, 3–4, 66–69, 71, 108, 193
Jacob-Lathrop-Jessey, 8, 13–14, 164
Jane Turner, 19
Jessey, Henry, 2, 7, 8, 19, 94
Jessey church, 7, 12–14, 197
Jessey memorandum, 5, 7
Jus Divinum, 154

K

Kensworth church, 144, 145, 152, 166, 167, 168, 184
Kerry church, 169
Kiffin, William, 13, 23–24, 27, 167, 173, 197
Kiffin Manuscript, 7, 9, 10, 71
Kilcop, Thomas, 12, 14
Killkenny church, 169
Kilmington church, 134
King, Daniel, 173
Kingston church, 152
Knollys, Hanserd, 13, 20–21, 36–37, 94

L

Langley, Arthur, 24
Lathrop, John, 4, 6–7, 74
Lathrop church, 5–6, 13, 165
lay ministry, 129–44

limited atonement, 194
Llanharan church, 28, 146, 164, 181
Llanigon church, 28
Llantrisant, 149, 150, 164
London Baptists, 58, 75, 76, 167, 170–71
London Confession of 1644, 12, 19, 78, 82, 131–32, 197
    authority of the church, 123–25
    baptism, 39
    Christology, 72–77
Longworth church, 169
Lord's Supper, 26, 30, 47, 195
Loughwood Church Books, 110–20
Lucar, Mark, 7
Luke, Samuel, 22
Luther, Martin, 135, 141–42, 143
Luton church, 169
Lymrick church, 169

M

The Marrow of Sacred Divinity, 56, 71
Marshall, Stephen, 41-46
Mennonite theology, Christology and, 75
Midland Association, 50, 76, 173–74, 200
Midland Confession, 76, 173
Miles, John, 150
millenarianism, 85, 94
ministry, 131–32, 145–51
missionary evangelism, 26–29
Morton church, 173
Munday, Thomas, 12
Munus Triplex Christi, 73–79
Myles, John, 28, 30

N

National Church, 60–64, 98
Newberrie church, 169
Newport Pagnell church, 169
Notae ecclesia, 36, 63

O

ordinances, 21, 34–36
ordination, 155–60
Original Sin, 24, 99, 194

Oxford church, 152

P

Particular Baptists
    associationalism, 188
    baptism and, 9
    Christology of, 71–77
    church discipline and, 97
    disputations, 22–26
    expansion of, 14–18
    missionary evangelism, 26–29
    preaching, 20–22
    publishing, 18–20
pastors, 56, 132, 151–55
Patient, Thomas, 17, 27, 173
Payne, Ernest, 164
Pearson, John, 173
Pendarves, John, 19, 94, 135, 172, 181
Pendarves, Thomasine, 19
Pettie France church, 145, 153, 158, 159, 160, 186
Pietism, 141
Pirton church, 152, 168
Poole, Elizabeth, 19
Poole, Robert, 32–33, 61–62, 195
Porton and Broughton Churchbook, 112
Prayer Book, 39, 69
predestination, 64, 194
Presbyterianism, 51, 190
priesthood of believers, 140–42
Prosser, Walter, 28
Proud, Thomas, 28, 47, 150, 181
Puritans, 2, 105
Putney sermon, 83, 88

Q

Quakers, 23–24, 117

R

Reading church, 166, 167
Rewcastle, Thomas, 111
Richard, William, 150
Richardson, Samuel, 85, 200
Ricraft, Josiah, letter to William Kiffin, 130–31

Rule of Christ, 31, 33, 103, 128, 197–98
Rutherford, Samuel, 40, 89
Rynsburgers, 10

S

sacraments, 35
salvation, 70, 76, 98
sanctification, 56, 67, 76, 127
Scotland, 16, 170
Seaman, Lazarus, 88
Second London Confession, 102, 187
separatism, 193
Shakespeare, J.H., 7
Sheppard, Thomas, 12
sola scriptura, 125
Somerset churches, 171, 186
Somerset Confession, 102, 111, 114
South Wales, 28, 164–65
Spencer, John, 12, 14, 20
Spilsbury, John, 6, 7, 13, 167, 173
Spittlehouse, John, 199
St Helen Bishopsgate, 20
St. Michael's Coventry, 25
Staresmore, Sabine, 5
Stassen, Glen, 51, 75–76
Stoke and Andover church, 116–17
Stukeligh church, 169
Subdean, Edmund, 112
suicide, 111–12

T

Taylor, John, 111
Teuxbury church, 173
Thistleworth church, 169
Thomason, George, 18
Throughton, William, 2
Tiverton church, 172
Tolmie, Murray, 2, 13, 129–30
Tombes, John, 23, 40–41, 45–46, 47

Torbet, R.G., 162
total depravity, 99, 194
Trinity, 24–25, 97
A True Confession, 71, 74–75, 98
Tyndale, William, 105, 203

V

visible church, 54–60, 67–69
Volkskirche, 39

W

Wales, 16, 30, 146, 164
Wallington, Joseph, 29
Wantage church, 152
Warwick church, 116, 167–68
Watford church, 30, 169
Watlington church, 152
Watts, Michael, 36
West Country Association, 76
Westminster Assembly, 35, 39-40, 52, 63, 87, 92, 131, 155
Westminster Confession, 76, 89
Wexford church, 144, 169
White, B.R., xviii, 6n, 11, 134, 158, 162, 169
women, 19, 143, 148, 189
Woolaston church, 169
Wright, Sara, 19
Wright, Stephen, 11

Y

Yarbrough, Sladen, "The Origin of Baptist Associations", 162

Z

Zwingli, Huldrych, 41, 105

www.ingramcontent.com/pod-product-compliance
Lightning Source LLC
Chambersburg PA
CBHW051053230426
43667CB00013B/2283